Fragments of the City

Fragments of the City

Making and Remaking Urban Worlds

Colin McFarlane

UNIVERSITY OF CALIFORNIA PRESS

University of California Press
Oakland, California

© 2021 by Colin McFarlane

Library of Congress Cataloging-in-Publication Data

Names: McFarlane, Colin, 1979– author.
Title: Fragments of the city : making and remaking urban
    worlds / Colin McFarlane.
Description: Oakland, California : University of
    California Press, [2021] | Includes bibliographical
references and index.
Identifiers: LCCN 2021012121 | ISBN 9780520382237
    (hardcover) | ISBN 9780520382244 (paperback) | ISBN
    9780520382251 (ebook)
Subjects: LCSH: Cities and towns. | Cities and towns in
    literature.
Classification: LCC HT151 .M388 2021 |
    DDC 307.76—dc23
LC record available at https://lccn.loc.gov/2021012121

30 29 28 27 26 25 24 23 22 21
10 9 8 7 6 5 4 3 2 1

Contents

Figures

Prologue

Imagine spacious landscaped highways . . . . They unite and
separate—separate and unite the series of diversified units,
the farm units, the factory units, the roadside markets, the
garden schools, the dwelling places (each on its acre of
individual adorned cultivated ground), the places of pleasure
and leisure. All of these units arranged and integrated so that
each citizen of the future will have all forms of production,
distribution, self-improvement, enjoyment, within a radius of
a hundred and fifty miles of his home now easily speedily
available by means of his car or plane. This integral whole
composes the great city that I see embracing all of this
country—the Broadacre City of tomorrow.

—F. L. Wright, 1932

The "integral whole," separated but united. So wrote Frank Lloyd
Wright, a figure who was hugely influential in twentieth-century debates
on architecture, planning, and urban development, in 1932. For all that
Wright's vision was a fundamentally American one, caught up as it was
with the classic image of suburban life, it speaks to a wider desire for
the "whole" that has gripped the history of thinking about cities. In this
view, cities are closely integrated spaces of flow and movement, blend-
ing urban and rural components with their functions neatly organized
and connected. They are portrayed as internally bound up with themselves; in a material and even social sense: whole.

Jump forward almost a century from Wright's comment to today and
you are more likely to read about the 15-minute compact walkable city
than a 150-mile radial urbanism, but the ambition for the integrated
whole remains. A recent piece in *The Guardian* newspaper, for instance,
wondered whether it might be possible to reach "peak city." Using the

example of Tokyo, the article's contention was that with most of Japan now living in cities, with a flatlining population and a relative absence of sharp inequalities, the city may have reached a stable, manageable "maturity."[1] Around the same time, a different piece insisted that "building a complete city is essential to sustaining growth."[2] The aspiration for "completion" is closely connected to a long-standing utopian ideal of the city as an integrated whole, meeting needs and wants.

The idea of the integrated, connected city functioning as a whole is central to the larger project of modernity. As Patrick Joyce has shown, the techniques and technologies of modernity had at their center objectives of consolidation, objectification, and abstraction that gathered so many fragments of things, space, and knowledge into efforts to cohere, govern, and control.[3] This includes forms of knowledge and governing that emerged largely in the nineteenth century and which underpinned liberalism in both metropoles and colonial cities alike—from maps and statistics to public health—alongside the development of municipal organization and bureaucracy, and the building of circulatory infrastructures and services from energy, water, and sanitation to neighborhood policing.

What, though, of the fragments, the shards, the scraps and ruins? What of the bits and pieces, the broken-off and discarded, the lying-around-and-who-knows-what-it's-for? According to the creed of wholism, they are the debris to be swept aside or tidied away, the troublesome sites of removal in the steps to the unitary city. Consider, in contrast, South African artist Sue Williamson, and her 1993 work on the infamous District Six "redevelopment" in Cape Town. District Six had been declared a "slum" that should be transformed into a "whites-only" area by the apartheid government in the 1960s, resulting in the forced removal of "coloured" residents to the Cape Flats from the mid-1970s. Here, writer Ivan Vladislavic reflects on a visit to Williamson's exhibition with his partner, Liz:

> *Mementoes of District Six* is a cabin made of resin blocks. Enclosed in each block is an object or fragment that the artist Sue Williamson collected among the *ruins* of District Six after the removals: a shard of pottery, a scrap of wallpaper, a hairclip, a doll's shoe. "It made me cry like a baby," says Liz. "You? Never." "Really, I'm no pushover, but it was just so moving, standing there like a kid in a Wendy house surrounded by these relics, worthless things made to seem precious, glowing like candles. As if each trinket and scrap had been a treasure to someone." We talk about trifles and their meaning.[4]

Mementoes of District Six contains everyday things that appear at once "worthless" or "trifles" and, at the same time, demand that we contemplate the lives and histories they were caught up with. Williamson's work is powerful not just because of what is there but because of what is *not* there. The people, the thick constellations of relations going on all around the ordinary objects of urban life, and how the "not there" is a product of a brutal geography of violence. The fragmentation of the city begets fragments: fragments of things, lives, and spaces. These are so often the costs of the "integral whole" and the fantasy of the "complete" city: the dominance of particular groups and aesthetics over others, and the machinations of urban value that define capitalist transformation. The utopian dream of the integrated, complete city leaves little room for the fragments.

We might ask, as Ananya Roy asks: "Whose urban experience is stable and coherent? Who is able to see the city as a unified whole? By contrast, for whom is the city a geography of shards and fragments?"[5] "Whole" and "fragmented" are not just different kinds of claims about the city—they point to radically distinct ways of experiencing and seeing the urban condition, even though they are often brought together in different ways. On the economic margins of the urban world, which are growing at faster rates than cities more generally, the rise in urban living typically does not lead to the integrated provision of amenities but to an urbanism of fragments. This book is about the fragments. The fragment is a form and idea that has always accompanied research and writing on cities—and we will encounter many instances of this across the book—yet there have rarely been efforts to examine what different manifestations of the fragment might bring to how we understand, express, and contest the urban condition. In exploring the fragment, the wholes are always there too, and not always as forms of violence, destruction, or exclusion. Sometimes the whole is what people are reaching and hoping for, and the fragments are what they are trying to escape. And fragments and wholes can be made into more than they initially seem to be.

In setting out this exploration of urban fragments, I am aware of how my own privilege has enabled not only a relatively stable and coherent experience of urbanism but also an opportunity for mobility and access denied to many researchers as well as most urbanites living on the economic margins. The way in which I have learned and come to see the urban world, for all its blindspots, provisionalities, and situatedness, is in part a product of the small and large privileges that are embedded within and accrue to a white man in a well-resourced university. I did not grow up in a wealthy or privileged context—we were a relatively poor family on the economic and spatial margins of Glasgow—but the opportunities I've had to travel across many sites in the urban world, as well as the geography of access and responsiveness that opens doors and informs relationships in different places, has shaped this book, and they are often denied to many researchers, especially in the global South. In addition, I have been privileged to have the help and support of many people in and beyond cities from Berlin, Kampala, and Cape Town to Mumbai and New York, whether fellow academics or residents or activists or people in municipalities and civil society groups.

As with any book, a disparate collective makes it happen, and I am thankful for the generosity, critique, and care of a great many friends and colleagues. I am grateful to Suzi Hall and to an anonymous reviewer for their helpful and insightful feedback on an earlier version of the book, and to the University of California Press—especially Kim Robinson, Summer Farah, and Kate Hoffman—for their support and advice. A big thank you to Ben Anderson, Jen Bagelman, Tariq Jazeel, Noam Leshem, Emma Ormerod, and Hanna Ruszczyk for their reading and insight, friendship, and humor. The work and friendship of many other colleagues near and far have shaped the book in different ways. Thanks go to Ash Amin, Vanesa Castán Broto, Steve Graham, Alex Jeffrey, Michele Lancione, Simon Marvin, Jon Silver, AbdouMaliq Simone, and Alex Vasudevan for their advice, support, energy, and scholarship. Thanks too to Michele for one of the images used on the cover of the book, taken on a memorable trip to Old Delhi.

The research in Kampala and Cape Town described in the book would simply not have been possible without Jon Silver, Joel Ongwec, Helen Friars, and Josephine Namukisa. A special thanks is due to Jon, who helped ensure that the work we did in both cities was both a success and a lot of fun. I am grateful to Ankit Kumar for his insight and energy when we worked in Mumbai together. The book may not have been possible without support from, initially, the Leverhulme Trust and later the European Research Council DenCity project (773209). The Department of Geography at Durham University has been a source of inspiration, and I am grateful to my colleagues for ensuring that it remains a generative, enabling, and caring place to work.

The biggest thanks go to Rachael, for her ever-present support and encouragement. This has been a tricky book to write, particularly in relation to its form, and I know the difference that our many conversations about it have made. I wouldn't have got there without her. I am deeply thankful to her, and to Keir and Arran, for their optimism, patience, support, smiles, and love. The final stage of the book was completed during COVID-19 lockdowns in 2020. I can only apologize to Keir and Arran for the Urban Geography lessons they suffered during home schooling. I hope I haven't put you off! My thanks too to Mum, Steven, Fiona, and Ryan for all their encouragement, and to David, David, and Garry.

This book is for my gran, to her memory and example, and to my wonderful wife and boys.

. . .

I would like to acknowledge that some parts of the sections on *Pulling together, falling apart* and *Political framings* were published, in different forms, in "Fragment Urbanism: Politics on the Margins of the City," *Environment and Planning D: Society and Space* 36 (2018): 1007–25; "The Poolitical City: 'Seeing Sanitation' and Making the Urban Political in Cape Town," *Antipode* 49 (2017): 125–48 (with Jon Silver); and "Navigating the City: Dialectics of Everyday Urbanism," *Transactions of the Institute for British Geographers* 21 (2017): 312–28 (also with Jon Silver). Some of the discussion in *Knowing fragments* draws on a chapter I published in Tariq Jazeel and Stephen Legg's edited collection, *Subaltern Geographies: Subaltern Studies, Space, and the Geographical Imagination* (Athens: University of Georgia Press, 2019), 210–30, entitled "Urban Fragments: A Subaltern Studies Imagination." I thank the reviewers and editors for their guidance on those publications. Finally, I thank Daniel Schwartz for the use of his photographs of Torre David, and Hubert Klumpner and Klearjos Eduardo Papanicolaou for facilitating. Renu Desai and Josephine Namukisa kindly gave permission for use of photographs from Mumbai and Kampala respectively. The Noah Purifoy Foundation granted permission to publish the poem "A Book Flown," and I thank them for that.

Reading Fragments

Writing in the late 1920s, Walter Benjamin described the anticipatory discovery at work in children's play. As Benjamin describes it, play for children emerges in the changing relations among perception, object, and action, and represents a creative remaking of the world often lost to adults. "Tidying up," writes Benjamin, "would mean destroying an edifice full of prickly chestnuts that are spiked maces, bits of tinfoil that are a hoard of silver, building bricks that are coffins, cacti that are totem poles, and copper coins that are shields."[1] Part of Benjamin's larger project was the multiplication of possibility that emerged from an attentiveness to what fragments might be and become, not simply in relation to play but in the violence of modernist transformation in the city or in the saturation of commodity capitalism. It was a style of urban pedagogy that worked with the disharmonious, the discontinuous, and what Miriam Hansen calls the "reinvention of experience."[2] This is partly why Benjamin, whom I will return to later in the book, so often worked with and wrote in fragments of text.

A very different context: when he was writing songs, the musician David Bowie would sometimes sit among fragments of text that he had gathered, some his own and some sourced from others, and piece them together, just as writers like William Burroughs have done with the "cut-up" montage method. Bowie created what he called "awkward relationships," which would sometimes startle or provoke him and which turned meaning, as Rick Moody has put it, into a nonsingular "wash of references."[3] This improvisatory method is, too, both a process of anticipatory discovery—albeit as conceptual art and music rather than children's play—and a practice of tidying up. Compare it to improvisation in, say, jazz, where the process of tidying up the fragments is different again. In jazz, composition is typically less random and scattered than Bowie's, more a learned language and method through which fragments of music are intuited.[4]

Just as there are different ways of working with fragments in music, art, or play, so too are there in writing. Imagine a book for a moment not as pages bound together, linear and symmetrical, but instead cast apart, the pages scattered across a room. The text might then be stitched together in all kinds of different ways, and in the process surprising juxtapositions could emerge. In their new relations, fragments of text may form, in the minds of different readers, quite distinct constellations of meaning and significance. I am not suggesting that writing a book, particularly one that includes a concern with fragments and their relationships to poverty, inequality, struggle, and politics, is akin to play or improvisatory art, but instead I am pointing to the long-standing experiments and tensions of relating fragments to a whole in efforts to express worlds.

The process of assembling text into a book is inevitably a practice of wholism. It is integrative, standardizing, structuring, and disciplining. It is a form of tidying up in which fragments are placed into position with inevitable consequences for how they might be read both in themselves and in relation to one another. This is, of course, an important and necessary step. But for a book about fragments that seeks, at least to some degree, to experiment with what writing in fragments might enable, it is a tricky process, and I have not found this question of form to be straightforward. I have been trained to work within and to value conventional practices of social scientific writing. Moreover, I have read books written in fragments that, to my mind at least, have just been *too* fragmented, too scattered and rangy, never seeming to settle and cohere, while I have read others that have used the fragment form to brilliant effect. At its best, and I will return to examples of this later, the fragment form reinforces the content and the arguments, conjures something of the atmosphere of what the book is about, and carries with it multiple lines of discussion that, while not necessarily integrating and unifying, cohere into a wider idea, narrative, and argument.

This kind of writing creates a tension between holding on to the "awkward relationships" between fragments that might be generative and suggestive, and the "tidying up" that might leave you wondering whether it was after all the right decision to strip out those fragments that didn't seem to fit. I have tried to steer a path between a conventional book structure and a highly fragmented text. It is inevitably a compromise, and in compromising, different people write into their own "comfort zones." I do not use the fragment form of writing to the extent of some of the examples I discuss later in the book (see the *Writing in fragments* discussions), in which text can be heavily broken up. My use of fragment writing is lighter and composed of often lengthy pieces and sometimes closely integrated narrative parts, brought together as thematic sections, partly as a consequence of my habitual writing tendency and partly in an effort to strike a balance between coherence and multiplicity.

I have three motivations for the use I make of the fragment form of expression in the book. First, writing in fragments enables a looser form of juxtaposition, a means to bring seemingly disparate and disharmonious ideas, questions, cases, and places together as entry points into the urban world. It is a form of writing that experiments with the combinatory possibilities of juxtaposition, which at times can be reinforcing and cumulative of a larger argument and at other moments disruptive, as a means of generating knowledge of the urban condition.

Second, while writing in fragments is a trade-off, in that it reduces the scope for extensive prose focused on singular discussion, it facilitates movement between a pattern of intersecting lines of thought. These lines create glimpses, evocations, provocations, fleeting images, and an atmosphere of displacement through which form can be used to reinforce content, in this case the idea of the urban world as incomplete, multiple, and always in the process of differently pulling together and falling apart. As we will see later, in the fragment form of writing the urban world often remains fugitive, beyond any one system of representation, and understanding emerges in the connective tissues across and between fragments. This is a form of conceptualization that is neither meta-narrative nor restricted to the local, but identifies a register in-between. It is a way of storying the urban world as a provisional and differential set of orderings, approached through multiple angles of vision, one that is open, mixed, and characterized by resonance rather than completeness.

Third, writing in fragments is an experiment in performing a damaged urban present, a mirroring of the discontinuities of the urban world. For different urban writers, and I will explore some of them, writing in fragments has in part been a method of bringing the text closer to an ontology of urban modernity and the urban condition, a use of textual strategy as a means to underline the fractures we see in cities. I have settled on a structure with the reader in mind, although some may find it too close to convention while others might think a more standard chapter form could have enabled the three motivations I describe above.

The book does not have to be read in a linear way. It does not follow a chronology or particular case study but is instead an effort to pursue the idea of the fragment—as material, knowledge, and form of expression, as I explain in the following pages—and its potential for generating understanding of life and politics in our increasingly urban world. It would, though, make sense to begin with the first section, *Pursuing fragments,* because here I introduce the four ways in which I think about fragments in the book, and contextualize the book's focus on the margins of the urban world. After that, I have set out a set of themes that offer points of departure for exploring the possibilities of different kinds of fragments in relation to material urban conditions, knowing the city, writing the city, politicizing the city, and researching the city. The reader can either follow that structure as I've set it out here or weave between the fragments, forming their own juxtapositions and lines of thought. The fragment form, after all, is just an intensification of what we all know about how we read any book: that it is dialogue, translation, and relational creation.

Pursuing Fragments

It is not, therefore, as though one had global (or conceived) space to one side and fragmented (or directly experienced) space to the other—rather as one might have an intact glass here and a broken glass or mirror over there. For space "is" whole and broken, global and fractured, at one in the same time.

—Henri Lefebvre, *The Production of Space*

Routes

What view might we gain of cities and the urban world if we look at them through the fragment? This is a book about fragments in the city. Or more accurately, about the relations fragments become caught up in and the ways in which they are used. Fragments not just as nouns but as verbs. Not just as things but as processes, doing different kinds of work, and sometimes in surprising ways. Fragments and their interactions, with residents, activists, artists, writers, and others. The fragment not only as a material entity but as a form of expression or a type of knowledge. I explore some of the diversity of thinking and acting with fragments in the city, and experiment with the fragment as a form of written expression. The relations formed around fragments can generate insight into what it means to be urban. They can help us to make sense of our increasingly urban world, and can become part of the possibilities of making and remaking the city.

As cities grow, they become increasingly unequal and fragmented. Much of what lower-income residents deal with on a daily basis is fragments of stuff: toilets that often seem to be broken or inadequate, water pipes that don't keep their pressure or quality, houses that demand constant labor and maintenance, everyday objects that stress and fracture, and so on. Urban life, for a growing number of people across the world, is more and more about the struggle of managing infrastructure, housing, and services that are unreliable or unable to meet basic needs. What I call "fragment urbanism" is the interactions different people have with fragments. It is a multiple and diverse process where bits and pieces of material things and forms of knowledge are caught up in all kinds of social and political relations, often oppressive and exploitative, sometimes progressive and generative.

As the world continues to urbanize, fragments are becoming more important. Before the COVID-19 pandemic, extreme poverty had fallen globally, but in cities urban inequality rose. Somewhere between a third and a quarter of all urban residents live in poor neighborhoods—often called "slums," or, less pejoratively, "informal" or "lower-income" neighborhoods"—or in transit housing settlements, squats, refugee camps, and in the interstices of the city: under bridges and flyovers, on pavements and in lanes, or balanced precariously on riverbanks or the edges of garbage grounds. More and more of urban life, especially on the economic margins of cities, revolves around efforts to collectively and individually work with, put to work, and politicize fragments. In this sense, fragments are both at the margins and at the center, both seemingly trivial and often overlooked, yet vital for how the urban world is lived and politicized.

There are many routes through which to think about the fragment; in this book I pursue four. I decided that rather than focus on one form of the fragment, be it material, knowledge, textual expression, or otherwise, I would instead explore how different approaches to, and instantiations of, the fragment would enable a particular understanding of the making and remaking of urban worlds. This decision facilitated the bringing together of unlikely urban domains that are not often part of the same conversation about cities and the urban condition, from protests over infrastructure in Mumbai and Cape Town, or forms of urban support in Berlin and Kampala, to artistic collaborations in Los Angeles, and the potential of methods like writing or walking in London and Hong Kong to locate and express fragments of different sorts. The four different routes I settled on—often overlapping, sometimes distinct—constitute an expansive, albeit situated and necessarily limited, reading of fragment urbanism.

First, I explore how marginal material bits and pieces come to act in different ways in the city. These fragments are not theoretical questions or conceptual abstractions; they are lived as individual, social, and political struggles. They are intimately connected to experiences of health, dignity, and the possibilities of urban living. They compose homes that are too hot, cold, wet, or flimsy, or just too much work, as well as partial and inconsistent water, sanitation, or electricity provi-

FIGURE 1. Everyday arrangements, Khar, Mumbai (Photo by author)

sions that are linked to illness, disease, and injury. In the neighborhood of Topsia in Kolkata, for example, Jeremy Seabrook and Ahmed Siddiqui describe an urban fabric of bamboo and wood-frame housing, industrial discards, roofs weighted down by stones, raised beds or makeshift doorway dams to block monsoon floodwater, aging plastic cans for drinking water, and so on (Figure 1 is a different example from Mumbai, showing some of the everyday metals, bricks, cables, and containers that support housing and infrastructure).[1] Fragmented homes and infrastructures, themselves the products of the political, economic, and cultural inequalities of the city, might break down, collapse, or—if they are on the wrong side of the law or the powers that be and their economic interests—be demolished altogether. At the same time, fragments can become enrolled in political contestation.

Second, I am concerned with how forms of urban material provision—a community toilet in a poor neighborhood, for example—which might start out life as a kind of "whole," then become fragments in practice, whether because they are subject to breakdown and demand constant maintenance, or because they are often so woefully insufficient in comparison to need that even when they are well-built integrated systems they are, in practice, always already fragments of provision. Even in cases where provisions in poorer neighborhoods—energy, sanitation, water, drainage, or transport, for example—seem to be, at least initially, relatively well functioning, in practice they are too often far from it, unable to provide for enough of the residents enough of the time, poorly maintained by the state. These forms of the fragment are sometimes ambiguous, moving between "fragment" and "whole" over time. Density plays a role here. Not because, as conservative urban voices sometimes claim, it is "too high": the issue is not one of optimum thresholds of numbers of people, but of the profound inequalities that force residents into marginalized, underprovided spaces in the city. Residents are often forced to struggle with overburdened fragments that barely cater to the numbers of people compressed into a small space. At the same time, densities of people become a resource to help people cope, or from which to form political formations that contest living conditions.

Third, I consider knowledge fragments—forms of knowledge, or ways of knowing, that are marginalized by dominant cultures, actors, groups, and power relations. The marginalization that increasingly accompanies world urbanization pertains not only to the realm of material stuff but to that of knowledge-forms and ways of knowing, from traces of historical memory and ongoing community festivals or art projects, to mapping projects or manifestos or alternative cultural imaginaries of a different urban future. Consider, for instance, whether the knowledges that lower-income residents have about how to manage and improve material fragments remains in the site—ignored, manipulated, or discarded by the powers that be in the city—or moves beyond the site to meaningfully influence policy and planning? Or, consider whether refugees from different spatial and cultural contexts, carrying with them their own histories, skills, aspirations, and concerns, have their knowledge and voice genuinely heard and responded to in city management?

Knowledge fragments are marked out as such in two broad ways. First, because of their position to or within a wider set of political, social, and cultural power-knowledge relations. Constructions of the urban whole involve a set of power relations that can exclude, subordi-nate, or otherwise transform knowledge fragments. Second, because knowledge fragments can be forms of expression that present clues to different ways of understanding the urban condition and its possi-bilities. Knowledge fragments can be provocations that demand recog-nition that the world is more than simply plural, but—as Dipesh Chakrabarty has written—"so plural as to be impossible of description in any one system of representation." The urban world as beyond any singular narrative or epistemology; to quote AbdouMaliq Simone, "multiple realities—visible and invisible . . . [through which] the urban is always 'slipping away' from us."[2]

Material fragments and knowledge fragments are often co-located. Edgar Pieterse, writing about cities in Africa, identifies "catalysts" for new directions in urban theory, policy, and practice from often margin-alized spaces: "I have no doubt that the street, the slum, the waste dump, the taxi rank, the mosque and church will become the catalysts of an unanticipated African urbanism."[3] We might think of the "cata-lysts" here as forms of politics and ways of understanding cities beyond the more familiar referent points. Writing about urban wastepickers in municipal garbage grounds in India, for example, Vinay Gidwani sug-gests that theory could be enriched by attending more closely to the lifeworlds of wastepickers and their interconnections to relations of capital, labor, and urbanism, through what he calls a "conjuring of the positive" from what has been "marginalized, remaindered, and stigma-tized" as a "primary intellectual and political task."[4]

The fourth and final way in which I use the fragment is as a form of written expression. The form of fragment writing deployed here, and I will explore this in more detail later, is expressed through vignettes of different lengths and kinds, from brief depictions and elicitations—often impressionistic rather than analytical—to, more commonly, longer descriptions and reflections on particular questions, themes, or cases, adding up to a set of juxtapositions across sites and issues.

By exploring these four uses of the fragment, I hope to tell a larger story—situated in my own angle of vision and told through a particular set of cases—about cities and the urban world. This is a story of people trying to cope with an inadequate and often unreliable urban fabric, striving to build and hold together vital forms of social infrastructure, developing political claims and approaches to contest their living condi-tions, and shaping political or artistic expressions that seek to escape or remake the fragments of the urban present.

The book is organized into seven sections that bring together a series of cases and discussions on a shared theme. In some places, the discussion will be more tightly woven across a set of fragments, owing to the substantive question at hand—for example, *Writing in fragments* includes sustained discussion of how a range of writers have sought to express cities and urbanism through textual fragments of different sorts, and *Walking cities* reflects on how walking does and does not reveal fragment urbanism. *Pulling together, falling apart* sets out fragment urbanism on the margins of the urban world in relation to a set of key ideas and processes, especially fragmentation, density, and social infrastructure. *Knowing fragments* explores the idea of the fragment historically and in different fields, from archaeology and classics to art history and critical theory, including how strands of postcolonial thought—and specifically subaltern studies scholarship—helps us to understand knowledge fragments. *Writing in fragments* examines how different writers have used the fragment form to express a city or the urban condition, from London to Paris and Johannesburg. *Political framings,* the longest sequence of fragments in the book, sets out a politics of fragments in six forms: *attending to fragments, generative translation, reformation, surveying wholes, occupation,* and *value.* This sequence of six is not intended as an exhaustive capture of the different kinds of possible politics at work here, but instead looks to consider the multiplicity of the encounter between fragment urbanism and the urban political.

The politics of attending includes rhythms of maintenance, improvisation, incremental improvement, and the often gendered labor of holding things together even as they break down and fall apart. Given that in many informal neighborhoods, people are forced every day, as AbdouMaliq Simone puts it, to manage the uncertain oscillations "between the provisional and incessantly mutating practices required to viably 'make do'," this politics of attending is an unfolding urban learning process that navigates, uses, and has to respond to changing relations among fragments, density, and place.[5] In addition to examples of attending to material fragments in Mumbai, I explore cases of attending to knowledge fragments in Berlin. In both cases, my focus is on how attending to fragments involves people coming together, trying to get by and to get on in the city. In contrast, the politics of generative translation relates to how fragments are translated as political objects that call the city as a whole into question, and here I draw on an example of the politicization of waste in Cape Town.

In the politics of reformation discussion I examine how artists take fragments that may have been destroyed—often as a result of different forms of political, economic, and cultural violence—and make them anew as social expression and critique. Fragmentation of different kinds enters into the making of different experiments in fragment urbanism. The politics of surveying wholes moves the focus more squarely onto the city as a whole, and here I focus on a social movement in Mumbai that campaigns for urban rights via data and state accountability. The fifth form of politics—occupation—also turns on questions of rights and recognition, but through the political tactic of massing in urban space, and here I turn to the politics of refuge in Berlin. I end the *Political framings* section with the politics of value, and with an exhibition at a city museum in Kampala. Value is a thread that runs in the background throughout the book: the question of who and which places are valued and which are not, by whom, in what ways, and with what consequences. The ways in which the city pulls together and falls apart—densifies and fragments—is in part a politics of urban value.

The section that follows, *Walking cities,* is a methodological reflection on the possibilities and limits of understanding fragment urbanism through walking particular routes in the city, and here I contrast walks through three cities: Berlin, Hong Kong, and New York. Finally, *In completion* concludes the book by reflecting on the key arguments and identifying some of the potential focal points for addressing and researching fragment urbanism, including in relation to the "connective devices" between fragments and wholes.

Fragment urbanism has produced some of the most important political moments for cities. It is from the fragment city, for example, that activists have confronted the bulldozers bringing down houses and sought a new political settlement, and where residents have rejected inadequate provisions as insults to their basic needs and dignity, or where refugees have organized among themselves to demand basic rights. The fragment city is a set of sites on the margins of cities across the urban world from which political movements have been partly shaped and drawn their agenda for change, from Brazil's participatory budgeting and city statute to the civil rights movement in the United States, and through which urbanites have articulated some of their most powerful calls to action and imaginaries of transformation. There is a wider story at work in which activists and residents fight back and contest a condition of having to live with, protect, and enhance fragments, or come together to rebuild in the face of demolition, or forge solidarities in what are often the most trying of circumstances. Fragments can take on new lives, becoming remade and differently instantiated in all kinds of interactions and sometimes unpredictable contexts.[6] As much as that is a story of violence, destruction, and struggle, it is also a story of possibility and hope.

On the Margins

I focus on those who either directly experience this urbanism most acutely, or whose work—as residents, activists, artists, writers, and so on—offers insight into the nature, struggle, and politics over it. The cases range across different kinds of "margins." The margins of the urban world are not fixed, nor do they entail a particular content or set of logics. They are multifaceted and changing, often combining economic exploitation and exclusion with social stigmatization and violence, and operating across material, cultural, historical, social, and political dimensions.[7] The margins are not restricted to a particular place or group. They are produced relationally, through historical fragmentation, the struggles and power relations around them, and the possibilities that emerge to address, negotiate, protect, or contest them.[8] My focus is not on the political and economic drivers of fragmentation processes, although those actors and processes will feature in the book. This is not because it is more important or relevant to study poverty and struggle in order to understand fragment urbanism than, say, the state, urban policymaking, real estate speculators, hedge fund managers, private sector providers, and so forth. They matter enormously and need to be part of our collective conversation about the inequalities and challenges of our urban present and potential futures.

Most of the cases I discuss relate to places in which people struggle in conditions of acute poverty, but the margins are not only economic. In some cases, the political margins—exclusion from basic rights to the

city, as is too often the case, for example, for refugees and asylum seekers seeking to make their way in the city, or people attempting to stop
or appeal housing demolition—may matter more than the fact of occupying an economic margin. At other times, social stigmatization, for
instance in the exclusion of particular groups and identities from new
government policies or provisions on the basis of, for example, gender,
sexuality, religious beliefs, or race or ethnicity, may be the central man-
ifestation of a margin. The margins are not experienced equally. They
are gendered, racialized, caste-differentiated, and differently lived
through ethnicity, age, sexuality, and more, as Suzanne Hall and others
have shown.[9]

The margins are diverse, both in how they are produced and in how
they take shape in what Michele Lancione calls the "making and
unmaking of precarious lives."[10] Yaffa Truelove has shown how everyday water and sanitation practices in Delhi are productive of particular
urban subjectivities that entrench inequalities and sharpen everyday
violence.[11] Women and religious minorities labor over the collection of
water and access to sanitation in ways that men often do not, while
often suffering harassment and violence. In urban India, segregation by
caste may have grown rather than reduced.[12] Estimates show that global
hunger has increased and that it is increasingly prevalent in urban areas,
often intimately tied to inadequate water and sanitation provisions, and
here children are especially vulnerable—one in three children in urban
areas is stunted, and often as a result more vulnerable to illness and
disease.[13] The world of work for the urban poor, which often takes
place in the unregulated informal economy, is another experience of the
margins, and is often oppressive, devoid of basic rights and provisions,
unpredictable, and exploitative. Laboring bodies at the margins are too
often used and discarded, trapped in poverty wages outside formal pro-
tections, and subject to the whims of employers.[14] This process too is
socially differentiated, encompassing everything from domestic labor,
waste work, and rickshaw driving, to construction work and brick-
making. Or, to move to a different context, Ananya Roy has shown
how housing displacement in the United States is driven not just by
gentrification but by a deep-rooted and variegated geography of racial
banishment.[15]

Often, different forms of marginalization operate together. The margins are relational intersections produced through fragmentation processes (on which more later) and attempts to cope with and respond to

those processes, and they take shape differently over urban space and time. They are intensifying as cities grow and become increasingly unequal, and understanding and addressing urban margins is vital for urban research, policy, practice, and activism—fragment urbanism is one important dimension here.

An Urban World

The discussions in the book are informed by fieldwork in various cities, including Berlin, Cape Town, Hong Kong, Kampala, Mumbai, and New York. This work has focused in different ways on urban poverty, inequality, and politics, mainly through interviews, walking methods, and documentary research. The privilege of being able to work across these different sites has given me the opportunity to produce an account of the urban world that, while situated and selective, is informed by quite different urban conditions. This includes, for example, discussion of fragmented sanitation provisions in Mumbai and Cape Town, collective efforts on a daily basis to reproduce infrastructures in Kampala that help residents get beyond fragmented provisions, and political occupations and connections formed among refugees, activists, and residents in Berlin.

The book further includes methodological exploration of fragments in different cities, from museum exhibitions in Kampala to the potential and limits of walking as a route to knowing fragment urbanism in Berlin, Hong Kong, and New York, or experiments in writing in fragments. I have also drawn inspiration from writing on other cities, from London to Johannesburg, and consider attempts to bring the ruined fragments of the city into artistic montages in Los Angeles and Dakar. Not all of the cases gathered in the book, then, focus on urban experience and politics on the margins—some, such as those on locating and expressing fragments through walking and writing, range across different kinds of urban conditions, sites, and processes—but throughout the discussions

I explore how fragments of different kinds feature in and express urban worlds.

In bringing different cases into juxtaposition, I develop a particular approach to writing about the urban world. I use the phrase "urban world" to signal two processes. One is the increasing centrality of cities, urbanism, and urbanization to the world. This includes, first and foremost, people. The world is continuing to urbanize, and the rate of growth is faster in low-income neighborhoods in what is often called the "global South" than it is anywhere else. This creates a fundamental challenge for research, policy, and practice: how to tackle the inequalities of urbanization, and how to live better together in ways that meet the needs and aspirations of growing numbers of residents? Beyond demographics, cities and urbanism are central to economic, ecological, cultural, and political change in the world. National and local states have come to see that the city is one of their most powerful engines of economic growth. Over several decades, a discourse of urban entrepreneurialism has taken hold, variously depicting the city as vital to creative, smart, innovative economies. We can debate the merit of those specific claims, but what is clear is that there is growing evidence that urban economic power, especially the power of finance and real estate, is a key driver of change in and beyond cities.[16]

So too has the political power of the city grown, and in particular the power of primary cities—from Milan, London, and New York to Mumbai, Bogotá, Kigali, and Tokyo—from which mayors, municipalities, and city coalitions and networks have gained stronger, more influential regional, national, and sometimes global voices. There is also a body of research demonstrating how the city can shape and transform key political questions and struggles.[17] The climate emergency is driven largely by cities, and ecological change is not only demanding radical changes to how people live in cities, it is threatening huge swathes of cities from Miami to Jakarta.[18] There is now an acknowledgment among global policy discourses and actors that the urban question is central to social and environmental futures, most notably in the emergence of the standalone urban Sustainable Development Goal (SDG) "to make cities safe, inclusive, resilient, and sustainable." The arrival of the urban in the global development agenda reflected many years of campaigning, and constitutes an important opportunity, as Sue Parnell has argued, to shape "how we think and act collectively in, on, and through cities."[19] As Ash Amin asserts, the challenge here is how to understand and intervene in the city and larger urban condition as an "ontology of world-making."[20] Understanding how the urban world is lived, changing, and politicized is a fundamental task not just for urbanists but for anyone concerned about the human condition and its futures.[21] Part of my argument is that fragment urbanism is an important stake in this debate.

Second, I use "urban world" as a name for the myriad forms of *being urban* today. Attending to fragments reveals some of the ways in which inhabitants are variously " 'written' into the fabric of urban life," performing different kinds of urbanism and possibility.[22] To focus on the urban world as so many ways of "being urban" means centering on how the urban is thought, experienced, expressed, and politicized across different spaces and through different actors, from residents and activists to artists, writers, and more. The material and knowledge fragments of the city exceed any one narrative, explanation, or lens on the urban world. Refugees forced from Syria ending up in Berlin live a particular instantiation of the urban world that differs from the experiences of low-income residents trying to develop coping strategies or forms of politicization in Mumbai or Kampala. Writing the urban world through fragments is a form of expression that works with "and"—through a generative archive of knowledge characterized by combination, resonance, and possibility, rather than analytical reduction, removal, and "tidying up."

The term "urban world" is not, then, only intended to refer to encounters between the urban and the global, which has been the focus of much debate in urban scholarship in recent years.[23] In contrast, my approach is to narrate a form of urban world that does not need a specifically "global" signature. I am not arguing against the use of terms like "global urbanism" or "planetary urbanization," which have become popularized in recent years. Indeed, the spirit with which I use "urban world" resonates with some uses of "global urbanism." Global urbanism is a useful shorthand for how cities are produced through all kinds of often deeply unequal and power-laden relations to elsewhere, and I have used it in my own work.[24] I use "world" as a grounded and revisable term for a field of fragment urbanisms. It signifies multiplicity and uncertainty, and the challenge of generating insight into a set of conditions that remain nonetheless epistemologically ungovernable. The world is thorny, sharp, ranging, dynamic, and shifting in its relations, producing different configurations, conflicts, and alliances, exceeding particular conceptual and analytic frames.[25]

The instances of fragment urbanism gathered in the book are a set of experiences and politics that resonate with one another rather than share a particular rationality or form. By "resonate" I have in mind a version of William Connolly's "resonance machine." For Connolly, "resonance" captures the amplifying interactions within and between different processes, which he calls the "rhythms of inter-infusion." Resonance is a useful term because it holds onto a sense of the particularity of context while recognizing echoes across the world.[26] It helps in appreciating that while the urban problematics of refugee struggles in Berlin or sanitation politics in Mumbai or Cape Town are radically distinct in their histories and contemporary configurations, there is nonetheless a reverberation between these experiences and politics that revolves around the struggle to live with and address fragmented provisions, or to bring knowledge fragments into greater prominence in the production, planning, and running of the city. As an experience at the urban margins, for example, fragment urbanism is a world process, in that there are resonances in conditions across urban space. But at the same time, it is irreducibly and radically multiple. Teresa Caldiera's invocation of a juxtaposition of singularities is useful here: cases that are particular but which also speak out beyond their locales and cities to stories elsewhere as part of a resonating urban archive, and which open up possibilities for understanding.[27]

The version of the urban world I develop derives not from a particular body of theory or practice, but from a loose and plural bundle of experiences, ideas, practices, and politics reflecting different ways of inhabiting or disrupting urbanism.[28] Writing the urban world here emerges from—as I outline in the next section, *Pulling together, falling apart*—working with ideas of fragmentation, fragments, densities, and social infrastructures, and the relations between and around them, as well as in different ways of expressing and locating fragments such as writing and walking that I examine later in the book. Rather than a singular understanding of the urban world, what surfaces is a provisional construction of urbanism that is differently pulling together and falling apart, at times destructive and at others generative.[29] This is a version of the urban world as a vast constellation of situated processes, as a provisional and sometimes difficult to discern and distill realm where differentiations neither add up to a neat total nor remain fixed, and which can provide clues to alternative urban futures.[30] The urban world surfaces as a pluriverse that is always moving, a "multiplicity of stories-so-far" and "coeval becomings," a "throwntogetherness," as Doreen Massey put it in a different context, of power-geometries that present all manner of openings and closures.[31]

The urban condition—or for that matter the city, or urbanization—does not operate, Ash Amin argues, like a "mechanical entity such as a clock" that can be made "transparent in all its workings," and any epistemology will at best only ever illuminate quite particular kinds of logics, systems, networks, and entities.[32] As the critique from a set of distinct positions has surely taught us—including, for instance, postcolonial, feminist, and queer debates—the ways in which the urban, city, or urbanization is conceived and takes place require at the very least a modest and provisional view, and one that tries to remain open to an expanding range of perspectives.[33] Fragment urbanism is a position that stays with the incomplete, power-laden multi-city, an urbanism that must work with "partial and adjusted insights" and the recognition that the "urban" is always plural and provisional.[34] I see this book as part of a genre of urban knowledge that, as Amin argues, posits a "modest and experimental style of knowing and acting in the world."[35] This is partly what Warren Magnusson gets at when he writes about the potential of "seeing like a city," which he argues "is to accept a certain disorderliness, unpredictability, and multiplicity as inevitable, and to pose the problem of politics in relation to that complexity."[36]

The urban world tends to be carved into imaginative geographies of global South and North, but those stubborn categories are becoming increasingly undone as archipelagos of wealth and poverty trouble at where and how the "South" and "North" show up, in ways that defy their status as geographical signifiers. As Jean and John Comaroff argue, the "hungry, unwaged, and unhoused" are increasingly numerous across the North.[37] Fragment urbanism is increasingly important to urban lives in the global North. The growing dominance of lean urbanization has left millions, from Athens to Glasgow or Detroit, struggling for basic urban life support like food, heating, clothing, and decent housing, and increasingly shunted to the spatial and economic margins of cities.[38] At the same time, increasing numbers of refugees, displaced by violence, intolerance, and minimal economic opportunities, are often forced into makeshift camps or other poorly serviced spaces and neighborhoods. At least one in a hundred people in the world have been forcibly displaced from their homes and live as internal or external refugees, and a record number of asylum seekers arrived in Europe over the past couple of decades, mainly from Syria, Iraq, and Afghanistan,[39] while two thirds of refugees worldwide live in urban areas.[40]

The interspersing of global South and North that we see in the distributions and experiences of inequality, wealth, and poverty prompt us to ask whether the categories of North and South are worth holding onto at all. The categories also starkly misalign with different regional formations, such as industrial and social transformations in East Asia or political change in the Middle East or Turkey.⁴¹. While for some, cities in the global South represent a particular "type" of human settlement, and "southern urbanism" is a set of tendencies that mark out cities in the global South as divergent from cities in the global North,⁴² it may make more sense to think of "the global South" as a "concept-metaphor," not a place but a signifier for critiquing and displacing inherited positions on what the North and South might be, and for developing new understandings and directions.⁴³

The question of South and North is also institutional, not only epistemic, and my own position in all of this is clearly one of privilege. I have been able to travel to multiple cities across the urban world, and to access knowledge resources and networks too often denied to many scholarly institutions in the South, and to some in the North. The arguments presented in this book were written with the support of an elite institution in the UK. I write too as a white man, and there is no doubt that the work I've been able to do, and the doors that have opened, have emerged in part from that. And so this is very much a book from the institutional and epistemic entanglements of a particular global North. As I try to reflect on how fragment urbanism operates in and from different places in the urban world, I have been guided by an effort to understand how it is shaped, experienced, and perceived in different cities by residents, activists, practitioners, writers, artists, and others, but this is nonetheless my account of particular aspects of the urban world.

The arguments in this book are informed by different traditions of urban thinking and research, including postcolonial, post-structural, and post-Marxist perspectives. This includes work ranging from subaltern studies and critical urban development to urban political ecology, and thinkers as different as Walter Benjamin, Henri Lefebvre, Gilles Deleuze, Elizabeth Grosz, and Rebecca Solnit. I do not adopt any particular theoretical tradition or perspective, nor is the work influenced by any one thinker, although at times in the writing of the book Benjamin's work was especially important. My approach has been to try to see the connections and synergies between different perspectives and traditions, notwithstanding their undoubted differences and, sometimes, downright contradictions. I have also tried to be open to other sources and voices beyond theory and research that shed light on fragment urbanism, including nonacademic urban writing, art, activism, poetry, music, and journalism. I have attempted, as much as is possible, to ensure that my interpretations do not render the cities in the text as passive illustrations of preestablished arguments I want to make, but as active and constitutive elements with at least some agency in the thinking and writing, even as the arguments and perspectives are surely animated by my own personal dispositions, politics, and background.

Pulling Together, Falling Apart

We discover possibilities for how human life can be reshaped out of its very vulnerability—out of the lengths that individuals go in order to piece together a barely viable urban existence out of fragments, and the kinds of abstractions they stitch together among characters of all kinds.

—AbdouMaliq Simone and Edgar Pieterse,
  New Urban Worlds

Materializing the City

As the monsoon rains soaked the ground in Mandala, Mumbai, they worked through the night and day rebuilding their homes. Women, men, and children, frustrated and tired of waiting for government approval, having had their homes demolished by the municipality nine years earlier, returned to claim the space they had once called home. After a decade of legal disputes and protests, a thousand families—around a fifth of those originally displaced—rebuilt their homes on the vacant land. Despite the support by housing movements in the city and local media coverage, the reoccupation only lasted a few days. The police returned with bulldozers to bring down the makeshift housing and leave the residents amidst the broken pieces.

In the low-income neighborhood of Namuwongo, Kampala, residents woke in the middle of the night to find trucks and tractors outside their homes. As the demolition got underway, and homes came crashing down, they roused their children, grabbed what they could, and got out. Local civil society groups provided temporary financial support for residents to cover rent in hastily arranged places nearby. The money helped, but it takes longer than a few months for people to get back on their feet after such an ordeal. When demolitions occur on the wetland or railway lands in Namuwongo, compensation is rare because much of the "occupation"—as with Mandala—is deemed "illegal" by the state authorities. In the absence of adequate compensation, here too the residents were left with little more than the shattered remains of their homes.

A few thousand kilometers away in Berlin, another set of constructions were underway. Refugee camps were hastily built in a pressured effort to accommodate Syrian refugees who sought to make the city a home, at least for a while. In Moabit, central Berlin, exhausted refugees huddled outside the State Office for Health and Social Services, waiting over the long cold winter to be registered and allocated shelter. The group, including children and pregnant women, slept on vacant land, sometimes for weeks. For a period, there were no provisions for toilets, food, blankets, or shelter, save one water tap of dubious quality. When I went to interview a local NGO at the site, conditions were improving. "You should have been here six months ago, because this was a slum," Christiane Beckman, a local activist, told me. If in Mandala and Namuwongo residents were left with homes destroyed, here refugees struggled without shelter and with paltry portions of "infrastructure."

In Kosovo, a neighborhood of Cape Town, a group of activists demolished five hundred "bucket toilets" delivered by the city council. The activists involved said they would no longer settle for substandard shared infrastructure, insisting that the state should provide the kind of "flush toilets" for each household found in wealthier and predominantly white neighborhoods: "We are not happy until one family, one toilet," one activist said. The demolition—an act not of mindless violence, as some authorities sought to describe it, but a political act of infrastructural sabotage—came on the back of a spate of radical protests in the city around the inequalities of sanitation provision. In these protests, activists rejected having to be subjected to working with overburdened pieces of sanitation—bucket toilets reminiscent of apartheid-era provisions—and instead claimed a different kind of urban settlement and provision.

These four distinct cases, from Mumbai, Kampala, Berlin, and Cape Town, are shaped by their own histories and struggles.[1] In each, there is a struggle to build or defend housing, toilets, and other basic provisions. The cases, all in cities in which I have conducted collaborative research of different kinds, resonate as a larger claim to the city that echoes across the urban world. They are claims that both depart from and use density as an urban force, drawing in social infrastructures of support. We know that the estimates of the numbers living in often precarious "informal" neighborhoods are unreliable, but the direction of travel cannot be doubted: from approximately 880 million in 2014 to over three billion by 2050.[2]

The key drivers vary from place to place, but there are some common causes at work, including: exclusion from land security and decent housing, leaving more and more people in insecure, rented homes; a lack of affordable food, infrastructure, and services, with the basics often becoming more expensive for lower-income groups; local and central states that lack the resources or political will to seriously tackle poverty and inequality, or which have cut public services and provisions in favor of market-based approaches; the operation of cultural power that exploits and excludes on the basis of gender, race, ethnicity, sexuality, religion, disability, or age, and more. Fragments on the economic margins of the city are expressions of inequality and poverty, and the legacies of powerful historical injustices—colonialism, structural adjustment, rounds of capitalist urbanization and disinvestment, cultural politics of race, ethnicity, and so on—that have shaped how cities have been historically produced and structured. The future of the city is becoming increasingly linked to the fragment city. But how does one live in the fragment city, how is it being contested, and what forms of knowledge, practice, and possibility emerge when we examine it?

Urban Life Support

Early one morning, Raksha made her way to the local municipal toilet block in Mankhurd, Mumbai.[3] From the cubicle next to hers, she heard a crash, followed by a woman screaming. The toilet floor had broken and the woman, Kalgana Pingle, a 41-year-old widow with two children, had fallen into the septic tank below. She died from head injuries and suffocation. Residents had tried to help her out with a long bamboo stick, but by the time the fire brigade arrived it was too late. In the weeks following, Raksha said, she would hear Kalgana's cries in her head, and for the first few nights she couldn't sleep. The toilet structure, said Raksha, had been poorly built and ill maintained. The septic tank had not been cleared for a long time, the block was old and unclean. Blockages were treated using chemicals that further degraded the infrastructure. The women's section of the block was built directly above the septic tank, so when the floor weakened through time a death trap had been created. The Brihanmumbai Municipal Corporation (BMC) sought to avoid responsibility, and pointed instead to the nongovernmental organization that had built the block through a BMC-run sanitation construction program.[4]

The collapse happened in Mankhurd, a low-income neighborhood in M-East. Most of Mumbai's poorest residents live in the northeast of the city, especially in M-East ward. While M-East is large and varied, it is an area with some of the city's lowest scores for "human development," the highest rates of infant mortality, and an "increasing social trauma

FIGURE 2. Toilet block in Rafiq Nagar, Mumbai (Photo by Renu Desai)

of visible inequity."[5] The most basic of provisions are often fragmented and unreliable. In the poorest neighborhoods, which are also some of the densest in the city, housing is rudimentary and people are frequently forced to find and use whatever available spaces they can as toilets, often at great risk, especially for women and girls who routinely suffer harassment and abuse, including near railway tracks, under bridges, at garbage grounds, and near riverbanks.[6] Where toilets are available, they typically take the form of one- or two-floor community toilet blocks of different sizes, structures often poorly maintained and unclean with frequently long queues and times of inordinately heavy use (Figure 2).

There are few cities in the world where the juxtaposition of toiling poverty and bloated wealth are so starkly materialized as Mumbai, and where inequalities in urban life support—basic provisions of decent housing, water, sanitation, energy, food, and income—are so glaring. The city is home to Bollywood and the stock market, and is one of the planet's most unequal in property prices, income, and access to infrastructures and services.[7] Historical processes of fragmentation have produced staggering geographies of density in the city. While an estimated 55 percent of the city's residents live in low-income neighborhoods and 10 percent are confined to a life on pavements—all squeezed into an astoundingly concentrated 8 percent of the land—the city is host to the world's most expensive private home, corporate India's celebrated Mukesh Ambani's US$700 million twenty-seven-floor mansion.[8] As Arundhati Roy has put it, wealth doesn't trickle down, it gushes up.[9]

A year on from Kalgana Pingle's horrific death, Raksha reflected, sanitation conditions had not improved in her neighborhood. The consequence of one block closing was even greater pressure on the other public toilet that remained, and a visible increase in open defecation in the area. The problematic of density and sanitation had intensified. The BMC provided a temporary mobile toilet with five seats each for men and women, but it was rarely cleaned, was infested with insects, the plastic floor became broken, and residents had to bring their own water. One woman badly injured her leg trying to walk down the steep steps to the toilet, and Raksha spoke of how her grandmother had been injured falling from the toilet. The exit pipe was left to drain into the open outside the structure. In response to one broken infrastructure, here was another disconnected and broken provision that barely provided for the neighborhood.

Eventually the toilet was removed and replaced with a state-built toilet, but this too was poorly maintained, had no light, and again the pipe was left to drain outside the toilet. Residents paid BMC road sweepers to informally clean the toilets. From her house in the morning, it takes Raksha around half an hour to walk to the structure and wait in line to use it: "If you have a running stomach you can imagine what happens." There are just two toilet blocks in the area for around four hundred households. However limited they are, these structures are important forms of urban life support. The difference, however, reflected Raksha, is that these provisions have become more intensely politicized. Raksha became a volunteer with a high-profile community-based organization that runs a successful toilet block in the west of the city, Triratna Prerana Mandal (TPM). TPM opened a discussion with BMC officials, albeit a slow and frustrating one for residents, and helped form a community-based organization. Their work sought to attend to existing provisions and to interrupt the repeated process of substandard inadequate systems being replaced by similar forms, and to push for new forms of urban provision that might adequately cater to the densities of the neighborhood.

When does an urban provision, such as a toilet block, become a fragment? A new toilet block is often welcomed as vital in a neighborhood in which there is significant pressure on existing provisions. It may be, initially at least, a kind of whole, functional and well connected to other infrastructures such as water, drainage, sewerage, and electricity. In practice, however, such provisions are often not well integrated with other systems. Very often, new toilet blocks lack sewer connections, and may be connected to septic tanks that are quickly overwhelmed.[10] The structure may then become blocked, and left out of use for a period of time. Or, the water taps may not work, or the electricity connections might be unreliable, meaning that at night—and for women and girls in particular—the block is difficult and risky to use, partly due to sexual harassment and violence.[11] In Mumbai, 78 percent of community toilets lack a water supply and 58 percent have no electricity.[12] In particularly dense neighborhoods where the use of the structure might be intense, other problems often quickly emerge. Doors become loosened from hinges. Cleaning provisions run low. Many don't have provisions for women to dispose of sanitary products. Sections of the block are closed off for repair work. Disputes might break out about responsibility for maintenance. In extreme cases, structures deteriorate to the point of collapse. The tragic story around Kalgana's death is not an isolated case.

In 1997, a group of civil society organizations, assessing sanitation to poor neighborhoods in Mumbai, asked a question that still resonates, despite the subsequent moves by the municipality to better involve civil society groups in sanitation production and management in the city:[13] "You call this thing a 'civic amenity'? The government's systems for building public toilets are designed to benefit the contractors, not the cities and certainly not the poor families who have to live with the stinky, sub-standard, broken-down toilet disasters."[14] The idea of the "civic amenity" connects to a long history of urban sanitation provisioning in cities across the world, and in particular to an imaginary of the whole in the modern city: integrated infrastructures, embedded in well-connected systems, able not just to meet the needs of all users but to support and enable urban life and circulation.

A fragment is not just a piece broken off or a portion left over. It can also—and I will return to this in more detail in the *Knowing fragments* section—be an *incomplete form* (noun) and a *process of breaking up* (verb). Provisions such as a toilet block often inhabit the edges between "fragment" and "whole." They are ambivalent structures. The biography of a toilet block in a dense, poor neighborhood—and, indeed, often in busy parts of city centers across the world—can be one of moving in and out of being a fragment or a whole. Fragments act as such not only as a result of their physical form but also because of how they operate in the context of the area, as partial and radically insufficient. Defining the status of a given provision, then, demands not an objective definition or imaginary of "the toilet block," but an investigation into how the form is differently instantiated over time and space. Urban geographical realities are pivotal here, not the semantic certainty of parsing out this or that object as a fragment. From the ground of how many residents experience toilet blocks on the economic margins of lots of cities, toilet blocks are, in practice, inadequate, incomplete, and breaking up: *fragments*. Or, at least, ambivalent fragments, shunting between something that is sometimes complete, integrated, and connected, and sometimes severed, partial, demanding repair, or unusable.

M-East is also host to Deonar, a large garbage ground located just a few miles from Mandala. The ground takes on 9,000 metric tons of waste a day, could accommodate 268 football fields, and rises to a height equivalent to between 18 and 20 floors, prompting aviation authorities to raise concerns about the proximity of circling birds as planes come and go from the city's airport.[15] The garbage ground was said to be "exhausted" in 2016, but the city's High Court allowed the municipality to continue using it while alternative sites were being developed, and while the municipality plans for a new waste-to-energy plant in Deonar from 2023.

Deonar began operation in 1927 and is the largest municipal garbage ground in India, a vast accumulation of waste with a huge urban economy of recyclers, organized through a complex arrangement of private companies, gangs, and municipal officials (Figure 3). This is where the solid waste of Mumbai comes to be recycled, where glass, plastic, metals, and even the occasional piece of gold or diamond jewelry are segregated, recalibrated, then redistributed through the informal and formal economies in the city and beyond. The site is a density of people, waste, and fragments, where work and livelihood are intimately tied to the embodied encounters with broken, discarded, ruined, and wasted organic and inorganic materials.

The garbage ground has always been a controversial site in the city, for all sorts of social, economic, and environmental reasons that collec-

FIGURE 3. Deonar waste ground, Mumbai (Photo by author)

tively hold its future in constant question, but it has rarely been so controversial as it has been in recent years. In 2015, for example, two large fires on the ground churned out enormous quantities of smoke and left a thick fog across swathes of the east of the city. The voices in the media demanding that the garbage ground be shut down intensified, and residents—particularly middle-class residents—led protests through the city, raising concerns over the health of their children and the seeming inability of the municipality to act. Few were sure why the fires started, although one rumor had it that it had been an act of sabotage between rival gangs of recyclers. For many of the residents who live—and make a living—as recyclers along the garbage ground, there have always been fires on the ground: it's just part of what people have to deal with living in a largely impoverished and neglected part of the city.

At Deonar, the wastes of the city are transformed and metabolized through bodies, air, and informal organizations of labor. While the smoke from the fire got the city's attention, residents are forced to deal with the wastes and ecologies around them every day, including inadequate sanitation and one of the highest rates of multi-drug-resistant TB in the city. Respiratory problems are exacerbated by a nearby medical waste incinerator. More than half of the residents in M-East, reports the Tata Institute of Social Sciences, have had heart disease, diabetes, respiratory problems including TB, and high blood pressure.[16] One NGO, Apnalaya, puts life expectancy in the area at a shocking 39 years, as compared to 73 for Maharashtra, the state of which Mumbai is the capital, more generally.[17]

Some women are forced to use the garbage ground as a toilet. Finding privacy poses risks of being bitten by aggressive stray dogs, falling into deep ditches, and sinking into the garbage, especially during the monsoons, as well as harassment, abuse, and rape. For many women, disposing human waste involves clambering over the city's solid waste, the same waste they might be later wading through in order to make a living. Everyday life entails an immersion in a back-and-forth between different forms of waste, hazard, and the generation of value from waste. Violence and risk are central to the ways in which human waste is metabolized, especially for women and girls.

Most people in nearby Rafiq Nagar, for example, are Muslim, in a city dominated by a Hindu-chauvinist political party, the Shiv Sena, and the neighborhood is "illegal" in the eyes of the state. "The narrow lanes of Rafiq Nagar are flanked by clogged drains and heaps of garbage," writes Shraddha Agarwal in *Counterpunch*, "the smell from the dumping ground hangs heavy in the air. Swarms of flies and mosquitoes hover everywhere." Agarwal describes how one woman—Kitabun Nisa Shaikh—has labored to make a living and care for children amid garbage collection and forms of exploitative manual labor, a precarious house that floods with wastewater during heavy rains, an abusive husband, religious violence, and family members with TB. "I was born in garbage, I'll die in garbage," she tells Agarwal.[18]

People were taken from the inner city and "dumped here on the dumping ground," one staff member from Apnalaya told me in 2016—this is "cleaning the city," and it is a religious politics: "Eighty-five percent are Muslim, the remaining are Dalits." Nearby Lotus Colony was originally a resettlement colony, the residents being displaced here from Worli, an economically better-off area closer to town. Now they live a stone's throw from the garbage ground. Kumar sees a wider logic of urban development in Mumbai at play in the co-location of the city's waste and displaced residents: "This is not a coincidence," he insists. There is some hope, he added, in alternative political parties like the Samajwadi Party, a socialist party that claims to represent minority groups, but they are up against a powerful and deeply ingrained politics embodied in the governing Shiv Sena.

In Rafiq Nagar, fragments are metabolized as a set of material, atmospheric, bodily, cultural, and economic entanglements that reproduce existing sociospatial inequalities, while at the same time providing residents an opening to—and at least some kind of foothold in—the city. It is true that people living in neighborhoods like Rafiq Nagar are skilled in using fragments of resource from water, energy, and waste in careful, calculated forms of reuse, distribution, and recalibration, often having to improvise and becoming what Gaia Vince calls the "most sustainable" of Anthropocenic urbanisms.[19] This view, though, is too celebratory, given the fierce experiences of fragment urbanism. It is a place of hazards and risk, and a place at risk. It is in marginalized neighborhoods such as Rafiq Nagar that residents often suffer the harshest consequences of rising sea levels, warming temperatures, flash flooding, landslides, the challenges of living with increasingly scare natural resources like water, urban air pollution (the Deonar fires being a case in point), and of course the growing threat of livelihoods and homes lost as cities seek to "clean up" in all-too-familiar ways. Here, everyday life and work casts fragment urbanism as a violent metabolics accompanied by the threat of removal and displacement, a de-densification that brings its own violences.

There is an archipelago geography of infrastructural provision in the neighborhood. Across the road from one of the entrances to Deonar, for example, is the *Jal Jeevan (Water is Life)* water plant. The small plant, paid for not by the state but by corporate social responsibility funding, provides a limited provision of subsidized clean water in the area. It was delivered with Apnalaya in conjunction with the Rotary Club and the Eureka Forbes Institute of Environment, and is run by a local women's group, Muskan Mahila Buchat Ghat (Smile Women's Savings group), which has been active since 2008.

The local women who run the plant explained that in an area where water pipelines are often contaminated by sewage, the plant is vitally important. The water is purchased from municipal water tankers twice a day. It is then purified through an impressive-looking piece of machinery at the back of the small store through several stages of filtration: a sand filter to remove visible matter, a carbon filter to remove oil or color pollutants, and then ultra-filtration blocks to remove micro-remnants. Then it is treated in a UV section to get rid of any final contaminants. In order to maintain the cleanliness of the water, residents are required to use the Jal Jeevan plastic containers and not their own. The women are constantly cleaning the plant, and disinfectant hangs in the air. Residents can pay in one of two ways, either by cash or "ATM," a machine and card system that allows members to use a separate tap and skip the queue. It is a highly particular sanitized infrastructure in the area, made up of a distinct assemblage of machinery, rhythm, atmosphere, symbolism, and regulation. When I spoke to the women in 2016, there were 500 registered customers, around 300 of whom used it regularly. It was rare for there to be queues, but some days the water might run out early or a municipal water tanker might fail to turn up, creating a buildup of people. The tankers are unreliable—if they don't turn up, the plant sometimes has to close. The municipality was planning on adding GPS trackers to tankers to make sure that drivers are not selling illegally, as part of the city's "smart city" initiatives.

Of course, this is a selective provision; many residents further into the neighborhood, or living along the garbage ground and who are usually poorer, do not use the facility, and live a different kind of sanitation and water experience from some of their nearby neighbors. The water is only marginally more expensive than other sources of water in the area (Rs. 10 for a 20-liter container of purified water), but this is a neighborhood with one of the highest child mortality rates in the city, where families often have to choose among buying either clean water or food or medicine. In the wider geography of water provisions and improvisations in M-East, the Jal Jeevan plant dramatizes the ambivalence of fragments: an apparent whole—a generally well-functioning provision—but which operates in practice as a fragment, sometimes ceasing operation and never quite being able to provide to enough people enough of the time.

The women running the plant were clear that while the plant was welcome, it was nowhere near enough—many residents couldn't benefit either due to where they lived or the costs, and the sanitation conditions in the area remain poor. Many toilet blocks lack water, and those that have it often have unclean water—sometimes black in color—which is used to "clean" it. The contrast between the purified water in the plant, with its own infrastructure of buckets, and the unclean water in public toilets, was keenly felt by the women. The key challenge, they reflected, was the municipality—its fractured provisions, and its lack of maintenance of what does exist.

Families in Rafiq Nagar earn roughly Rs. 100–150 per day, a substantial amount of which goes to water and kerosene. While Mumbai gets an average water supply of 200 liters per person per day, the city's "slums" receive less than 90 liters, and often nothing at all.[20] The metabolic violence of the highly prescribed and patchwork geography of provisioning are felt differently across the neighborhood. Back in 2011, the *Hindustan Times* "Hunger Project" featured a story about local resident Aasma Sheikh. She was the mother of Gulnaz, a severely malnourished child. Malnutrition here is common, a product of poor sanitation conditions and often crippling poverty. Aasma was prescribed medicines to treat the illnesses that she, Gulnaz, and her other children suffered from and which were exacerbated by malnutrition, but the cost of water meant that she could not afford to buy them. She had to spend Rs. 30–40 on water per day, and was faced with the choice: water or medicine. Tragically, the child later died.

Following the *Hindustan Times* report, state women and child development minister Varsha Gaikwad visited Rafiq Nagar, but no change followed and the deaths from a combination of malnutrition, poor sanitation, and low incomes have continued, including occasional diseases such as TB and cholera.[21] In fact, local NGOs have insisted that the situation is getting worse. The attention, sadly, comes and goes, and the struggles of many residents, who live day-to-day to meet basic metabolic needs from a set of often untenable and unevenly distributed provisions on small incomes, continue. One activist at an NGO described Rafiq Nagar as "mindless urbanization," a critique not of the residents themselves but of the state for allowing a situation in which there are people without resources and places lacking decent, reliable infrastructure and services. It is likely that we will see more plants like Jal Jeevan crop up (it is not the first in M-East), paid through corporate social responsibility, before we see the necessary substantial state investment in the water and sanitation needs of residents living in the neighborhoods around the garbage ground.

Volumetric Urbanism

The geography of fragment urbanism is as much vertical as it is horizontal, from the drains, pipes, sewers, and septic tanks beneath the ground, to the mountain of waste at Deonar, to neglected and dilapidated housing blocks that stretch above ground. The forty-five-floor Torre de David building in central Caracas has been a home for squatters since 2007. The building, which was intended as an office and commercial complex but was never completed following the Venezuelan banking crisis in 1994, has been described variously as a self-organized community, a vertical slum, a massive squat, and as a potential model for the future use of empty buildings.[22] In this vast space, residents have improvised and organized social infrastructures to run the building, socialize its spaces, run gyms and churches, and develop economic activity from shops to hairdressers, drawing on their previous experience of incremental housing in the city's barrios.

As Urban Think Tank, an architectural group based in Caracas led by Alfredo Brillembourg and Hubert Klumpner, have shown, all manner of fragments have been used, adapted, produced, and set in different contexts and roles. Fragments of materials have been used to strengthen stairs, balconies, and hallways. Some residents have used "scavenged trusses, PVC pipes, and unmortared bricks, to varying degrees of stability and durability."[23] Windows found in the building have become mirrors. Walls have been broken down while others have been built up, through simple partitions or in red brick, to create privacy, while some residents have installed floating ceilings. Some of the building's air conditioning units have been dismantled and their parts reused. Arno Schlueter et al. argue that "the only truly static element in Torre David is the concrete structure—everything else is in flux," a lively space of active construction and adaptation, and a particular form of what Donald McNeill has described as "volumetric urbanism."[24] Across the building, a delicate and variegated interplay of fragments, architecture, and social rhythm has emerged as an ongoing set of collective undertakings (Figure 4).

This has also involved negotiating all manner of risks. Urban Think Tank describes some of the risks that residents deal with every day, many of them connected to the verticality of the structure:

> Many floors remain partially open to the outside, with no dividing walls; glass panels of the façade have been removed to increase air circulation, leaving gaping holes to the outside. And while some residents have implemented their own safety measures by erecting short brick balcony walls, the possibility of a fatal fall calls for constant vigilance. This ubiquitous danger is compounded by unexpected holes in the floors, encountered throughout the building. The stairs lack handrails, although residents are in the process of constructing their own. Elevator shafts remain open in many instances.[25]

Part of Urban Think Tank's work has been to support existing infrastructures and suggest others to residents, such as rainwater harvesting, while also looking to replace "shoddy and dangerous construction materials and methods" with "a factory-built kit of components, whose assemblage is familiar to barrio residents and which accommodate small-scale development and dramatically enhance building quality."[26] As Torre de David indicates, improvisation can be important for the making and remaking of fragment urbanisms. From toilets to vertical neighborhoods, fragment urbanism is often a process of dealing with hazards, calculating risks, and having to improvise. In conditions of sharp inequality and profound poverty, improvisation is not a process to romanticize. We hear plenty of boosterist talk about improvisation from all kinds of state and nonstate actors in cities, whether in relation to urban creativity or innovation businesses, or proliferating interventions self-described as urban experimentation, entrepreneurialism, living labs, incubators, and more.[27] In the context of urban poverty and marginality, improvisation is frequently a forced urban experience.

The squat is a neighborhood and set of communities, with all the tensions and possibilities that brings. In this deeply fragmented city, it is also a viable form of urban inhabitation. In addition to the growing

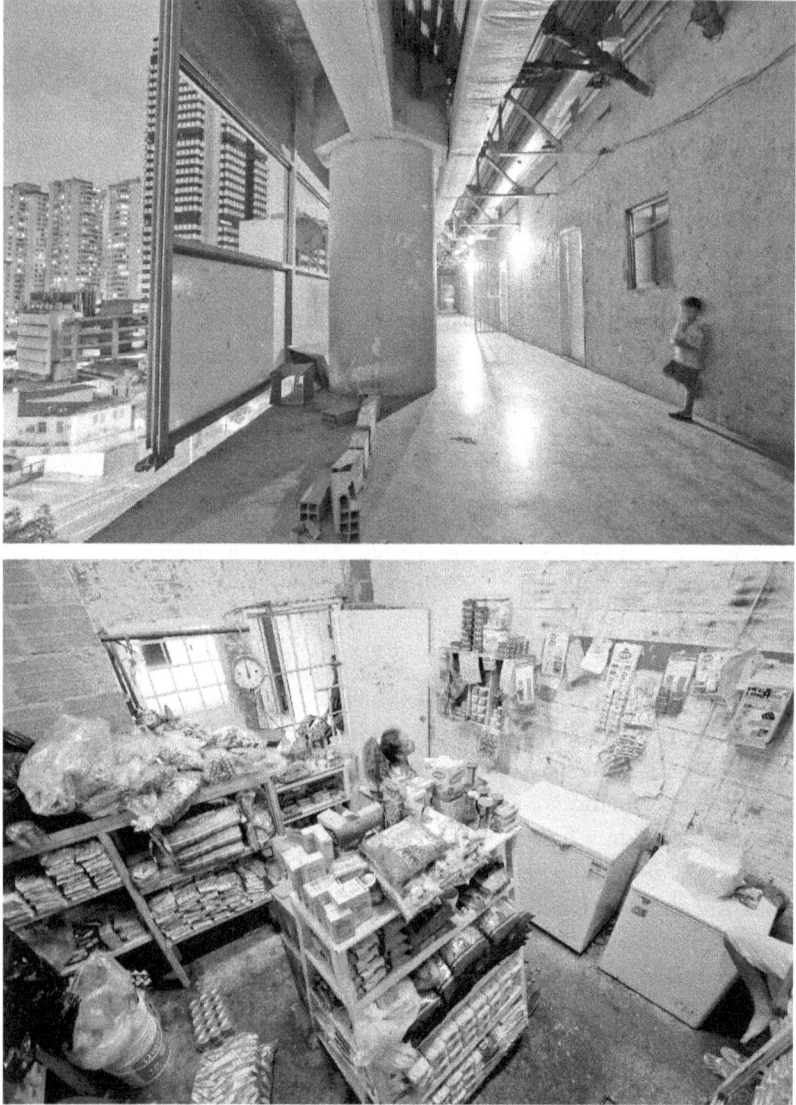

FIGURE 4. Inside Torre David (Copyright Daniel Schwartz)

housing market that priced out the urban poor, in Caracas the state, private sector, and wealthier groups have intensified the material and social architecture of fragmentation in the past quarter century: "Contemporary Caracas . . . is among the most fragmented cities in its politics, economy, culture, and urban fabric. Major roadways cut through the urban fabric, isolating communities from one another. Fearful for their safety, people gravitate to shopping malls, bubbles of civic life insulated from the violence of the street."[28] As markers of urban inequality, these "bubbles" are volumetric geographies expressing distinct forms and realities of urban living.

Fragmenting Cities

Cities are continually falling apart and coming together. The city is a fundamental theatre for the drama of fragmentation, a pivotal site for its production, spatialities, and politics.[29] Think, for example, of how the city has in so many places become carved up and divided into "gated enclaves," often securitized and fenced off, or made exclusive through processes of gentrification and real estate speculation that push land and housing prices to points where lower-income residents are shunted out, or how urban space and living becomes "splintered" due to the privatization or commodification of infrastructures or public spaces that have become increasingly expensive.[30]

The research on urban "fragmentation" is vast, from accounts of segregation in colonial and militarized cities, or histories of political and economic transformations that have sought to ideologically remake urban areas, to the emergence of spatial fragmentation as a signature feature of the post-Fordist neoliberal city.[31] Research, for example, on how cultures, economies, and practices of securitization fragment urban space and socialities, from "fortress LA" to "fortified fragments" of housing, neighborhoods, and public space in São Paulo.[32] Or the considerable research on the fragmentation of infrastructure and services through what Stephen Graham and Simon Marvin describe as the collapse—insofar as it ever existed—of the "modern infrastructural ideal" of universal provision, driven by the economic restructuring of water, energy, transport, telecommunications, and more.[33] As Henri Lefebvre argued, capitalism actively requires the fragmentation of urban space in order to sustain itself, from the shuffling and displacing of densities of labor to the targeting of particular places for speculation and economic surplus.[34]

Fragmentation is increasingly driven by real estate speculation of different kinds, and by economies, cultures and politics of expulsion, demolition, and selective inclusion.[35] While global real estate makes up 60 percent of the world's assets, 75 percent of which is in housing, for growing numbers of people city life is increasingly about watching on as exclusive urban forms sprout up around them while they scrape by in often poorly provisioned neighborhoods.[36] New upmarket apartment blocks in Mumbai may intensify vertical densities in some areas while pushing lower-income residents into poorer areas, including often already highly dense informal neighborhoods.[37] For Andy Merrifield, writing in *The New Urban Question,* there is a global process of "neo-Haussmanization" at work here, a contemporary incarnation of the redevelopment of Paris in the nineteenth century but one that entails a predatory speculative real estate and financial capitalism operating on a global scale.[38] As Merrifield vividly argues, a small elite feeds off the city for massive financial returns— a process he refers to as a "parasitic city"—in which land, housing, and infrastructure are increasingly subjected to forms of "speculative urbanism" that drive up prices to access and leave growing numbers of residents with often substandard provisions.

This shuffling of densities is masked by a particular kind of "density fetishism" that provides certain kinds of "greenwashed" densities for the relatively well off and leaves the poor in often dense, underprovided suburbs of often fragmented homes and infrastructures.[39] Fragmentation is a simultaneously economic, political, social, and ecological transformation of space. As Hussain Indorewala has argued in relation to Mumbai, the economic exclusion of the urban poor from profitable areas of the city is accompanied by the production of "scarcity" of land—which in fact often reflects the locking-up of land for "higher end" economic gain rather than the physical availability of it—and ecological damage:

> To profit from land, the first step is to make it *appear* scarce. So how will Mumbai produce "affordable" housing? By filling up salt-pan lands. How will we build metro yards? By levelling and concretising our forests. How will we carve out highways? By reclaiming the coast. How will we house our millions? By snatching away land from the poor and stacking them in penal conditions. Meanwhile, all the land that lies under-used such as the defunct

mills, the port, BKC [Bandra-Kurla Complex], on the mainland, will make way—"more gainfully"—for commercial complexes, luxury housing, and shopping malls.[40]

Such speculation also includes the fragments of previous rounds of capital accumulation—dilapidated industrial units, decaying factories, crumbling warehouses, and office blocks—now plugged into new forms of creative labor, startups, and "incubation" spaces, backed up by city governments, including advertising, art, media, software, fundraising, and sharing economies. As Richard Williams has put it, "The spectacle of creative workers bashing away on their laptops amidst industrial ruins of the city is one of the twenty-first century's great urban clichés."[41] We see cases of this across the world, from Amsterdam to Berlin and Sydney, and they too sometimes lead to shifts in land and property costs that result in social and spatial fragmentation. Sometimes, the speculation fails, and we end up with capitalist ruins that were never realized in the first place, and perhaps—like Torre David—even reappropriated for other ends.

Fragmentation is also shaped by a contingent set of cultural and social prejudices across race, ethnicity, gender, sexuality, religion, caste, and other vectors.[42] Both the causes and the consequences of fragmentation—in material, spatial, social, economic, and political terms—have been shown to be the articulations of place-specific histories and context, even as they shaped in part by translocal relations that might stretch across the world.[43] Take, for example, Kampala, a city I will return to later. Kampala is not a megacity, nor is it especially prominent in the trajectories of global urban policy or research debate, but it is a vital East African metropolis that is quickly growing (it has an annual population growth rate of 5 percent and over three million residents).[44] Redevelopment plans connected to the establishment of a new port, and attempts at "beautifying" the city—particularly through the all-too-familiar clamping down on street traders and other ongoing "urban renewal" processes, connected to a rise in the costs of housing—reinforce precarious conditions for many residents.[45] Street hawkers face harassment from Kampala Capital City Authority (KCCA) officials tasked to stop street trading in the central city, while lower-income young men often face harassment from the police.[46] The KCCA has increasingly focused on projects that "try to appeal to Uganda's urban middle class and elite, managing the city in their interest."[47]

Yet 60 percent of Kampala's residents live in over thirty informal neighborhoods across the city, with 39 percent living below the poverty line.[48]

Life in the city, for many, is a shared experience of fragmented basic provisions, the ongoing threat of evictions, and a sense that the dominant renderings of the city's future are not for them.[49] As Sarah Wallman has shown in her work on Kampala, while in some areas "most of the permanent houses have electricity, piped water, water closets, nearby soak-pits, hedges and/or security fences," in others—sometimes a street or two away—few of the semipermanent and more precarious housing and virtually none of the temporary structures have any of these.[50] The poorest houses are "congested with poorly constructed latrines and 'bathrooms' and the daily clutter of charcoal stoves, old plastic bags and piles of rubbish," with toilets "made of sacks, rags or papyrus reeds that seldom have roofs or doors," using curtains—*kanga* cloth—to cover entrances, often using open drains that run through public spaces.[51] The geography of fragment urbanism plays a role in the prevalence of illness and disease that Wallman reports, with her respondents often positioning malaria, dysentery, diarrhea, pneumonia, flu, and TB near the top of frequent health problems (all linked to inadequate sanitation in particular).[52]

Fragmentation in Kampala was exacerbated by the Structural Adjustment Programs (SAPs) imposed by the World Bank/IMF,[53] which played a role in underinvestment over decades, impacting for example the challenges faced in relation to the HIV/AIDS epidemic.[54] HIV prevalence increased from 6.4 percent in 2004–5 to 7.4 percent in 2012–13, and is higher in urban areas and among working-class groups.[55] As Rosalind Fredericks has argued, "The severe neoliberal experiments that African cities have undergone at the hands of international development loans operate through wasting spaces and bodies in the pursuit of economic growth that rarely materialize."[56] At the same time, social and spatial fragmentation in the city has been shaped by war, ethnic conflict, crises, and migration in Uganda and neighboring states, which has driven refugees into the city, including into segregated state-designated areas, and typically to neglected neighborhoods and precarious, low-paying informal jobs. For example, one Congolese refugee, Bridget, told Will Monteith and Shuaib Lwasa, "Kampala is not like Congo, here you have to buy everything— even drinking water . . . I remember we used to stay the whole day without eating because we did not have money. The rent also is very expensive; to get even a single room you have to pay Ush 100,000 [US$28] and the landlords keep increasing the price."[57] Fragmentation in Kampala both shares characteristics with other cities globally, and is locally distinct from the process in cities ranging from Mumbai and Lima to New York.

Fragmentation proceeds through changing geographies of densification and de-densification. As the world becomes increasingly urban, the dominant trend is for cities to expand rather than densify. As Shlomo Angel and colleagues have shown through population data and satellite maps, sprawl is outpacing densification across the world.[58] They have charted the rapid expansion, since 1990, of "new urban peripheries," and their findings suggest that these peripheries may have absorbed more newcomers than the older parts of cities.[59] They find too that from 1990 to 2014 cities have on average *doubled* their geographical areas in ways that planners did not anticipate or prepare for.[60] This is part of an urban explosion of what Roger Keil has called, building on Henri Lefebvre, "disjunct fragments" of peripheries and suburbs, a dynamic pattern of urbanization that transcends conventional distinctions between urban and rural, formal and informal, center and periphery.[61] The World Resources Institute has identified three interconnected drivers: developers speculating on land on the urban fringe as a way of extending real estate economies into new terrain; a lack of specificity in state or city policy and regulations on where new housing or other developments should be located; and a generally weak set of property rights among residents and landowners on urban peripheries.[62] Land speculation is of course not only a feature of city centers—indeed, as vital as the central city is in driving social and spatial fragmentation, it is only one site through which capitalist processes of what Neil Brenner and Christian Schmid have called "planetary urbanization" proceeds.[63]

Two key reinforcing processes of densification are at work here. In the first, cities continue to become spatially unequal, i.e., lower-income groups are increasingly forced into slivers of land in the city as the costs of land and housing increase elsewhere. In the second, more and more people are moving from rural and agricultural spaces and livelihoods into cities, and typically into poorer neighborhoods that are urbanizing faster than cities more generally. Of course, not all low-income neighborhoods are dense. But across the urban world, lower-income neighborhoods, typically on the spatial and economic margins, are relatively the densest parts of the city (and especially so in Asia). This density is typically expressed horizontally through one- or two-story shacks and other sometimes precarious buildings, but is also sometimes vertical, from the sloping hills of Latin American favelas to stacked structures in Asia.

If density is often important in fragment urbanism, this does not mean, as some on the political Right like to argue, that there are "too many people," but that urban capitalism is dividing up urban space in a more intense and unequal way than it has before. Some estimates suggest that as many as a third of urbanites end up in some form of lower-income neighborhood, increasingly located on the suburban peripheries of cities.[64] Add to that both the lack of political will and in some cases the economic inability for local and national states to respond to this process, and the result is horizontally denser neighborhoods with fewer and fewer adequate provisions.

Density here is not simply an abstract calculation of people set against provisions in place. It is a lived and political set of processes in which the connections between fragments and densities are remade. Residents work with each other, with community groups, with nongovernmental organizations, with political parties, with municipal officers, with artists, and others to organize to manage fragments, for instance a broken toilet or drain or water provision, or to make political claims about those fragments. Residents often enhance precarious fragments of infrastructure over time by individually or collectively building or maintaining provisions, or using forms of social reciprocity among neighbors, friends, and family in providing services, or by drawing on forms of vote-bank patronage with political parties, often shaped by religion, class, gender, and caste.[65] And residents pursue and become caught up in the politicization of fragments, whether through social movements or short-term political acts and claims, or in the ongoing work of community-based and nongovernmental organizations. As I will later show, artists and others sometimes find ways of re-expressing the relations between fragments and density to generate debate, reflection, and political claims.

In materially fragmented neighborhoods, the very reproduction of everyday life in the city often demands being able to connect with and use densities, such as in the form of social connections, rumors of threats and opportunities, temporary protesting crowds, or ways to make a little extra money or develop new networks. Think, for example, of initiatives such as the high-profile case of the Orangi Pilot Project (OPP) in Pakistan. For decades, the NGOs and community groups linked to OPP have designed and built low-cost simplified sewerage systems in communities in Karachi, weaving urban densities into new configurations by connecting formal civil society organizations and new material systems. Here, instead of large sewer pipes, a smaller system of collector pipes connecting homes and running next to streets was co-constructed and paid for by community groups. By 2011, 90 percent of the sewer lines in Orangi had been constructed and financed by residents, improving public health and helping to foster other community spinoff activities, for example around youth issues.[66]

As the OPP indicates, sanitation is a powerful example of the role of density in fragment urbanism. Sanitation has been called a "demon of density, because the inadequacy of bits and pieces of sanitation—toilets, drainage, water, waste collection, and so on—for large concentrations of people in often small slices of urban space, can be devastating for health and well-being, as well as for livelihood, education, gender inequalities, and exclusions around race, ethnicity, caste, and religion. The language of "demons" may be theatrical, but the problem posed by fragments of sanitation in dense informal neighborhoods is difficult to overstate.[67] Almost 25 percent of the 2.6 billion people lacking adequate sanitation live in urban environments, mostly in informal neighborhoods, and that grew by 100 million urban residents between 2000 and 2015[68]—there is a huge struggle ahead to meet the United Nations Sustainable Development Goals (SDGs) of providing adequate sanitation for all by 2030.[69] At the same time, the demands on the fragmented infrastructures and services that do exist are becoming more intense as cities variously expand and densify.[70]

Dhaka, for example, has some of the highest densities in the world, with informal neighborhoods of over one million people per square kilometer. Only 25 percent of Dhaka is connected to sewers, and most people depend on pit latrines, septic tanks, and informal drainage and sewers. Neighborhoods like Korail—which is spatially central in the city but economically and politically marginal—lack effective disposal of human and solid waste, with many residents employed informally in recycling fragments of waste. In Mumbai, only 47 percent of informal neighborhoods have access to toilet facilities, compared to 83 percent for the city as a whole, and the ratio of toilet seats to people varies across the city from 58:1 to 273:1 in the poorest neighborhoods like Rafiq Nagar in the northeast, where there are only a few unreliable public toilets and inadequate hanging latrines (Figure 5). Here, the toilet becomes a profound site of inequality and poverty, vividly revealing the inadequacy of fragments to meet the needs of a dense neighborhood, shaped by economic, political, and social fragmentation processes.

At the same time, the OPP is a reminder of the potential of urban density for addressing fragment urbanism. While civil society groups need the state to support their work, especially in building big infrastructure projects such as trunk sewers, the OPP nonetheless serves as a reminder that residents and activists can come together to organize

FIGURE 5. Latrine in Rafiq Nagar, Mumbai, May 2012 (Photo by Renu Desai)

ways of providing rudimentary sanitation that is both affordable and practical in a dense space. They were able to mobilize the know-how and ways of seeing that are often shunted to the margins of urban policy and planning, in a new context and relationship for improving material conditions. Furthermore, by demonstrating success they were able to bring elements of the local state on board to help support their work. For all that urban densities can be exclusionary—organized, for example, around social differentials of class or gender or religion or caste—they can also be vital resources for reproducing everyday life, organizing new possibilities, and politicizing poverty and inequality. Sometimes, this is about forming collectives that might translate existing materials into new configurations, a kind of "urban piracy" that appropriates and recasts the inherited city.[71] Then there is also the everyday, small calibrations and negotiations.

Writing about Mumbai, Vyjayanthi Rao argues that the high densities we often see across urban Asia demand constant forms of "adjustment." Adjustment is an important feature of urban life in Mumbai, from negotiating energy or water to making room on overcrowded trains.[72] These different configurations of fragments and densities constitute, in part, the *urbanism* of fragment urbanism. As Rao puts it, "this juxtaposition of densities of bodies, infrastructures, and affects makes possible incessant intersections that characterize the ontology of the informal."[73] Here, both material fragments and knowledge fragments intersect with densities—density both as context and actively constitutive in claim-making, organization, and politics—in ways that both provide insight into poverty and offer provocations for more progressive urban conditions.

This focus on dense urban life positions urbanism not just as a trajectory of expansion but as a multiplicity of loosely coalescing interactions that enable or disable, enhance, alienate, exploit, or inspire different forms of urban life, housing, infrastructure, and politicization in the fragmenting city.[74] On the one hand, this is a lived challenge of coping with insufficient provisions for numbers of people in place, and we can add to that the thorny politics of working out who gets what access how and when, which is often unequally differentiated by gender, race, ethnicity, class, and other vectors. And, at the same time, density is a resource, not just an abstract number or thing or calculation between people and provisions, but a multiplicity of people, experiences, and politics that can and is configured and reconfigured in ways that help people manage fragments as well as make political claims in relation to them. Yet too often this form of density is portrayed as a congested mess that needs to be removed, regulated, or escaped from.[75]

Fragmentation and densification are urban bedfellows. Indeed, the very right of certain kinds of urban density is now increasingly at stake. The densification of a city through elite apartments and attached commercial activity fits the dominant script set by powerful urban actors in real estate, development, and policy areas. The densification of the city through often extremely poor group and migrants occupying often small slices of space in substandard housing, with fragmented and perhaps even entirely absent infrastructure and services, fits less well and can be met with violence.[76] Simply inhabiting certain spaces is increasingly a political act, whether the residents would wish that politics or not.

The relations among fragmentation, space, fragments, densities, and politics reveal the city not only as incomplete and multiple but, as a result, and notwithstanding the huge daily challenges residents and activists routinely face, a variegated site of changing possibilities. These relations, as I will show later, can provoke new ways of seeing or thinking through, for example, art interventions, residential collaborations, or activist politics. They might be caught up in forms of occupying urban space to demand more just conditions, or in claims to moral and legal rights. They might help to form new connections between people on the margins and others in the city, or develop new directions for urban knowledge. Fragmentation processes are partly constitutive of different expressions of fragment urbanism. In the process, the context of fragments—the what, where, and when of fragments—matters to why and how they become individually and collectively put to work and politicized.

Social Infrastructure

There is nothing new about social infrastructure. It is as old as the city itself, and increasingly vital to how residents cope with fragments in the city. For most urban residents, the fact that material infrastructure is always already fragmented demands that formations are in place in order to assure, maintain, and reproduce basic provisions. Most of urban history has been characterized by people having to, or choosing to, fill in the gaps of faltering infrastructures, even to become infrastructure, including through the laborious and very often gendered work of locating and distributing water, cleaning and maintaining waste systems, tweaking and tinkering with lighting, and so on. In forming social infrastructures, whether temporary or long-term, from civil society groups and social movements, to political party bases and youth groups, people weave densities into particular configurations and purposes.

In urban research, social infrastructure has received less attention than material infrastructure. Material infrastructure has become an important lens through which urbanists conceptualize the urban condition and research cities. The "infrastructural turn," as Ash Amin has described it, has positioned material infrastructure as a "lively" presence in the political, economic, cultural, and environmental reproduction and transformation of the city rather than as a passive backdrop.[77] There is a rich vein of work here: from research on the pivotal role of infrastructure for basic provisioning such as water or in shaping urban ecologies, or critical inquiries into infrastructure privatization, removal, and demolition, to a growing focus on infrastructure's relations to digitalization and automation.[78] While the "social" features across all these counts in different ways—from how materials animate social imaginaries and collectives, to how social vectors of race, gender, class, and religion might shape infrastructure distribution—the role of social infrastructure has had less attention.

We can think of social infrastructure as a practice of connecting people and things in relations that sustain urban life. It is made and held stable through repeated work. It is a connective tissue, anchoring urban life across the urban world, varying in form and content.[79] If the urban environment is "full of machines," as AbdouMaliq Simone argues, the machinic is as much people as it is materials, "anticipated and parsed into varying measures and used by different constellations and densities of actors and things."[80] The term "social" in the couplet "social infrastructure" underlines the fact that in many cases, infrastructures are "peopled," to echo Simone's arguments around "people as infrastructure."[81] The term "social capital" is less useful here. As Eric Klinenberg argues, social capital describes the extent of people's interactions and relationships, and is less focused on the forms of care, support, or coordination that bring a social glue to responses to fragment urbanism.[82] Social infrastructure can be thought of as a way to stretch long-standing research on urban poverty and "assets"—physical, financial, human, and so forth— by focusing in on practices of connection that support the experience and geographies of urban living.[83] Social infrastructure is not a place, nor is it necessarily a set of formal organizations—as it is in Klinenberg's *Palaces for the People*—but a range of connections between people and things that helps to reproduce everyday life, shaped in relation to both material and knowledge fragments.

These connections include, as I will try to show, forms of care or coordination through which residents work, in ways that inevitably include some and not others, to cope with fragments, and to get by or get on in the city. It can be a loose connection between neighbors at a site (as I will show in relation to Kampala) or residents across a city (as I later discuss in relation to refugees in Berlin), or a closer set of bonds across family and friends. It is, then, sometimes a form of social reproduction, and sometimes a way of becoming exposed to knowledge or rumors about particular conditions in the city, or to connect to other people who might be able to offer advice or help on issues as different as training, job opportunities, cultural exchange, and so on. Social infrastructure is a necessarily flexible resource that responds to and anticipates the contingencies of everyday life. This multiplicity is why I prefer the term "infrastructure" here to capital, reproduction, or network, even though there may be elements of all of these in different expressions of social infrastructure. Infrastructure focuses our attention on the urban basics while remaining open to a range of organizational forms, while the social places people and knowledge in close relation to those forms. The use of "infrastructure" is also to signify that when material infrastructure is fragmented, social infrastructure can become profoundly important.

Care and Consolidation

Social infrastructure is a process made and remade every day as an architecture of subsistence and possibility. It acts primarily as a coping device, put to work in different ways according to the relative socioeconomic positions people occupy and the resources they can mobilize, and revealing significant differences in the nature of fragment urbanism within the neighborhood. Densities matter here. Density is both a resource for social infrastructure, because residents often find themselves in contexts where there are many hands to call upon, and an obstacle to it, as residents find that social infrastructures—like material infrastructures—can only stretch so far, and that some are closed off to them, often because of resources and connections that they don't have. Here, I examine two examples of social infrastructure from Kampala: *care* and *consolidation*.

Namuwongo is a centrally located neighborhood, in an industrial zone, partly built on a wetland and adjacent to an unused railway track leading to Port Bell (the port being one of the city's redevelopment aspirations). In a city in which newcomers account for over half of the total population, Namuwongo has become a crucial space in which migrants are able to find cheaper sources of housing, connections to kin, and economic opportunities.[84] An estimated 15,000 people live in the area, with few services and infrastructure, leading to patchwork combinations of infrastructures that struggle to provide for its density.[85] The occasional enforcement of building controls within ten meters of the

railway track and wetland locations has meant that the threat of demolition and eviction continues to cast a long shadow over the future of
the area.[86] Almost 80 percent of residents are fearful of their dwellings
being demolished and over 70 percent consider their dwellings to be
semipermanent or temporary, following partial demolition by the Kampala Capital City Authority (KCCA) and Rift Valley Railways near the
tracks and enforcement by the National Environment Management
Agency (NEMA) of the wetlands.[87] The few attempts at development in
Namuwongo have tended to be small scale and led by NGOs such as
Hope for Children.[88]

Residents in Namuwongo weave together a range of skills, knowledges, and economic pursuits. The six people I describe here, based
on work with Jonathan Silver and Joel Ongwec in 2015, reflect that
(Figure 6).[89] Jennifer works in different ways to earn income, from
bead-making to catering. She has also set up a woman's group and helps
local families apply for scholarships to schools. Ali moved to Namuwongo to be with his sister when he first arrived in Kampala from eastern Uganda. He started by selling fruit and eventually established one of
the most popular stalls at the neighborhood market. Josephine moved
to escape insecurity and conflict in northern Uganda. She has benefitted
from informal contacts with women in the neighborhood who have
helped her with selling fruit and vegetables in the city, a difficult and
precarious livelihood with little income. Basic needs—charcoal, paying
for toilets, simple foods—take up almost all her daily earnings. The
Pentecostal church has helped with school fees for her family. She and
her neighbors often help each other, from looking after each other's
children to finding a reliable bricklayer to repair the house after a storm.

Isamail sadly passed away in May 2015 due to poor health, at the age
of 36, leaving behind his wife and four children. He was a matatu (privately owned mini-bus) driver who traveled the route between Namuwongo and the city center. The matatus are an important and cheap
form of travel for residents, but work was not always certain for Isamail.
He had no guarantee that a matatu would be available for him to drive
every day, or if he'd be well enough to work. If he did work, the driving
involved long, tiring hours often stretching between 5 a.m. and 10 p.m.
Like many residents, Isamail struggled to take care of his health, pay for
medical treatment, provide for his family, and maintain a steady income.

Masengere was a chief in his village in western Uganda, and was
from 1991 a local party chairman in Namuwongo for the ruling branch
of the country's dominant political force, the National Resistance

FIGURE 6. The residents of Namuwongo involved in the research. Top row: Josephine, Jennifer, and Ali. Bottom row: Masengere, Ismail, and Amiri. (Images compiled by Colin McFarlane, Josephine Namukisa, and Jonathan Silver)

Movement (NRM), until he died in March 2020. He played a vital political role in the area, and with his stamp could provide the approval needed for a wide range of local issues or economic pursuits from job references through to identity documents. Finally, Amiri is young and stylish, and understands the challenges many young people in the area struggle with. He lost both parents when he was young, stopped school, and started to earn money by collecting and selling scrap materials in and around the local area. Through the help of his uncle he was trained as a carpenter, producing an impressive range of different wood products in his uncle's workshop at the edge of the neighborhood, while living with friends in a tiny, rented dwelling in the "Soweto" section, the densest and one of the poorest parts of Namuwongo.

How, then, does social infrastructure operate and vary as a means of coping with and advancing urban life in a dense, fragmented neighborhood? *Care* matters here. Friends, family, and neighbors come together to secure essential needs, share, and support each other during heightened moments of crisis, or to advise and identify new opportunities. Each of the six residents both called upon and enacted a social infrastructure of care in different ways.

Through past experience as an elected chairwoman in the nearby town of Jinja, her struggles as a widow to sustain a family, and her links to a range of individuals and organizations, Jennifer finds herself at the center of all kinds of moments of care. She has worked with the local Pentecostal church to build sanitation facilities for collective use by the congregation, helps out her family members to start businesses, and seeks out sponsorship for children to attend school. She plays a prominent role in a women's group, which includes the making and selling of crafts for sale, and a savings group covering everything from everyday essentials such as food or fuel when times are tough, through to exceptional needs such as funeral costs and, in some cases, saving toward a small business. These social infrastructures of care are at once social and material, ranging from food and fuel to craft skill training, basic services, school access, and contacts for informal employment.

Jennifer and others like her play pivotal roles in the architecture of social infrastructures of care in Namuwongo. This is also an architecture of urban densities, weaving and reinforcing particular kinds of connective relations between people as part of the reproduction of everyday life. The close configuration of density in a small territory is itself important to the reproduction of care, for example in the informal daily conversations with people that Jennifer has as she moves around the streets and lanes in her part of the neighborhood, seeing how they are getting on, identifying problems and providing contacts to help. Yet care should not necessarily be seen as a species of altruism. As critical accounts of care have shown, the carer subject-position is not disconnected from wider social power relations, and may in fact reinforce status.[90] Jennifer has positioned herself as locally important, and as such often benefits in a range of ways, from the parents for whom she has secured a school place, through to selling handmade beads to local contacts and through word of mouth. The time and work that Jennifer puts into creating and sustaining social infrastructures of care is also an investment in herself and in a wider reciprocity upon which some of the rhythms of urban life turn. This story of reciprocity repeats-with-difference in neighborhoods globally.[91] For example, reciprocal exchanges form the basis of informal insurance systems in which people borrow, lend, buy, or sell among themselves, as has been documented in classic anthropological works such as Carol Stack's *All Our Kin*, which highlights the social infrastructures of reciprocity, debt, and circulation of objects, favors, and services in poor neighborhoods.[92] Very often, social infrastructures of care are profoundly gendered. The connective densities that are woven are predominantly composed of women, and in this case often of widows.

Social infrastructures of care vary considerably, even among nearby neighbors. For example, Josephine's caring infrastructure is less extensive than Jennifer's, yet all the more important because Josephine and her children are less able to secure basic necessities. Social infrastructure enables Josephine to work, for instance as neighbors look after her children, and at times of intensified crisis social infrastructures are vital for her survival. In situations of crisis the social infrastructure can spatially widen, including as far afield as rural family hinterlands, pulling in distant family to supplement the support of local densities of neighbors and friends. On one occasion while selling fruit in town she seriously injured her leg, and family from her village in the north of Uganda sent food, while locally neighbors and friends helped when they could. Again, there is a reciprocity here: Josephine will occasionally look after the children of neighbors, and she had also taken responsibility for the care of her niece, who has HIV and was unable to secure treatment in the village where she had lived. This meant another mouth to feed in a context where food is often scarce and where she can seldom scrape together the money to get her children into school, placing yet more pressure on her and making the social infrastructure of care all the more important. Amiri's relative security in his carpentry job is assured through his uncle. He has moved in and out of essential social infrastructures of care, and spoke of a growing realization that he lives in an urban space in which caring infrastructures are necessary, from providing basic urban provisions, to finding employment through contacts or looking out for each other when the police are in the neighborhood.

Beyond care, social infrastructures of *consolidation* can serve to enhance new opportunities and positions, and help residents to get beyond struggling with material fragments. Of all the residents, Masengere was the one whose position in the wider area was relatively secure. Such was his relative security that he was the least concerned of the six residents about possible future development, a security reinforced by his ability to use political power to maneuver into a better position than most and the fact that he resides outside of demolition target areas. Still, even his consolidated position had its limits; he spoke, for instance, about his belief that the area will eventually become too expensive for current residents, adding that KCCA ought to pay compensation to those who will lose their homes. What's striking is that with a more consolidated position, Masengere was in a stronger position to shape through urban densities and fragments, whether by accepting or rejecting small transformations to the urban landscape or by holding some sway over new investments and activities in the area. Here, then, social infrastructure is at the same time a deeply political infrastructure, linked to local political parties and political power plays. Again, gender plays a vital role here, and his was quite a different power from that which Jennifer holds.

The social infrastructures of consolidation vary just as those of care do. The stories described here are not consolidated to the extent that Caroline Moser identifies in her work on low-income neighborhoods in Ecuador, in which the built environment is consolidated alongside improved livelihoods and education.[93] For Jennifer, consolidating her economic security and social position was about learning how to make jewelry using beads, and here external NGO training had been vital. Consolidation allowed, Jennifer reflected, a more secure position in relation to food: "This is a big problem. There is nowhere to plant your own food, so you have to buy it and that's more expensive." Josephine, in contrast, remarked that there didn't seem to be opportunities for the kind of training Jennifer had. NGOs and government programs are thin on the ground.

Josephine can never be sure that she will have enough money for food from one day to the next, let alone costs for school fees or starting up a local business, which she one day hopes to do. Consolidation here is always out of reach, not because of a lack of social infrastructure but because of the lack of state investment, the harassment of street hawkers, and the failure to support their livelihood opportunities. The KCCA severely restricts Josephine's hopes of consolidating, and she connected the municipality to gender, opportunity, and urban space: "KCCA does not find a way of collaborating with women who sell goods in town. They don't think of the women."[94] Josephine is developing plans, however, and spoke of setting up a business to buy fish in the town and sell it back in the village.

Amiri learned skills that helped bring a measure of consolidation through training from his uncle in woodwork, but it would be wrong to give the impression that he was simply in a position of growing security and confidence. Uncertain futures press up against consolidating practices. Like Jennifer, Amiri is aware of how the city's inequalities limit opportunities, and he alluded to a felt threshold in the capacity to consolidate further: "I sometimes feel positive about changing things, but then I think no: I cannot change anything." To some extent, this is about the KCCA and the limits it puts on urban opportunities—"If you have a small plot of land, the KCCA will say it doesn't meet standards and move you on"—and about the impact of urban change more broadly: "All of the changes made have hurt someone. Change is never smooth." He is acutely aware of a lack of jobs for young people.

Amiri's position reflects the wider "intergenerational bargain" through which young people's life chances are supported by reciprocal responsibilities of care from adults.[95] As stable employment opportunities recede for many young people in increasingly competitive and precarious global labor markets, family care can be vital or even the only forms of support for a "lost generation" of youth that Alcinda Honwna has characterized as remaining in a state of "waithood."[96] Uganda has the highest poverty incidence among young people (between 18 and 30) in sub-Saharan Africa, with 94 percent living below US$2 per day in a society in which 78 percent of its population are under 30 years of age.[97] This reflects the broader urban African experience for many young people, left struggling with fragment urbanism, shunting repeatedly from limited social infrastructures of care to efforts to consolidate some measure of often precarious economic security.[98]

For Ali, in contrast, the ability to work with customers, to build rapport, to negotiate to buy the best products for the right prices to sell in his stall—all are capacities that have helped him consolidate a relatively stable economic position. He decided to pay an extra 10,000 shillings a month (around $4) to acquire the front stall, visible upon entry to the market from its main entrance, in order to take better advantage of bottlenecks of urban flows and increase the number of customers. The decision paid off and his turnover increased. Again, gendered power relations are vital here: his capacity to weave and sustain these relations, predominantly among other men, is predicated in part on his being a charismatic male figure. His vision for Namuwongo revolved around growing business opportunities, including connections to the rest of the city and its hinterlands. He was enthusiastic about the new road KCCA had built through Namuwongo. Indeed, he connected the construction of the road, in the same breath, to a more secure neighborhood—less materially fragmented and dependent on social infrastructure, more able to channel its densities into economic growth.

Ali was in quite a different position from Isamail in this respect. Isamail struggled to consolidate his position due to poor health and the unreliability of available taxis when he was well enough to drive, and so his income stream was far more unpredictable and his ability to ensure provisions of food, water, schools fees, and other costs for himself and his family were more curtailed. He was planning to start a retail shop selling food, in an attempt to find other ways beyond depending on limited social infrastructures. In the end, not only was Isamail far from consolidating any security, social infrastructures of care were not enough. His death made it harder still for his young family to consolidate into the future. The tragedy of the loss of a parent can lead to all kinds of other impacts, for instance with children often dropping out of school, having to spend more time on household labor and caring duties for siblings—especially for girls—or migrating to live with relatives.[99]

Social infrastructures of care and consolidation are vital and closely interrelated formations through which residents work with, cope with, and seek to move beyond fragment urbanism. Each individual reveals a quite different story of Namuwongo and Kampala. Jennifer's centrality to social infrastructures of care enhances her ability to consolidate, while Josephine's relatively limited social infrastructure is both vital but also reflective of the struggle she has in seeking to consolidate daily life and longer-term speculations. She lives only a few lanes from Ali but is economically living on quite a different urban margin from the margin he occupies. The limits placed on Isamail's social infrastructure by the political economies of health, services, and infrastructure left him bereft of life-sustaining support. We have, then, a situation of urban multiplicity, in which the relations between material fragments and social infrastructures take on different configurations for distinct residents, living in quite different manifestations of the urban margins in close proximity to one another, enrolled in and making different geographies.

Knowing Fragments

However splendidly the fragment gleams, what fascinates us even more is the darkness surrounding it.

—Glenn Most, *On Fragments*

In the Relation

Noun: a piece broken off, an incomplete part, a portion left over.

Verb: the act of breaking up, of separation, fragmenting.

The fragment operates in the relation. It is both thing and action, being and occurrence, dearth and potential, noun and verb, presence and absence. Fragments are instantiations, made and perceived in the relations of here and now, but shaped by their fragmentation histories and the identities attached to them. They are things in and of themselves, and always made in process through relations to other things, carrying too what they may have been or could otherwise become. They are forced into forms of action even when they are not quite up to the role, just as they act as hints or lures to that which was or could be. Fragments are often middle-aged, neither origin nor complete, their purposes realized through different angles of vision. Some may see a given fragment as a redundant remnant, others will see some yet-to-be realized role, or an active provocation and statement. They can be suggestive of historical conditions or testimonies to discontinuity.

Fragments are often understood as the *products* of fragmentation, as nouns rather than verbs. They are the overlooked bits and pieces, merely the debris of capitalist urbanization, a distraction to the real drivers and action of urban change.[1] Yet fragments can act as verbs; active and varied actors in the making, remaking, and politicization of the urban margins. Fragments are caught up with residents in all kinds of relations, rhythms, projects, collectives, personal ambitions and opportunities, and routes through and beyond the city—an urban "method," as AbdouMaliq Simone has put it, that emerges from, but which is also not simply reducible to, "the shards of broken lives and broken infrastructure." This method is a rhythm of endurance and possibility.[2]

The term "fragment" has two key routes into English, specifically late Middle English, the form spoken between the Norman conquest of 1066 and the late fifteenth century. The first is from the Latin words *"frangĕre"*— to break—and "fragmentum," and the second is from the French term, "fragment." While the earliest use of fragment as a noun, according to the *Oxford English Dictionary*—obviously largely limited to English—is in the eleventh century, it wasn't until the sixteenth century that it became popularized. A key moment was the publication in 1531 of Thomas Elyot's popular treatise, *The Boke Named the Governour.* Elyot was a powerful and wealthy diplomat, member of Parliament, and humanist whose three-volume book set out, among other things, a status-quo description of forms of hierarchical government, heavily influenced by Greek and Roman traditions, with the monarch at the top.

In the book, the use of fragment related to Elyot's description of idolatry, and his view that it was not quite extinct but persisting, remaining in "fragments" in every region of the country. This, then, was the fragment not as a material thing but as a form of knowledge and practice. Elyot recognized a power in fragments: they might endure not in spite of being fragments but because they were.

As a noun, fragment appears to have been used from the late sixteenth century as both a "thing"—a broken piece, a portion of writing, a segment of land, a found object such as a chunk of pottery—and as a form of knowledge. Less common, at least according to the *OED,* is the use of fragment as a verb. Here, the instances appear in the written record much later, and especially from the early nineteenth century, in relation to forms of organization and ways of being, from revolutionary councils to Christian spirituality. While I use both forms of fragment— as noun and verb—it is the latter sense that I am especially interested in. Fragments as materials or knowledges that act in the urban world in all kinds of ways.

In the seventeenth century, there was a development of the fragment form of writing, influenced for example by Montaigne's earlier *Essais,* and in the late eighteenth century the fragment idea surfaced in Romanticism through, for instance, the German writer Friedrich Schlegel, for whom the fragment could be a kind of whole unto itself, such as with a miniature work of art.[3] But it is in the mid to late nineteenth century—from the 1840s to the 1890s—that the *OED* locates peak use of the term "fragment" in written English. From that highwater mark the term has become steadily less prominent in recorded use to the present day, dropping toward the lower levels of the early eleventh century. But during that heyday in the second half of the nineteenth century, we see the term appearing in all kinds of ways: as fragments of pottery in Samuel Bartlett's 1879 *Egypt to Palestine,* as a descriptor of portions of property in Edward Freeman's 1871 *The History of the Norman Conquest,* in descriptions of the "New Atlantis" in Benjamin Jowett's 1875 translation of Plato's *Dialogues,* or as a critique of the idea that Christ's teaching could be fragmented in Hugh McIntosh's 1901 *Is Christ Infallible and the Bible True?*

If these texts are a barometer of how the term was understood—and we could of course question how representative they are and whether they relate to wider everyday uses of the term—we can see that, first, the fragment has often been both noun and verb, and, second, that while there are diverse uses of it, the forms of use remained quite specific. A fragment emerges as a piece of some*thing*—whether of papyrus, paper, clay, granite, or land—or a form of knowledge, whether a way of seeing a question or issue, or as a not-quite-disappeared knowledge-form or practice.

It has also been, less commonly, a description of an effort to break something up, for instance in McIntosh's aforementioned use in relation to Christian theology. McIntosh connected the idea of the fragment to the inviolability of scripture, arguing that those who sought to isolate, remove, or break any one part would necessarily leave it "broken as a whole." This latter use points to two ways of using fragment as a verb: one to describe the *act* of breaking something up (throwing an object across a room, for instance), the other to describe the *process* of breaking up (the moment of the pieces coming apart)—while the noun refers to the piece itself. And finally, across this history, there is the fragment as a form of expression, for instance through relatively short pieces of writing in the emergence of the essay form. Rather than select one of these different versions of fragment—as a material thing, as a form of knowledge or way of knowing, and as a form of textual expression—I explore how all three generate insight into cities and the urban world. There is also another quality running through these accounts that is valuable, and that is the fragment as a disruption of that which is taken to be known or given.

This sense of the fragment as a kind of discontinuity emerges too in critical theory in the twentieth century. Theodore Adorno's well-traveled line from *Minima Moralia*—"the whole is the false"— has a certain completeness that echoes Schlegel's earlier notion of the fragment as a whole unto itself, "a partial performance of its own truth," as Ian Balfour has put it, a kind of sovereignty in the power of its claim: "complete in itself, discursively airtight."[4] More generally, the fragment was important to how Adorno developed his critique of modernity.[5] We see it in his elaboration of negative dialectics and in his writing on the nature of conceptualization, including his critique of systematic thought and reductive categories, and his attention to the role of the nonconceptual that has not been "pre-digested by the pre-existing concepts."[6] We see it too in his analyses of Beethoven's music, his writing on Freud, and his inverted use of the Leibnizian monad. Rather than seeing the monad as symbolic of the whole, Adorno positioned the fragment as the *discontinuity of history,* a disharmony through which the whole slipped away, and pointed as examples to the "fragmentary artwork" of Picasso, Proust, Kafka, and Joyce.

For example, Adorno argued that fragments in Beethoven's music were not to be overlooked, that beauty could be attributed to fragments that didn't identify with the whole, that in fact resisted the totality.[7] More than this, the fragment for Adorno was the more truthful form of art, in that the irreconcilable was a central part of the modern itself.[8] It was perhaps in critical dialogue with Walter Benjamin that Adorno developed his "preference for the fragmentary over everything that has been completed," and especially in the sense Benjamin understood the fragment via German Romanticism, in which the fragment, precisely because it is incomplete, retains the force of truth.[9] And there are Benjamin's writings throughout the 1920s and 1930s, which remain powerful illustrations of the fragment form of writing as a means of juxtaposing, unsettling, and critiquing the economic, political, and social coordinates of urban modernity. Both Adorno and Benjamin worked with a sense of the generative possibilities of forms of critical thought that retained a speculative and playful commitment to the unfinished and incomplete, forms of thought and writing that lingered with fragments of knowledge rather than what Adorno called "ready-made concepts": "If we measure a thought immediately by its possible realization, the productive force of thinking will be shackled as a result."[10] Here, the fragment surfaces variously as a provocation, an invitation or lure to speculation, and a form of expression.

The connection between the fragment and discontinuity is important. Fragment urbanism emerges as discontinuity, in that it is both the product of a damaged urban world and at the same time an unfolding process in which we can see possibility at work. Those possibilities emerge even in some of the most trying circumstances in the urban world, as residents work with fragments through different relations or claims. Discontinuity signifies both the destruction and possibilities of history and the present, and the irreducibility that accompanies living in the fragmenting, incomplete city. The fragment—whether as material thing, knowledge form, or mode of expression—is a shorthand for the city and urban world as discontinuity, always operating between destruction and reformation, provision and absence, power and marginalization, constraint and possibility. It is a reminder of the always already multiple nature of the urban, in which the city and urbanization are at once predictable and stubborn patterns of inequality but also generative processes of difference, surprise, and alterity.

Across these historical accounts, there are multiple registers of the fragment: as a *thing,* a *knowledge,* an *act,* a *process,* a *disruption,* an *invitation,* a *form of expression;* and these different uses seem to have often been co-present. The term "fragment" then is both multiple—these related but distinct uses, across all kinds of empirical concerns—but quite specific, used repeatedly, in English at least, in relation to one of these areas. This is quite different from related terms such as "part," which has a much larger and more diverse history—from quantities of measurement of space, time, or books, to bodies, things, speech, and duties or concerns, or partings, separations, and partialities—and has been used in and with a far wider range of contexts and issues. In relation to forms of expression, "part" is more often connected to speech than fragment, which tends to be more closely associated to texts, perhaps because the term fragment has so often been used in the fields of archaeology, history, and the classics (see below).

It is for these reasons that I work with the term fragment, and not another related term, such as splinter, shard, part, or trace. The term "splinter" has proven important for understanding the relations between fragmentation and urban inequalities. In *Splintering Urbanism,* Stephen Graham and Simon Marvin examined the "splintering" of public space and provisions in the context of urban infrastructure. They demonstrated how neoliberalism, and in particular the relations among privatization, liberalization, and the application of new technologies, shaped a globalizing process of "unbundling" infrastructure.[11] "Splintering urbanism" has come to mean a process of infrastructural fragmentation, and the splinter a product of capitalist transformation, but in the process the potential agency of the "splinter" in urban politicization and experience has fallen from view. It has lost, curiously, some of the generative relations and possibilities that urbanites can and do enact with splinters of infrastructure. Fragment is a more open term.

Similarly, the term "shard" carries a specific imaginary that contrasts with the definitional flexibility of "fragment."[12] A "part" refers to any kind of portion or division within a whole, whereas fragment carries a deeper sense of ambivalence to the whole. The term "part" does not capture the sense of forms that do not straightforwardly connect to a preconstituted whole. Dipesh Chakrabarty, for example, has written about fragments and wholes to show how activists in colonial India not only resisted the social "whole" as constituted by colonial elites, but saw themselves as embodying knowledge-forms that sought either to develop an alternative kind of "whole," or for which the idea of the whole simply carried no meaningful value.[13]

The term "trace" is a useful descriptor of those histories that linger in particular areas of the city. Chakrabarty uses the term in his argument that histories of subaltern labor can only be located in narratives of capitalist transition as a Derridean trace.[14] Here, the trace "constantly challenges from within capital's and commodity's . . . claim to unity and universality."[15] As with a trace, a fragment both contains the marker of that which it is not,[16] and—as Gyanendra Pandey has argued—can act as a "disturbance," "an appeal" to the possibility of difference.[17] Nonetheless, I use the term fragment rather than trace both because trace is always fixed in a minority position in a given set of relations, unable to become much more, and because of the greater sense fragment conjures of a force—material or knowledge—acting in the world.

Presence-Absence

In the variegated history of the fragment, the relation of presence and absence is caught up with the cultural power of the fragment form. The connection between the fragment and the sacred loom large here. There is a long history of religious fragments as hallowed or sanctified entities. The connections between fragments and spirituality reflect a wider set of religious preoccupations with the "whole," and with relations of presence and absence.

We might think, for example, of scholarship on the significance of the fragmented possessions of, or even bits of bone belonging to, important religious figures, or broken objects that have been said to be associated with them, from textiles and ceremonial texts to artifacts and shrines. As historian Julia Smith has shown in relation to Christian relics, the social consequence of relics often lies not in theological insight or clerical statement but "from the subjective understanding of those who gathered and cherished them."[18] That said, in this "cult of relics," not all fragments are made equal. For example, fragments of the Cross said to have been used in the crucifixion have been in rumored circulation since at least the fourth century.[19] In these histories, the fragment is inexorably tied to a profound sense of the "whole." It is, after all, part of the very purpose of religion to explain why and how humans are part of a deeper whole, through materials and experiences that may register as fragments but which become points of passage to a whole that is said to have always been there.

This relationship between the fragment and the spiritual is an indicator of an important quality of fragments more generally, which is that they are often defined in a relation of presence and absence. As Jacqueline Lichtenstein shows, this refers to two ways of seeing the fragment: as a thing in and of itself, and as "a sign that refers to something else, to the absent thing."[20] In Christianity, an example here is the breaking of the bread: a process of making fragments that are also at the same time wholes in their connection to the body—as materiality and spirit—of Jesus Christ.

Some of our understanding of religious relics comes from the field of "fragmentation studies" in archaeology, which operates at the intersections of archaeology, anthropology, and material culture. Fragmentation studies is not only the study of found fragments but also an effort to make sense of *deliberate* fragmentation, ways of attaching cultural meaning to fragments. Deliberate fragmentation has played important roles in forming collective memory, reinforcing social relations, and shaping new forms of social categorization and personhood. If this field entails a kind of biographies of things, its focus tends to be on the midlife period of an object, which is the point at which it takes on its significance, i.e., after it is broken and before it is settled into a context. Fragmentation studies have focused on practices associated with different moments in this midlife period, including *enchainment,* i.e., the reuse of fragments that remain connected to a previous use, and *accumulation,* the concentration of fragments into social and material relations. This, then, is always a relational biography, concerned with the making, reuse, and exchange of objects.

Fragments here are always more than materials, in that materials can become symbols or carry the aura of a pre-fragmented form or social role. While some objects are made with the principle that they will break or be later fragmented for some other use, others do not relate to a whole, and perhaps cannot relate to a whole. In their research on the prehistoric Balkans, John Chapman and Bisserka Gaydarska show how each fragment that was shared in a social system in deliberate fragmentation comes to stand for a whole—synecdoche—either as a potential or as an actual element of a whole that relates objects and personhood.[21]

The rub, however, is that the archaeological and historical record do not always allow us to understand, specifically, the content of the social, cultural, or spiritual power attached to a fragment in a particular place and time. Many of the studies are, therefore, speculative and meaning can be lost in translation. Drawing on a rich body of work in classics on fragments of text and their historical circulations, for example, Nora

Goldschmidt has examined the fragmentary translation and nontranslation of ancient Greek texts in modernist writing that engage with the processes of textual and cultural transmission.[22] Forms of translation and transmission can have profound impacts not only on how fragments are understood, but in how they are perceived in what are inevitably collective conversations across space and time: "The texts of the past come to us in pieces and filtered through the temporally disparate voices of others."[23] Fragments are found and lost and translated and take on different significances in distinct contexts. They are, then, very often *composites,* their identities in flux over different timelines and geographies.

The relation of presence and absence can take on a kind of mystery, and one—as Glen Most has argued—that can be peculiarly seductive, inviting a kind of detective work and cultural fascination.[24] Indeed, as Most argues, the very status of the fragment as an idea has itself fluctuated over time in the classics and related fields of inquiry. Ancient scholars looked for complete manuscripts. It was only later, from the fourteenth century and into the Renaissance period, that classical scholars realized they had to look to fragments to extend records of thinkers or periods. For German Romanticists of the late eighteenth century, fragments of art could generate new ways of thinking beyond established forms and genres. For example, Friedrich Schleiermacher's 1807 commentary on the fragments of Heraclitus focused on fragments of ancient Greek philosophy that helped establish rigorous ways of analyzing fragments of text.[25]

It wouldn't be until the middle of the nineteenth century, however, before scholarship on ancient literary fragments really took off—dovetailing with the growing use of the term in the *OED*'s recorded history—when it became a key identifier of German classical philology (including August Meineke on fragments of Greek comic poets and Johann August Nauck on Greek tragic poets). Oftentimes this work involved painstaking research to identify and contextualize fragments, eventually creating a culture of scholarship that positioned fragments as a legitimate space of research inquiry and knowledge formation.

For example, William Tronzo, in his edited collection *The Fragment: An Incomplete History,* examines how fragments have been understood and researched in art history.[26] There is a long historical and global association of fragments and art, from fragments of antiquity—parchments, sculptures, paintings, and so on—assembled in city museums, to remnants of partially forgotten poems, songs, myths, stories, or folklore. Tronzo tracks two important understandings of fragments in art history.

First, there are "remainder-fragments" and "creation-fragments." The former are those that are received, broken off from a whole, and the latter those that are created, taken from a context and used to force a new idea or sentiment. Second, he shows how the relationship between the fragment, power, and temporality is not fixed. We might tend to assume that wholes are enduring and fragments ephemeral, but—Tronzo argues—art history has troubled at this relation, and shown the opposite more often to be true. Wholes might deteriorate, change shape, become transformed, while fragments, even when they are seared off, can be obdurate, while at the same time conjuring all kinds of speculations about their absences.

"However splendidly the fragment gleams," writes Most, "what fascinates us even more is the darkness surrounding it."[27] But while some writers have filled in the ellipses or missing gaps in historical fragments of art or text with suggestions that effectively fabricate meaning, it's also the case that recovering original meaning is in any case sometimes impossible, given the radical shifts in context and perception. Indeed, Goldschmidt is as much concerned with stressing the *un*translatability and *in*commensurability of scraps and fragments from ancient Greek texts as she is with arguing for common points of understanding and identifiable meaning.

Moreover, as with fragmentation studies in archaeology, some fragments are deliberately made as such. Goldschmidt uses the intriguing term "quasi-fragment," which might be used to emphasize non- or partial translation or transmission. Here, historically, writers purposely mimic the fragment form in order to work with nontranslation as an idea. Others might use epigrams or aphorisms as deliberate efforts to provoke significance in ways that are radically open to different readings and uses. Goldschmidt is particularly concerned with how these (non)translations and (non)transmissions reverberate into modernity. The past comes to us mediated and in pieces: "Fundamentally, the modernist fragment was engaged in dialogue with the wealth of textual and material culture from Greco-Roman antiquity coming to light in the period and the activities of classicists which attempted to process it, from papyrology to philology and from epigraphy to lexicography."[28] Fragments are densities of other fragments from all kinds of places and moments, in which the absences might remain elusive. Nonetheless, scraps and relics are not dead inheritances but lively presences, and often powerfully so, even while their instantiations, meanings, and significances can be ambivalent and difficult to read.

The same can be true of ruins. As Noam Leshem has shown, the making and unmaking of ruins can be a deeply political question. In *Life after Ruin,* he develops a spatial history of the ruination of the Arab-Palestinian village of Salama, later named Kfar Shalem. He examines the ways in which ruins, presents, and futures become folded together but in ways that are often uncertain rather than fixed, replete with small and sometimes large tensions that aren't resolved. The mosque that remains in the village decades after the 1948 war which is, over time, pulled into all sorts of distinct relations to do with community life or legal imperatives or acts of violence, from youth centers to vandalism. The synagogue which in its very material form, for example in plaques on the wall that commemorate other places and atrocities, at once echoes yet remains cut adrift from, and even sometimes at odds with, the project of Israeli state building. Or the Arab housing that remains a signature of pre-occupation pasts while at the same time being a home *now* that has morphed and become layered with all manner of mundane material and cultural registers, and yet which may well be demolished by the state. And so on.

Leshem's account is one of displacement and exile, not just of *people* but of *places* caught up in a kind of reoccupation and recomposition, replete with traces and echoes of other times and lives. Here, ruins are on the move through material, cultural, political, and legal registers that are themselves remade in sometimes unexpected ways. Leshem's focus is Tel Aviv, a particular kind of city to be sure, and one in his account that is often so many "fragments, shattered objects and incomplete accounts," in which "consolidation is rare."[29] As much is absent as is present, but that relation cannot be straightforwardly read from the material fragments and historical traces.

Sometimes in cities the ruin becomes a signature of an atmosphere that typifies a time. For Orhan Pamuk, Istanbul is one such case, caught up as it is in a relation of *melancholy,* where melancholy is a particular cultural connection to ruin through which history holds residents in the shadow of the past even while they move into different futures. In his 2006 book on Istanbul, Pamuk argues that moving between, on the one hand, dominant cultural narratives of Istanbul and, on the other hand, the labyrinthine micro-histories of the city's neighborhoods, allows the writer "to 'discover' the city's soul in its ruins."[30]

As Leshem and Pamuk differently show, far from being discarded, historical buildings—not always fragments, of course— are actively constitutive of all kinds of presents. This includes mundane sites in the city.

In his study of St. Ann's Church in Manchester, Tim Edensor shows how a 300-year-old church is always *becoming*, enrolled in changing techniques and technologies of maintenance and repair, as well as shifting cultural aesthetics, economic rationalities, and spatial connections. The church, Edensor concludes, is not simply an historical architecture but "testifies to a continuous and ongoing emergence that is antithetical to certain versions of heritage that fix meanings and narratives."[31] And there is, of course, a vast tourist industry wrapped around the marketing of some remnants, relics, and ruins, often speculating with lost histories.

Across the fields I have briefly pointed to here—theology, archaeology, classics, art history, geography, and history—the fragment is a noun and a verb, a thing, knowledge, act, process, and form. It is a composite carrying all kinds of histories and geographies, and a quasi-object differently known and put to work depending on context. The ways in which it comes to register is unstable. Geography and time play constitutive roles; the contexts and travels through which the fragment is made, practiced, enrolled in social or cultural meaning, read, lost, found and found again, analyzed and argued over. In these routes and encounters the relations of presence and absence that both accompany and disrupt fragments gain and lose their clarity and shift in their significance.

The Gap

As a relation of presence and absence, the fragment also emerges in the intimate relations among materiality, memory, and urban life. When I was growing up, we lived for a period in Pollok, a council estate in south Glasgow. We stayed on the third floor of a four-story housing block, on a street of tenement flats that to my eyes seemed to stretch on forever, across the road from the school I attended and the church we went to. We played in the open grass in front of the flats, or in the school, and most of the shops we went to were just a short walk away. We chatted with friends and neighbors at the entrance to the building and looked on, probably a little suspiciously, at strangers who passed by, especially if they were around our age, wondering if they attended the rival school at the bottom of the hill. There were always people around and things going on, and while it was possible for people to opt out of the comings and goings of the neighborhood, most people knew a little, if not a lot, about each other.

Here, everyday life, in echoes of some of Jane Jacobs's writings, created a loose sense of community, sociality, and safety, and we saw a broad range of life and ways of living in that small space.[32] It was also a poor and underserviced neighborhood, where people sometimes struggled to put proper food on the table, where there was alcoholism, conflict, an occasionally hostile atmosphere to difference, and sporadic violence. In growing up there you had to know how to negotiate daily life: to know when to be outside and when not to be, who to avoid and who to be seen with—everyday habits and calculations that could be the difference between finding yourself in a spot of trouble or dodging it.

A few years ago, I went back to the old place and was shocked to find that our building was gone. The entire street had been demolished. I thought back to rumors of how the housing blocks had subsidence and the street might be knocked down, and I was aware too that significant demolition had taken place in Pollok in the time since I had left, but all of those bricks and mortar and life had never realistically seemed temporary to me. Pollok was the first of the four large postwar peripheral housing estates on the periphery of Glasgow—along with Castlemilk, Drumchapel, and Easterhouse—and like those others it was no low-density suburb: instead, it was designed with "higher densities than previously considered acceptable for such projects," built as a mixture of four-, three-, and two-story flats and houses.[33] It densified an area of the city that was previously largely farmland and uninhabited, thereby transforming a large swath of the southern city, and communities grew up around it.

However, the thick set of amenities needed to ensure that neighborhoods would thrive—good transport links, community spaces, youth groups, jobs training, sports centers, cinemas, theatres, cafes, and so forth—largely did not materialize, and housing and streets were often poorly maintained. The quality of housing deteriorated over the years, and the area suffered from health and social problems. By the time I was living there as a boy in the late 1980s it was hard to argue that the plan had been a success. From the 1990s onwards, large areas of Pollok and surrounding areas were demolished—especially the four-story blocks— and many residents left, sometimes to other parts of Glasgow, but more often beyond to the New Towns of East Kilbride, Cumbernauld, or Bishopton, coastal areas like Irvine, or—following families like ours— to more established nearby towns such as Paisley. Much of Pollok's demolished public housing was replaced by private housing, not especially expensive in relative terms but nonetheless outside the price range of many of the previous residents.

This is a familiar story of the slow fragmentation of working-class spaces over a period of decades, which meant, gradually, that much of Pollok was left to contend with inadequate housing, infrastructure, and services. Many criticisms have been leveled at Glasgow's postwar housing strategies and its larger de-/re-densification plans, often arguing that authorities were more concerned with shunting working-class families out of sight than with building decent housing.[34] Yet Glasgow also had to contend with budget cuts from the central state that other post-industrial British cities suffered, especially in the Thatcher-Major years of Conservative governments running through the 1980s and 1990s. The city struggled to meet the significant needs of communities in large postwar housing estates. The ambition and scope of projects like Pollok belonged to a previous era in British cities, a postwar moment in which the state took on large-scale social improvement ambitions and sought to rally a new vision of the city that transformed urban living and redistributed social geographies.

Looking down the street previously occupied by buildings and densities that had been so familiar, I was struck by the brute fact that instead of a four-story block of flats, there was nothing. Or, not quite nothing: more of a gap, an absent presence, a space with a deep echo of a once-lived cacophony of routine and event. I looked at the spot in the middle of the air where we once lived, in what would have been three floors up, not quite able to reckon with this empty rectangle where I once slept, opened Christmas presents, fought with my brother, did my homework. All that vibrant activity—friends, homes, neighbors, areas where I played, memories that were so deeply ingrained—no longer had a territory, now replaced by smaller buildings in a mix of houses and apartments.

The city, as AbdouMaliq Simone has put it, "is a constant reminder of what could be but isn't."[35] Many urban residents can tell similar stories of unexpected and disruptive absent presences in cities. They are stories of urban transformation that remind us that cities are never complete, that the densities we see today may be gone tomorrow, turned to fragments and perhaps eviscerated altogether. A place bristling with "sheer life" now might be, as Ash Amin and Nigel Thrift have argued, "broken and abandoned" later, then perhaps remade in a quite different way.[36] This is a familiar story in another sense: one of disinvestment and demolition, a story of the city as a space structured by histories of fragmentation that repeat-with-difference globally. Not all densities of people and things end up, like that street in Pollok, turned to fragments not of things but of memory, disappearing almost without a trace. Instead, fragments very often persist in one way or another, hinting at stories of other material arrangements and urban lives.

Knowledge Fragments

While all fragments defy any easy distinction between material and knowledge, there is a difference between material fragments and knowledge fragments. A knowledge fragment is a form of knowledge or way of knowing. "Knowledge" refers to an understanding that individuals or collectives have created about a given issue or set of conditions, and a "way of knowing" refers to how issues or conditions are perceived, and is often more deep-rooted. Both material and knowledge fragments, as I discuss them, are often pushed to the margins of the city, but I am not suggesting that there are particular kinds of knowledge that "belong" to marginal spaces. Alternative knowledges and ways of knowing the city can be found anywhere, from activists setting out new political claims from a peripheral informal neighborhood to groups of young people speculating about a different kind of city while wandering bored through a shopping mall.

Knowledge fragments have no pre-given geography. While spaces on the economic margins of cities are likely to be conceptually and politically important for knowledge fragments, these are not the only spaces in the city where we might find knowledge fragments. What marks out a knowledge fragment as such is its marginal relation to how the city is understood, a marginal relation that is also a relation of power, given that the focus of attention on urban questions often reflects the dominance of particular actors and their ways of seeing and narrativizing the world. Unsurprisingly, knowledge fragments and economic margins often coincide.

One useful resource here lies in how the "fragment" has been developed in subaltern studies scholarship.[37] Fragments of knowledge are fundamental to the subaltern studies project because they present clues to other histories and to forms of conceptualization and methodology, often only hinted at in archives, that speak to a different way of conceiving some of the categories of historical investigation, including agency, struggle, insurgency, consciousness, politics, class, even history itself. At stake in attending to knowledge fragments is not empirical variation alone, but new "vantage points." Partha Chatterjee, for example, uses the idea of "fragment" in *The Nation and Its Fragments* as a shorthand for forms of difference and resistance in Bengal that cannot be adequately understood within mainstream representations of nationalism.[38] Conventional accounts of the struggle for Indian Independence and the formation of the modern nation either excluded or actively subordinated fragments around caste, gender, and religion, especially Islam, missing the ways in which anticolonial projects operated with referent points outside of largely European understandings of categories like "nation" and "modern" and "community." Gyanendra Pandey, in *Routine Violence: Nations, Fragments, Histories,* focuses on contemporary versions of Indian nationalism to show how nationalist discourse can be used to spark violence against minority groups.[39]

Pandey shows, for example, how minority groups are recovered as the targets of incorporation, including Dalits, who are assimilated in ways that reproduce caste hierarchy rather than in ways that seek to challenge it. As Pandey elsewhere wrote: "The 'fragments' of Indian society—the smaller religious and caste communities, tribal sections, industrial workers, activist women's groups, all of which might be said to represent 'minority' cultures and practices—have been expected to fall in line with the 'mainstream' (Brahmanical Hindu, consumerist) national culture."[40] It is these minority groups that constitute the fragments in Pandey's critique of Hindu nationalism, and in this sense there is a broad similarity between Chatterjee and Pandey's accounts of how certain discourses of nationalism can serve variously to exclude and subordinate particular ways of knowing or forms of identity.

A knowledge fragment is marked out as such by Chatterjee and Pandey in two broad ways. First, because of its position within a wider set of political, social, and cultural power-knowledge relations. Fragments emerge in the making of dominant cultures and polities, and can therefore shift over time depending on how those power relations change. Second, the fragment can be a form of knowledge, expressed for example as a piece of drama or a collection of poems or a political protest, that presents clues to a different way of understanding history, or the nation, or community, or citizenship. Dipesh Chakrabarty locates subaltern struggle in relation to the "fragmentary and episodic" rather than the pre-given abstractions of the general and continuous routinely put to work by historians.[41] Antonio Gramsci is an important influence here. For Gramsci, the aim was for the subaltern, working with the revolutionary intellectual, to transcend subalternity by becoming a unified political force that can better understand and challenge power and the state.[42] For Chakrabarty, however, it is important analytically and politically to stay with those forms of subaltern struggle that do not necessarily coalesce into a cohesive force—this, after all, is partly what marks those struggles out as subaltern. "Can we imagine another moment of subaltern history," writes Chakrabarty, "where we stay—permanently, not simply as a matter of political tactics—with what is fragmentary and episodic, precisely because that which is fragmentary and episodic does not, cannot, dream of the whole called the state and therefore must be suggestive of knowledge-forms that are not tied to the will that produces the state?"[43]

Notice here that Chakrabarty connects knowledge fragments and the "whole." But it is a whole, for subaltern political agitators at least, that remains obscured. Subaltern struggle cannot "dream of the whole," and so they constitute knowledge fragments in two senses: first, in their status as marginalized or silenced forms of knowledge and episodic political action on the edges of conventional historical archives; and second, because they are animated not by critique of a conventional political whole where the state in particular is vital, but by different centers of gravity. Chakrabarty pushes the notion of fragment to disrupt commonplace conceptions of both the fragment and the whole: "Not 'fragmentary' in the sense of fragments that refer to an implicit whole but fragments that challenge not only the idea of wholeness but the very idea of the 'fragment' itself," because if the fragment is not framed as part of a whole then it needs to be understood differently, a provocation that challenges, contests, and pushes different positions.[44] This sense of the knowledge fragment as something that can take on different and even unpredictable meanings is useful for thinking of fragments as verbs, enrolled in generative relations in the city.

For Chakrabarty, the "fragment" is part of an orientation toward the social world as beyond any one system of representation.[45] Here, knowledge fragments are provocations that demand recognition that the world is more than simply "plural," but is "so plural as to be impossible of description in any one system of representation"; instead, the challenge is to "learn from the subaltern," or as we might put it here, to learn from the fragment: "To go to the subaltern in order to learn to be radically 'fragmentary' and 'episodic' is to move away from the monomania of the imagination that operates within the gesture that the knowing, judging, willing subject always already knows what is good for everybody, ahead of any investigation."[46] Chakrabarty discusses, for instance, Gyan Prakash's book on bonded labor in Bihar, *Bonded Histories: Genealogies of Labour Servitude in Colonial India*, and uses it to argue that some peasant knowledge-forms in colonial India understood power not in relation to the state, labor, and class struggle but to ghosts and spirit cults.[47] However, such ontologies tend to be understood through the prism of a system of representation that takes the modern subject and political struggle as an implicit framing device, meaning that peasant knowledge-forms and (episodic) political action always remain analytically and politically subordinate to the modern.

In this move, Chakrabarty insists that the world is incomplete, multiple, and replete with possibility not because it happens to be very diverse, but because of radically distinct yet coexisting ways of understanding worlds, cities, and so forth. Tariq Jazeel makes a similar argument in relation to what he calls "singularity."[48] For Jazeel, singularity names an approach to knowledge production and conceptualization. His point of departure is that there is enormous scope and potential in attending to alternative knowledges and ways of knowing, and to being open to what they might provoke. As he shows, singularity is not about defining and subsuming knowledge, but is instead "a point at which a given object is simply not defined."[49] These undefined "objects"—ways of knowing or seeing, forms of practice, modes of inhabiting, structures and styles of expression, and so on—can emerge from any source, perhaps in surprising ways.

From this perspective, knowledge fragments are a lure to ways of thinking about the urban and the city, often obscured or radically distinct from dominant and mainstream ways of knowing in policy, research, and practice. This is not the same thing as claiming that knowledge fragments are necessarily subaltern. The subaltern nature of any act or group or individual or space cannot be defined in advance other than to say that it is that which, as Ananya Roy has put it, drawing on Spivak, exists beyond recognition and identification and "marks the silences of our archives and annals."[50] Of course, the tendency to equate subaltern with a more generalized conception of the marginalized has been one of the flashpoints of debate around the use and potential of the category of subaltern. Rather than conflate the two, I see the knowledge fragment as a wider category that names socially and politically marginalized knowledges that may or may not be subaltern and which are both increasingly important to the constitution of urban life, yet often unaccounted for in the run of most urban debate, policy, and practice.

A knowledge fragment may be a marginalized space or group that is regularly identifiable but has not yet been taken seriously as a challenge to conventional ways of understanding cities and the urban condition. The history of urban thinking has demonstrated that conventional categories can be understood in new ways through engagement with other ways of knowing those categories. Take a category as fundamental to the city as infrastructure. Understandings of the production of material and social infrastructures in various parts of the urban world have challenged urban researchers to rethink the basis upon which infrastructure becomes politicized. If critical accounts of infrastructural change have been shaped by a focus on Western Europe and North America, and with that the connections between privatization and inequality, accounts elsewhere have shown that the public-private relationship is often very different, and that privatization is often one of many other political, economic, and cultural logics shaping the nature and politics of infrastructure.[51]

As with material fragments, the knowledge fragment is not straightforwardly equivalent to the particular. It is, instead, the relations in which the fragment is caught up. It is the particular instantiated through what is abstracted from it. That which is abstracted is not a transparent compression of the fragment and what it means. Given the limits of any translation and the frameworks that govern it, it can only ever be a partial grasp, which does not mean that abstraction translation cannot be generative or ethical.[52]

It is useful to hold on to the idea of the knowledge fragment as a marker of how cities and the urban are understood and represented— ways of knowing that arise from living and being and imagining and making the city that have been at the margins or even invisible to much of urban research, policy, and practice, and which may point to new knowledge. The knowledge fragment acts as a kind of lure, an invitation to pause and stay with difference, even as that difference might slip away. Engaging with knowledge fragments—as with material fragments—can provide clues and directions to different ways of understanding cities and the urban condition. In the context of marginalized spaces in the city, ways of using or politicizing or reimagining material fragments always entail forms of knowledge and ways of knowing, and indeed may generate new kinds of knowledge. Nonetheless, the heuristic separation of material and knowledge fragments remains useful, because—as I will show—there are moments when the politics of fragments rests primarily in the realm of how a particular situation is known and understood.

Connecting fragments to wholes does not necessarily mean integrating residents into preexisting liberal wholes. In some cases, the city demands an encounter with alternative knowledge fragments and wholes, which therefore requires a careful, reflective set of engagements about how to support different residential experiences and perceptions without simply integrating them into preexisting frames of knowledge, policy, and practice.

The challenge, as the accounts above indicate, is not only in "seeing" knowledge fragments but in the politics of how they are engaged with and used. For Theodore Adorno, there is a kind of desire for mastery at work in forms of conceptualization that incorporate and subsume difference: "The intrinsic aspiration of all mind to turn every alterity that is introduced to it or that it encounters into something like itself and in this way to draw it into its own sphere of influence."[53] In his elaboration of "negative dialectics," Adorno presents a compelling case for the intellectual potential of the knowledge fragment.[54] Adorno had in mind, for instance, Freud's focus on those phenomena that seemed to exceed existing conceptualizations, such as dreams, slips, neuroses, and so on—areas where dominant forms of thinking have not become embedded, "things that pass unobserved or by what people prefer to regard as undeserving of scrutiny."[55]

The challenge Adorno set forth is: How do we comprehend the fragment, but not subsume it? Rather than attempt to bypass the contradiction, Adorno's position is—as much as is possible—to defend an approach that is anti-synthetic: "[I have] the gravest possible objections to the concept of synthesis . . . a violent antipathy."[56] However seductive conceptual systems might be, whatever "energy" they generate in their promise to capture relations in total, any conceptual work gains by being "guided by the resistance it encounters," i.e., by the material realities of the world and not just by concepts themselves.[57]

Writing in Fragments

For far too long we have busied ourselves with thinking
about ways to change the city. It is about time that we let the
city change the way we think.

—David Kishik, *The Manhattan Project*

If one takes this exteriority of relations as a conducting wire
or a line, one sees a very strange world unfold, fragment by
fragment: a Harlequin's jacket, or patchwork, made up of
solid parts and voids, blocs and ruptures, attractions and
divisions, nuances and bluntness, conjunctions and separations, alternations and interweavings, additions which never
reach a total and subtractions whose remainder is never
fixed.

—Gilles Deleuze and Claire Parnet, *Dialogues*

Montaging Urban Modernity

As a form of fragment writing, the vignette consists of a set of styles, including brief depiction, elicitation, provocation, and juxtaposition, ranging from short reflections to longer explorations of particular themes, cases, or questions. It is a form that is often more impressionistic than analytical, performing a relay of glimpses into issues that matter on their own terms, but where that mattering tends to deepen not through extensive prose but via the juxtaposition of issues in other vignettes. It is often accompanied by a certain rhythm of writing, typically fast in tempo and creating fleeting images, and an experience of moving around, rather than delving into, particular questions. It is a form of writing more suited to the "and" than to the "is," more concerned with multiplicity than the singularity of focused discussion. Perhaps more so than more extensive prose, it is a form that generates a less contained conversation with the reader, more open to tangents of interpretation.

The fragment form of expression generates a set of intersecting lines that, through juxtaposition, have something cumulative to say about the state of things. The fragments might clash and form something unexpected, even as the author guides them in particular directions. In urban thinking, the most notable example of this is Walter Benjamin's luminescent and unfinished text on nineteenth-century Paris, *The Arcades Project*. Across his writings, the city Benjamin conjured—whether it was Paris, Berlin, Naples, Marseilles, or Moscow—often registered through a set of disjointed textual fragments, thrown into juxtapositions that gave a sense of the cinematic quality of urban life and city transformation: the city as both coherent and fragmented, singular and radically multiple, permanent and fleeting, predictable and nonlinear, densifying and falling apart, ordered and disruptive. Benjamin pursued a pedagogy of fragments that drew in difference and alterity as part of a wider project of disrupting what is known and taken-for-granted, jolting us into new ways of seeing and acting. Through juxtaposing fragments of text and disrupting a singular narrative, Benjamin presented the city through different angles of vision simultaneously, producing a montage of difference. As with other writers I mention below, Benjamin's writing in fragments brought form into dramatic performance with content: in a sharply divided, violent, destructive, and unequal urban world, he seems to say, persisting in fragments is often the only way in which life can proceed, and at the same time where possibility might emerge.

Benjamin, who, as David Ferris has put it, lived a life "among the fragmented and fragmenting edges of modernity," argued that the urban modern—what was portrayed through infrastructure, technology, fashion, or politics as "progress" and "coherence," a form of wholism—was in fact violence, exclusion, and exploitation.[1] A "world in fragments," as Susan Buck-Morss has described Benjamin's analysis, in which the passing of time constitutes "not progress but disintegration."[2] The *Arcades* took Haussmann's nineteenth-century transformation of Paris as a central point of reference. Here was a vast illusion of the whole-as-progress, powerfully operating to distract attention from bourgeois power and social inequality. Paris had become a commodity-saturated dreamworld, a phantasmagoric relay of commodity display, fashion, and technological exhibition.

Benjamin's method of writing in a montage of fragments mirrors and performs the heterogeneity and discontinuities of urban history and experience.[3] Through montage, the fragment emerges not just as a series of disconnected bits and pieces thrown together but as an ontology of urban modernity. As Jacqueline Lichenstein presents it in another context: "This conception of the fragment puts in question the very idea of a unified totality . . . Indeed, it might be thought paradigmatic of what we used to call *modernity*. It leads towards a new conception of totality as a non-unified totality, fragmented or dismembered—however paradoxical that notion."[4]

Like the poet and flaneur Charles Baudelaire, whom he admired so much, Benjamin was a kind of urban "ragpicker," interested in "the refuse and the detritus of the great city," and in using this urban detritus allegorically to reveal the horrors and possibilities of contemporary life.[5] He repeatedly juxtaposed images—both visual and discursive—of aging arcades, discarded clothes or toys, fading advertisements, fleeting encounters, ways of seeing and moving through the city, and myths and stories of the past, to provoke new ways of thinking about what the present might otherwise be. For Benjamin, fragments were not just bits of the whole or even symbols of the whole, but entry points into other ways of remembering the past, making the present, and building the future. Fragments, or "thought fragments" as Hannah Arendt, writing about Benjamin, called them, had conceptual significance and potential.[6]

This is an urbanism of pre-given scripts but also of affordances. Part of Benjamin's aim was to interrupt the narrative form of history and present, and to do so by allowing the "rags and refuse" of the city to forge critical ways of seeing urban modernity. Allegory was a vital part of his pedagogy of fragments. Allegory takes a fragment, disconnects it from its context, and gives it a new meaning alongside other fragments.[7] As Howard Eiland and Michael Jennings argue, it is a method well suited to seeing the city, because it entails exploration of the "multilayered life of the city, with its many threshold experiences and its tendency to incorporate older forms as traces within the framework of the new."[8] Allegory involves "weaving webs of the fragments of narratives" in the "ruins of the city," a process that "excavates the fragments and then recombines them," of "unravelling and then recasting in fragments."[9] Through allegory, insight is produced through empirical points of departure, not as symbols—where the general is revealed *in* the particular— but where the general is revealed in dialogue *between* particulars.

Benjamin produced constellations of images. One result was to generate synchronic parallels, for instance between the growing grip of Nazi urban industrialism in the 1930s and Haussmann's nineteenth-century state-sponsored projects in Paris, or between Hitler's seizure of power and that of Napoleon III (both took power, then used a vote to legitimize it).[10] Here, at junctures Benjamin called dialectics at a stand-still, "it is not that what is past casts light on what is present, or what is present its light on what is past; rather, image is that wherein what has been comes together in a flash with the now to form a constellation."[11] "In the dialectical image," writes Susan Buck-Morss, the present as the moment of revolutionary possibility acts as "a lodestar for the assembly of historical fragments."[12]

Yet none of this was entirely decided or clear-cut, and in places the process of writing in fragments seems to be one of Benjamin staging the ambivalences and inviting a conversation with the reader around something he's not quite certain about himself. The task, as Benjamin described it in 1927, was to display the city's presents and futures as they are "brutally and distinctly visible among the people and their environment,"[13] and to allow readers to dwell between insight and uncertainty, as a way of both living with and making sense of the "picture-puzzles."[14] Those "picture-puzzles," as Benjamin's longtime friend and interlocutor Theodore Adorno argued, stayed with Benjamin and derived from a commitment "to immerse himself without reserve in the world of multiplicity."[15]

In his 1928 essay "One Way Street," for example, Benjamin refused both linear narration and any division of macro and micro, and was concerned instead with "the same phenomenon viewed in different ways."[16] An experiment with often discordant fragments, "One Way Street" presents textual fragments of the urban modern, and sees Benjamin continually shift the narrative around, from bemoaning the decline of social interaction in an increasingly commodified Germany or reflections on the craft of writing, to passages on books, art, how children read, or how the urban experience so often depends on the contingency of timing and encounter. As Rebecca Solnit has written, the short narratives in the book "are like a warren of streets and alleys," and its form "seems to mimic a city": "a subversive confection of short passages titled as though they were city sites and signs—Gas Station, Construction Site, Mexican Embassy, Manorially Furnished Ten-Room Apartment, Chinese Curios."[17] Solnit is right to state that Benjamin's textual fragments, so often "beautiful aphorisms and leaps of imagination," are less about defining the urban moment and more about "evocation" of its mood, tendencies, and political conjuncture.[18]

"One Way Street" was published not long after the release of Walter Ruttman's brilliant silent film, *Berlin: Symphony of a Great City,* a captivating montage of urban industrial modernity—from trains, factories, and streets to crowds, movement, and metropolitan rhythm—located in Benjamin's home city. As Esther Leslie has argued, the film's syncopation and montage influenced Benjamin's attempts to find a language to describe Berlin in his own work.[19] "Benjamin's autobiographical writings of the city," she elsewhere wrote, "arrange fragments of Berlin in filmic analogues: scenes, sequences, edits, close-ups, details, moments montaged together . . . a string of disconnected, non-chronological snapshots."[20]

Benjamin's work is part of a much larger tradition of attempting to understand the urban modern in a way that is, as Jean and John Comaroff have put it in a different context, neither an "all-embracing meta-narrative" nor "microscopically, myopically local," but the "awkward scale between": a critical theory "immanent in life itself," which "may occur anywhere and everywhere."[21] For David Kishik, the aim in this approach "is not to be *in* a city but, as strange as it may sound, to *be* a city, to let it affect us—with no fear or remorse": "For far too long we have busied ourselves with thinking about ways to change the city," Kishik boldly writes, "it is about time that we let the city change the way we think."[22] This idea of "being a city" derives, Kishik suggests, from the "sheer life" of the city ("sheer life" is a term Benjamin uses in passing to describe the buzzing landscapes of Paris in the *Arcades*). Immersion in the sheer life of the city enables an account of how the urban world is produced and lived as it continually pulls together, falls apart, and becomes remade through projects small and large.

In *The Manhattan Project,* Kishik attempts to imagine how Benjamin, had he lived through World War II, would have understood New York, working in much the same way he once did in Paris. He positions Benjamin in the Public Library in Manhattan, working through a dense and diverse archive of twentieth-century New York. If the preoccupations of the *Arcades* were arcades, Haussmann, Baudelaire, Marx, gaslight, advertising, and fashion, in New York Benjamin's fragments, Kishik speculates, might include Robert Moses, Hannah Arendt, Andy Warhol, neon, graffiti, hip-hop, and of course the shopping mall. Instead of focusing on the dense, commodity-saturated dazzling city center as a locus of the urban phantasmagoria, Kishik's imaginary Benjamin locates the phantasmic in the American twentieth-century obsession with the suburban ideal, an ideal that, Kishik argues, both abandons the rest of the city and lacks the vitality of the street: "Phantasmagorias never die; they just relocate to a new zipcode."[23]

As much as Kishik's arguments are inspired by the *Arcades,* among other sources, there is a shift at work here that requires a rethinking of the work of the fragment from Benjamin's writings. In the *Arcades,* Kishik rightly argues, fragments—for all that they open out imaginative and political possibilities—are "tragic reflection" or the "experience of disaster," because they remain sutured to modern urban commodity capitalism and often brutal state power.[24] Commentators who find redemptive and hopeful forms of fragments in Benjamin's work often end up referring to his writing *outside* of the *Arcades.* In contrast, the imaginary Benjamin of New York is less determined by ruin, loss, and catastrophe, and more by possibility and openings. While possibilities emerge in all sorts of spaces—Kishik points to some forms of modern art, fashion, hip-hop, film, and dance, for instance—it is the in-between spaces of the city's streets, its sheer life, that constitute its "potentialities."[25]

Sheer life, argues Kishik, is a kind of *infrastructure* of the city, where infrastructure here is not only material systems but a liveliness very much of the city street, a liveliness that is at once bodily and social, biological and cultural, private and public. Part of Kishik's point is that the life of the city cannot be reduced to written regulations and laws, or to architectures and housing, or to blueprints and city visions, but is instead found in the great layering and overlapping of occurrences and interactions. The street is vital in Kishik's account in various ways: as a city in miniature, as an example of the *actuality* of the city, or as a space of potentially living differently. From early films focused on life in the street, to Andy Warhol's films or Tehching Hseih's art, Kishik examines a series of works focused on the "actualities" of city life. These works "see" sheer life precisely because they cease to categorize it.

But this isn't simply empiricism or anti-conceptual posturing. There is a more profound claim at work here, which is that we only begin to understand what urban life is when, paradoxically, we recognize that we lose sight of its coeval and experiential multiplicity in the very effort to "pin it down." No surprise that Kishik partly takes this line of thought from Benjamin, given that the latter—as Andy Merrifield has argued—wrote from the position that however saturated urban life was with commodification, that commodification was at the same time never total, because the city in the end was always too elusive, multiple, porous, and improvisatory. For this reason, and notwithstanding the mood of destruction that we often find in the *Arcades,* Merrifield insists that Benjamin's city is "a city of hope, a place full of pedestrians, sexiness, and bustling streets."[26]

I locate my own use of fragments not so much in "sheer life" as in urban densities. When I use the term "density," I have in mind not just the busy, diverse, and experimental city center street—the kind of street that exists more and more in a romantic urban imagination rather than in practice—but instead a wider set of experiences of "throwntogetherness," to borrow Doreen Massey's felicitous phrase.[27] Density matters to the remaking and politicization of fragments around the broken toilet block or at the public water pipe that needs constant attending to. It matters as groups mass together to protest the inadequacy of state-provided fragments of infrastructure or services or housing, or when the state bulldozes those same provisions into fragments. It matters in the ways that activists and refuges pull together to protest, or share resources, or try to settle disputes. It matters to how artists pull bits and pieces of stuff, or elements of marginalized knowledges, into dense configurations not only of people but of objects and ideas that provoke a different story about a place and its struggles. Set against these different relations between density and urban life, "sheer life" is too narrow a term, and in a sense too demanding of the people caught up in fragment urbanism, who are after all sometimes in the desperate position of just trying to make sure urban life remains viable at all in the face of violence or dispossession, or the struggles of poverty.

Without Closure

In his montage method, inspired by Benjamin, Allan Pred brought fragments into relation with one another to enable "combinatory possibilities" that distills new ways of seeing.[28] In his close and concentrated juxtaposing of verbal and visual fragments from all kinds of sources in his work on Sweden—newspapers, anecdotes, song lyrics, jokes, ethnographic research, aphorisms, photography, cartoons, and more—Pred connected the industrial modernity of nineteenth-century capitalism to the hypermodernity of late twentieth-century capitalism. His aim in doing so was to "bring alive" the text to "multiple ways of knowing and multiple sets of meaning." His commitment to textual fragments entails ways of seeing from different angles of vision. By hurtling fragments together and assembling montages of everyday life, Pred gave his accounts of the modern, as Derek Gregory has put it, "an intensity of experience quite alien to most conventional human geographies."[29]

Pred's approach was to "force discordant fragments to whisper and shout at each other in polylogue," so that the reader might find associations:

> One may, in other words,
> attempt to illuminate,
>   by way of shock,
> attempt to jolt out of position
>   by suggesting a totality of fragments,
> attempt to destabilize

> by way of a stunning constellation,
> without insisting upon a closure
> that does not exist.[30]

Or, to take another example, in 1991 the journalist Peter Jukes produced a remarkable book, *A Shout in the Street,* that follows a broadly
similar approach to that of Benjamin's *Arcades.* Jukes uses the fragment
form to assemble a vertiginous range of sources, bringing together multiple fragments from sources across different scholarly and nonscholarly
registers. Unlike Benjamin, who focused in the *Arcades* on one city,
Jukes develops a comparative dialogue across four cities: London, Paris,
Leningrad, and New York.

Jukes clusters the book around a set of recurring themes—poverty,
bodies, commodities, crowds, power, and mobility, all themes for Benjamin too—which he draws out in relation to often powerfully revela-
tory images and textual fragments. The fragments of text are sources
from all kinds of writers, from Charles Dickens and Virginia Woolf, or
Benjamin and Jane Jacobs, to Le Corbusier, Frank Lloyd Wright, and
Richard Sennett, all set alongside the poetry of Charles Baudelaire, the
music of Bruce Springsteen and Bob Dylan, the writing of Leon Trotsky,
the photography of Teresa Watkins, and graffiti in the Bronx. Through
them, he weaves a remarkable urban historical geography, a concentration and constellation of urban scenes, analyses, and provocations.

The book is organized around the cities, starting with London and
ending in New York, while some of the sources—Baudelaire, for
instance—run through all of the discussions. Jukes combines a careful
focus on context with a wider effort to create resonances across the cities. Four essays frame and bring together the fragments: street as
museum (London), street as market (Paris), street as forum (Leningrad),
and street as thoroughfare (New York). These essays both reflect on the
fragments that preceded them, interpreting them or using them as provocations for particular discussions on urban change and perception,
and reach out comparatively across the four cities.

Key themes recur. The de-/re-densification of London over time, for
example, is a testament to the city and national state's repeated focus on
abolishing not poverty but poor places; London as an historical geography of production and accumulation, rarely redistribution: "Landscapes of poverty" are made "into playgrounds, but only for those who
can afford it."[31] The history of London is presented as one of profound
discontinuity, its geography regularly torn apart amidst changing forms

of architecture, planning, wealth, and war. The essay on Paris, in contrast, reflects on the streets following Haussmannization, and returns again and again to the play of private desire, consumption, and the crowd. Much of this discussion hinges on male consumption of commodities, styles, and women. Being visible and being seen becomes central to the production of what Benjamin would call, in the *Arcades*—following Baudelaire in particular— "urban types"; shorthands for nineteenth-century forms of urban life shaped in part through power, seeing, and performance. The emerging power of advertising and spectacle are significant here.

The story of Leningrad is different again—one not of the *social* crowd but of the *political* crowd and of street fights—while in New York it is a thoroughly American story of mobility and transformation, of space derived through and for motion, and of the city's streets as orchestras of cars, commerce, and unequal multiculture. Throughout, the historical geographies of these four great cities are presented fundamentally as processes of fragmentation, of cities carved up and divided even in the face of—and in fact sometimes because of—efforts to bring a kind of unity, connection, or holism to the city, from Haussmannization in Paris to Moses's New York. What's especially powerful is how Jukes's use of textual fragments renders visible the ways in which fragmentation operates through simultaneously economic, social, political, and material registers. The production of urban types and new forms of fashion, display commodification, and café culture in Paris were dependent, he shows, on the demolitions that enabled the wide boulevards delivered through Haussmann, and the state power and violence behind it, as Benjamin too so insisted.

Jukes looks on at the fragments he has assembled from a conceptual distance. His concern is not so much to assemble fragments that he endorses or that reflect a particular normative position—indeed, some of the sources are in contradiction or even socially or politically regressive—but to rummage around in different archives of knowing the city at particular times. He is interested in how certain motifs, images, and discourses became attached to particular urban moments, whether the Parisian flaneur or the Dickensian view of Victorian London as narrow, crowded, sometimes "grotesque," deeply unequal, and always full of stories.[32] He is sometimes critical of the accounts and depictions in the fragments. He often reflects on how sites described in the historical fragments later became something quite different and unanticipated.

And yet the conceptual distance Jukes deploys, which is important to his form of observational analysis, leaves him as an author curiously missing from the text. His methodologies of knowing fragments, and the implications of the author in producing an account through fragments, slip from view. In some forms of fragment writing, such a removal is rejected from the outset, and with powerful effects, and it is to examples of these that I now turn.

Points of Departure

Ivan Vladislavic's *Portrait with Keys: Joburg and What-What,* is a wonderful example of the fragment form of writing centered around one city, Johannesburg. The text is a careful and often deeply personal reflection on racism and inequality in the city, and the attendant geographies of security and confrontation around them. The book consists not of quotations and essays, which is the method of Jukes, Benjamin, and Pred, but of 138 vignettes from the city, cutting across different space-times and issues. If this form is a kind of journeying through multiple points in the city, it is no surprise that Vladislavic provides a set of possible "itineraries" at the end of the text, which he calls "thematic pathways," through the book.[33] This thematic index lists themes and page numbers around a set of issues that he describes as being "symbiotically" connected.[34] There are twenty-nine in total, ranging from "ghosting through" and "painted walls" to "security," "walking," and "water."

It is a thoroughly spatial and temporal account of the city. Vladislavic situates his book in the textures of the city, and from it weaves an account of unease, transformation, and inequality. The start-stop rhythm of the vignettes has him always moving around, shifting back and forth through history and across neighborhoods, connecting encounters with family and friends to moments of eviction and displacement, to security and anxiety, to labor inequality, to begging and stealing—a city that is "a fiction that unravels even as I grasp it."[35] While some histories have been removed, even brutally, from the city, other histories force their way to the surface, such as the tramlines tarred over in the 1960s that are now becoming visible on broken surfaces, or the old cinemas now converted to junk shops, or the histories of gold prospecting now mirrored in the speculative prospecting of downtown high-rise real estate.

The vignettes facilitate a flexibility in the writing. Vladislavic reveals, for example, the rise and fall of a particular part of the city through vignettes centered around aspiration and, later, disappointment. People and places are changed through shifting logics and circumstances, even while their previous traces and histories persist and translate. Johannesburg is a "frontier city" of evermore elaborate and politicized spatial securitizing and defending, caught in a grip of race- and class-based politics, both moving up and out as it grows, and forming barriers all the time, so that former paths come to abrupt ends against new walls and fences.[36] Material fragments everywhere tell stories of previous geographies—Vladislavic often writes of "ghosts" of former urbanisms—such as the broken or decaying metal hinges from gates now buried into remote-controlled barriers. The city that emerges is fugitive and full of surprises, but also always often one of conflict, and sometimes waiting things out until the dust settles.

The style of fragment writing I am using is closer to Vladislavic than to, say, Pred's more poetic form of writing that managed to so elegantly perform different possibilities, meanings, and politics in words, sentences, and segments. I use vignettes of different lengths, some short and others longer, more sustained excursions into particular questions, themes, or cases, grouped under particular themes in the different parts of the book.

Vladislavic's style of short, energetic, and sometimes surreal vignette-writing is not, of course, uncommon. Luiz Ruffato's powerful book, *There Were Many Horses,* is a series of sixty-eight fragments, typically two or three pages long, consisting of instances across one day in São Paulo from before sunrise to after sunset.[37] The fragments take radically different forms, each providing a glimpse into the multiplicity of life in the city—some are extracts from menus, prayers, or horoscopes, others relay a stream of phone answering-machine messages or run through lists of books on a shelf, and there are others—most in fact—that tell stories of individual lives of struggle, fear, uncertainty, crime, exploitation, or hopes lost. It is a powerful and often moving set of lenses on the profound inequalities and hardships of the city, and the strains that living in and making a living in São Paulo place on daily life and relationships. The city that emerges is a brutal one, in which people are ground down, their aspirations lost to struggle or tragedy, where violence and catastrophe lurk in even the most mundane spaces and encounters, where longings are often unfulfilled and painful memories haunt buildings, streets, and neighborhoods. In Ruffato's stories people's lives are often falling apart—livelihoods lost, relationships breaking down, energies dissipated—and the fragment form mirrors the struggle of living in the city. At the same time there are stories of care, kindness, friendship, family support, social infrastructure, joy, and laughter, and spirituality fills everyday life.

Perhaps more than anything else, what emerges is a city of fleeting moments and encounter. São Paulo is here a city in motion, of people on the move and encountering one another, of places and memories rushing past, of people warily attempting to read a hugely complex and multifaceted city that exceeds their grasp, trying to figure which risks to take or avoid, working out who to trust and connect with and who to move past. Ruffato plays with punctuation and fonts to create pauses, emphases, shifts, and diversions that communicate a sense of the cacophonous city going on all around people and with which they may or may not at any moment become differently entangled. What the fragment form allows here is a sense of all of this happening, for the city's inhabitants, in the movement of the moment. Here, the book seems to say, is the incessant city that Paulistanos are forced to deal with, and all they can do is muster what differential know-how, networks, and resources they can to move with it:

> são paulo streaks of lightning
> (is são paulo the out-there? is it the in-here?) . . .
> rattling down Rebouças Avenue
> the traffic light shifts green to red
> cars and cars
> bums peddlers boys girls
> cars and cars
> thieves muggers hookers dealers
> cars and cars
> another day
> tuesday
> weekend far away
> the streetlights headlights lights on the electronic panels
> of the buses
> and everything is the color of tiredness
>   and the bodies are even more tired
>   more tired
> my calves are killing me and my head is killing me my[38]

The relationship between the fragment form and the city on the move is a device we see in other city writing, including, for example, books based on moving across urban space. Iain Sinclair's *London Overground: A Day's Walk around the Ginger Line,* is a fast-paced and often personal text made of vignettes, and part of a series of similarly styled books he has written on London that are informed by long walking excursions. Sinclair persuades an old friend to walk with him along the new Overground train line. What results is an often intimate conversation between Sinclair and the city, where "the city" is configured not just by particular encounters and sights on the way but by the memories, writers, and controversies they provoke. It is a brilliantly erudite, loquacious, and—like much of his writing—often very funny account.

Sinclair's text both follows the geographical route of the line and jumps all over the place. At one moment we are in the midst of a personal reflection on Angela Carter's work, a writer who clearly left a big imprint on Sinclair, whose novels revealed London as "a beautiful monster . . . deformed, heavy-bodied, flighty, vulnerable," and which "inform and inspire our city."[39] In another moment Sinclair is provoked to think of Patrick Keiller and his films of the city, or later the poet John Clare, or the painter Leon Kossoff, or J. G. Ballard. In other places he is attacking particular architectural failures they encounter on the walk, or describing how streets and areas have changed, for instance through the shifting property values along the line. Fragments of text from places, lives, and histories, woven alongside fragments of space, from discarded things or abandoned places to "those urban secrets allowed to survive between eras: a crack, a cranny, old bricks brushing our shoulders."[40] It is not just the author who drifts, but the prose and Sinclair's particular histories of the city.

The fragment form of writing helps to give Sinclair license in his writing, a capacity to imaginatively roam, a freedom to bring seemingly disparate and disharmonious issues together. It is an exciting disruption of the conventional barriers of writing, this refusal to stick to any particular line (other than the train line itself), and it calls to mind the experimental energy of Pred's faith in the "combinatory possibilities" of fragment writing. Nonetheless, a wider statement on London runs through the book: the city, Sinclair sometimes grumpily complains, seems to be losing its depths and possibilities to crude and unconvincing speculative capital, or to just plain badly thought-through interventions. The material and social legacies of Thatcherism and its austere afterlives are frequently encountered. Clapham Junction, for example, one of the sites on the route, is "overprescribed, a little shaky on its feet," only just about making space for the "casualties of cuts and expulsions who are barely tolerated, as invisibles, in the microclimate of station-conforming blocks with pointless water features and thrown-up overnight estates."[41] The city emerges as increasingly divided. The Chelsea Harbour "regeneration," for instance, with its luxury apartments and boats, may have only been partially successful (on its own terms) but nonetheless "trades in separateness . . . built as a set, refusing cultural memory."[42] The Earls Court Exhibition Centre, which opened in 1887 and which was the focus of major statements about the nature of London and Britain, from Empire and modernism to New Labourism, is—predictably—slated for "development into the standard blend of residential flats, retail outlets and a convention centre."[43]

Sinclair, and his walking mate, are—like the city—always on the move, and just about everything seems to be fleeting or in question. The city is a point of departure and a provocation for Sinclair's sojourns into art, writing, poetry, or interrupted commentaries on the contemporary moment. At the same time, in doing so he returns again to the city, and to the specific place and moment of the walk, whether it is the Hampstead he "never quite qualified for . . . financially, culturally, sartorially," or the places just beyond the walk, such as St Pancras Old Church, a "whole area up for grabs" of "railway terminals, redeveloped warehouses, Euro shopping zones, canal veins ghosting towards the Islington tunnel."[44] He is not only writing in fragments, he is—like Benjamin—continually encountering them in the city.

The story is also a metabolic and embodied one. His companion is seemingly always hungry. Toward the end of the walk Sinclair is so tired that "walking becomes dreaming": "Legs could not remember a time when they weren't keeping my weight off the pavements. Those grey Camden flagstones were another sky. Tarmac was treacle. My soft cartilage was so worn down that I could hear the grinding of bone on bone."[45] The walk, then, is always already a mix of multiple imperatives: the immediacy of place is also the immediacy of memory provoked by place, the damning condemnation of place is caught up not just with socioeconomic transformation but with the experience of encounter and navigation. "Wanderers are amateurs of geography, literature, statistics," he writes, "scavenging researchers, provokers of exploitable accidents. They behave like suspended detectives with no proper brief . . . Walking is the only tool of interrogation."[46] Textual fragments, here, are a collage from all kinds of origins, a density of translations coordinated into a holding pattern of intersecting lines.

I describe Sinclair's account above as both intimate and embodied. This matters. For a start—and I will return to this later when I discuss walking and fragments—Sinclair's capacity to roam the city is enabled by his being a white male. The city, as an idea and set of spatialities, is not neutral, but actively constituted by inequalities of gender, race, class, age, bodily ability, and so on. His practice and his writing, and I recognize this too in my own methods and writing and will return to it, are enabled and shaped by the historical production of inequality in the city. His emphasis on the embodied nature of his walks points to something else about the nature of knowledge production on the city, which is that it is based not just in this or that theoretical tradition or epistemology, but in the contingent—and, again, unequal—encounters with the city, and how they have been shaped in the context of Sinclair's own experiences as a Londoner.

The intimate and the embodied, and the inequalities around them, are vital parts of how we come to see and write the city. These are points of departure, and just as much as abstraction or conceptual work. The fragment form allows Sinclair to push this intimacy and bodily connection, as he jumps around fragments not just of places but of memory and text, often with little concern for narrative other than the chronological arc of the walk itself. In urban scholarship, it is important to point out, concerns with the role of the intimate and the embodied—and the personal, professional, institutional, and geopolitical privileges that inevitably accompany them—are not often written into accounts of the city and urban change. Much of the creative and political thinking here that has been done has been done by feminists.[47] Sinclair's method is one approach for making more space for the intimate and the embodied.

Fred Moten's *Black and Blur* works too with entangled fragments of text, and with the blurring of all kinds of places, practices, and histories, but with a focus on Blackness that implicates the author and reader from the outset. Like Sinclair's *London Overground*, Vladislavic's *Portrait with Keys*, and Kishik's *The Manhattan Project*, Moten's book is an extraordinarily eclectic concoction of encounters, from jazz, rap, film, and art to social theory, philosophy, and historical transformations, from C. L. R. James and Cedric Robinson to Deleuze and Adorno. And like those books, his text is equally transgressive of borders of place and knowledge-forms, equally open to lines of flight. Indeed,

Moten opens the book, in the preface, declaring that his effort is one of "trying hard not to succeed in some final and complete determination."[48] The form is a kind of "escape," an "ode to impurity," a political commitment to showing that racial slavery and freedom are always yoked together in a resonant "durational field" rather than simply as historical events, carried forward into art, music, and politics.[49]

The book is organized around twenty-five chapters and fifty sections of different lengths, ranging from the music of Miles Davis to the art of Theaster Gates. Music, for example, emerges here as both freedom and unfreedom, a force that comes together and repeats, which can be disciplined, but which can be improvised, a simultaneous dispossession and possession. Musical forms and political identities in Black culture, he argues, are forged in historical injury, trauma, and dispossession. The form of the book—a dissonant montage of theorization and encounters with Blackness—is itself a performance of the irreducibility of the traces of history, including slavery, domination, and self-determinations, where "being black is only being black in groups," "dissonant," "atonal," "atotal," and "experimental."[50] Music is vital to Moten's writing, not just as a source for analysis but as a style of thought. For example: "I've barely written about hip-hop . . . [but] my work is grounded in it . . . I emerge from it."[51] Moten describes hip-hop, via a discussion of Rakim and Gayatri Spivak, as education through the noncoercive rearrangement of desire: a desire to listen, dance, to act out individually and in common a life and sociality that is always entangled and blurred.

Hip-hop, like jazz, is itself a montage of fragments. As Franklin Sirmans argues, hip-hop "takes apart and reassembles," putting techniques from the past and elsewhere into new uses.[52] Sirmans sees a similar move in the montage paintings of Jean-Michel Basquait, the New York artist who died at just twenty-seven but who left behind an astounding range of work. Basquait, Sirmans argues, recombined Western painting, traditions of African art, neo-Expressionism, and a politics of decolonization. His art was both modernist and a "barbed critique" of modern art.[53] Basquait's work was as much urban as global, as much about race and class as it was about geopolitics and colonialism.

In the late 1970s, US hip-hop, Sirmans argues, was passing through a moment of innovation, albeit with, or maybe because of, simple materials—turntables and a microphone—while Basquait was embarking on his work with similarly mundane technologies: paper, pens, and a Xerox machine. Like hip-hop, Basquait's montages combined image and text—"with words cut, pasted, recycled scratched out, and repeated," producing work that sometimes looked like "a torn piece of wall"—critiquing the political moment through themes of war, racism, class politics, colonial power, and postcolonial subjects.[54] For Kimberley Parker, Basquait "presented a vision of a fragmented, colonized self in search of an organizing principle," connecting events from Haiti as well as African American history and troubling at questions of mimicry, power, and identity.[55] His habit of working with themes of presence and erasure, writing words that are crossed out and difficult to read, for example, suggests cultural trace, the often violent unmaking of cultural forms, practices, and identities that nonetheless persist in translation.[56]

As with Moten's writing, Basquait's art was influenced by jazz—Charlie Parker, Miles Davis, and others—alongside hip-hop, paying tribute to Black cultural invention but without losing sight of the exploitation and ongoing violence that shaped it. As Sirmans points out, there is also a cultural mixing at work here, an historical and material Creole formation that recalls the collages of Richard Saunders using found objects, and the work of the Italian art movement, Arte Povera, in the 1960s and 1970s. Arte Povera, a loose collective operating through painting, sculpture, photography, and more, worked with throwaway detritus rather than with themes of race, music, and culture, but what's common here is a commitment to the always already blurred relations between origins and sources, and the distinction to established forms of expression, narrative, and dominant value.

Fragments and Possibility

What is at work—across the different texts described in this part of the book—in the effort to express the world in ways that avoid a "completeness" or linearity, or a neatness of categorization? As Eric Santer has argued, there is a larger critique at play here of the "Enlightenment faith in progress . . . [from] fantasies of plenitude, purity, centrality, unity, and mastery," and the violences that enabled and flow from them. Instead, he argues, there is a proliferating intellectual discourse of "shattering, rupture, mutilation, fragmentation, to images of fissures, wounds, rifts, gaps, and abysses." Santer is surely right to connect the appeal of the fragment with disillusionment with the promises of Enlightenment, and with modernity and particular ideas of the "whole" too. For Marshall Berman, for example, the expansion of modernity from the start of the sixteenth century to its grip in the twentieth in the form of an expanding "modern public" became increasingly shattered "into a multitude of fragments," so that the very idea of modernity lost its "vividness, resonance and depth . . . its capacity to organise and give meaning to people's lives."[57]

And yet there is also more at work here. In the writing of Benjamin and Adorno, for example, the appeal of the fragment was in part borne out of their own individual historical experiences—in the shadows of World War I and the Depression, and with Nazism, World War II, and the Holocaust—but also in the political potential of the fragment. Fragments can slip out of the grip of power. Sometimes, fragments name something beyond, or at least on the edges of, the control of ideology, economy, and power—a flicker of alternatives and a suggestion of something else. In an essay on Benjamin, Adorno wrote that "hope appears only in fragmented form."[58] Greil Marcus puts it this way:

> If the technics of [the] antimodern were unlimited in their capacity for oppression, brutality, and evil, for erasing the very understanding of the modern of what it meant it meant to be human, one thing that linked Benjamin, Aragon, Adorno, and Chtchelgov (and, for a moment, Ruttman, before he became a Nazi) was the philosophical conviction, or instinct, that the totality had to be resisted, even chipped away, even defeated, by the fragment: the street, the sign, the name, the face, the aphorism, the evanescent, the ephemeral, the worthless, the unimportant, the meaningless.[59]

Across many of the accounts above, the fragment as a form of expression is at once a description or performance of the damaged present, and a generative potential, whether through written or artistic montage or through music. The present emerges, at different historical moments and places from Benjamin on Paris and Vladislavic on Johannesburg to Ruffato on São Paulo and Basquait on late twentieth-century New York, as fragmented, as *persisting in fragments,* as if to say that in the violence and transformations of the urban world, this is the only way in which conditions *can* proceed. Fragments of different kinds too: of knowledge, sociality, materials, places, and things.

In these accounts, fragments in their different guises—as textual forms, as material bits and pieces, or as cultural traces—are both a form of expression and a name for how a world produced through violence nonetheless continues even as it weaves the ongoingness of violence into the textures of expressing and living. In this reading, the "whole" is not so much something that did not or cannot exist, but sometimes just inconceivable, a kind of impossibility: in the face of exploitation or destruction, and in the face of efforts to assemble (and ensemble) ways of getting by and getting on, the whole is so often something that is simply gone, disappeared, beyond realization, sometimes brutally so.

Drawing on Santer, Veena Das's account of the ethnographic knowledge-making of violence uses the idea of the "fragment," but in a different direction from Santer. For Das, the fragment is not a part that can be assembled into a totality, but "the impossibility of such an imagination":

> Instead fragments allude to a particular way of inhabiting the world, say, in a gesture of mourning. I have in mind a picture of destruction, such as that sketched by Stanley Cavell in his writings on philosophy, literature and film. Cavell takes up Wittgenstein's famous comment—of his investigations destroying everything that is great and important, "leaving behind only bits

of stone and rubble" . . . What is it to pick up the pieces and to live in this very place of devastation? This is what animates the lives and texts in this book.[60]

Living with devastation, where the idea of the whole appears to be an impossibility, but finding a way of going on. Das's careful accounts of survivors of violence from the Partition and the 1984 massacre of Sikhs following the assassination of Indira Gandhi in India show that people often go on not through recovering "grand gestures" but "through a descent into the ordinary," in which trauma and violence are "folded into ongoing relationships" in fragile, intimate everyday textures, and where stories about violence might in a sense be *spoken* but rarely *voiced*.[61] The book's accounts of violence against women are powerful but at the same time—because of that power—point to the limits of language in expressing or describing those violences and traumas amidst efforts to "pick up the pieces." As Gyanendra Pandey has written, in conditions like these—conditions shared by " 'partition sufferers', African-Americans, slaves, untouchables and women"—"certainty of knowledge, the clarity of History, and the consistency of ideological 'truth'," fall away and in their place emerges the possibility of stories distinct from "the historians' history that we have come to privilege," but which is now confronted instead with knowledge fragments beyond learned forms of graspable legibility.[62]

For all that fragments, whether they are objects or knowledges or texts, are so often the product of violence and damage, or subject to neglect, exclusion, or misappropriation, there is also a sense in the accounts above that it is perhaps the fragment, and not the whole, that persists. Jean Baudrillard's *Fragments: Cool Memories III, 1990–1995*, the third text in a series, uses the fragment form to make a similar argument. The text consists of fragments of varying lengths, from a single sentence to a page or so, with no chapters, index, or contents list. The entries are often gloomy and cynical, weaving around a range of issues, from contemporary reflections on war or sport or discussions of sense-making in media and culture, to reflections on sex and relationships, politics, and professional practices such as writing or conferencing. Baudrillard uses the fragment form of writing in an attempt to destroy any linear conception of continuity of expression, in order to mirror what "the system has done to reality," which is to transform and distort it so that it persists but in ways that "no one knows what to do with."[63]

There is a sense in Baudrillard's text that even when everything else seems to fall apart, when the reader is dragged into a maelstrom of representation and simulation, that the only things we will be left with are the fragments, "like the flies in a plane crash which are the only survivors because they are ultralight": "[T]hey alone will survive the catastrophe, the destruction of meaning and language . . . the lightest items sink the most slowly into the abyss. It is these one must hang on to."[64] There is, for Baudrillard, a kind of democracy of expression here, in which each insight resonates with at least some reader, and opens out a potential future discussion that is foreshadowed but uncertain and not pursued: "Fragmentary writing is, ultimately, democratic writing. Each fragment enjoys an equal distinction. The most banal one finds its exceptional reader. Each, in its turn, has its hour of glory."[65]

Of course, in practice fragmentary writing is a series of decisions about what to include, where and how, and is always a process of seeing from somewhere. Is Baudrillard right to suggest that writing in fragments is more open than more linear forms of structured writing? I doubt the form of writing is the key variable here. What matters most is how form is related to content, argumentation, and sensibility in the writing. Nonetheless, the form can play a role. My hope is that the form of writing I pursue in this book, which is to be sure a lighter form of fragment writing composed mainly of longer pieces of text that are less broken up and more integrated than some of the examples of writing described above, underlines the potential of fragments to generate insight amidst the radical differences that characterize the urban world. Part of the reason Walter Benjamin often wrote in fragments was to capture the "schematic form" of urban life and possibility.[66] In these schematics was not just a critique of the present but resources from the past that might form constellations that provoke alternative futures. Fragments in this light can become caught up in politically charged relations, prodding and prompting at an urbanism of violence and possibility, juxtaposition and dialogue, affordance and lines of flight.

Political Framings

The "fragment" . . . is not just a "bit"—the dictionary's "piece broken off"—of a preconstituted whole. Rather, it is a disturbing element, a "disturbance," a contradiction shall we say, in the self-representation of that particular totality and those who uncritically uphold it. The fragment is, in this sense, an appeal to an alternative perspective, or at least the possibility of another perspective.

—Gyanendra Pandey

Attending to Fragments

In Mankhurd, Mumbai, the nongovernmental organization CORO for Literacy works with volunteers who inspect state-provided community toilet blocks in informal neighborhoods. CORO's network of Mahila Milan (Women Together) groups monitor the conditions and maintenance of municipal public toilet blocks. I spoke to CORO in late 2015 as part of ongoing research on sanitation in the city. Each of these activists—over twenty of them, mostly women—take a checklist to toilet blocks and scrutinize them, identifying improvements to be made, from physical conditions to the ways in which women are treated by caretakers. The inspection activities involve the slow work of bringing localized shortcomings with particular toilet blocks—broken toilets, poor maintenance, and inadequate services to toilets (water, electricity, drainage, etc.)—to the public, private, and civil society groups responsible for running them.

One of CORO's inspectors—Shekhar[1]—described the checklist process for inspecting community toilet blocks. Toilet blocks are scored from A to D. If a toilet block is rated "D" it is blacklisted and, eventually, the group running the block may have their license removed by the Brihanmumbai Municipal Corporation (BMC). The blacklisting system, he went on, has its drawbacks in that some BMC officials have used the threat of a poor rating to elicit bribes. It also means that inspectors like Shekhar take on a new authority in the neighbor-hoods they live in. When the work of attending is able to work well, fragments—damaged, broken, inadequate, or dysfunctional toilets—are repaired and enhanced. But it is a laborious and sometimes frustrating process, in which activists often become embroiled in site-specific disputes set within particular histories and power relations. The inspections reveal and attempt to address a range of concerns that are variously shaped by, exacerbated by, or partially addressed through local power relations, structures of ownership, forms of intimidation and violence, collaboration and solidarity, social relations of caste, gender, and class, and social infrastructures.

Some blocks are run by municipal officials who have vested interests. There is occasional intimidation. One inspector pointed out that after a public meeting on a particular toilet block he received a phone call from the owner—an individual who owns several blocks—warning him not to create problems. Another complained to a local politician who then confronted her and warned her off. There were speculations about whether the inspectors might be benefitting from the payments residents make for using local toilet blocks, and distrust deepens when residents further suspect they are paying more than they should, or wondering if they should be paying at all (some blocks are supposed to be free of charge), not to mention whether the payments actually are used for maintenance instead of something else entirely.

Some operators treat the blocks as commercial enterprises rather than local services—toilets as "cash points," in Mike Davis's memorable phrase.[2] For example, owners have occasionally responded to poor inspection reports by firing the caretakers rather than investing in better conditions. One of the challenges here then, at once political and ethical, is holding caretakers to account while recognizing that caretakers are themselves often marginalized, lower-caste residents. Throughout, volunteers like Shekhar, Rupali, and Sheela exchange experiences, often through WhatsApp, sharing what works or asking advice on particular issues as they come up.[3] The state becomes part of a changing set of relations that involve different actors, including private landowners, residents, and civil society groups. In the process, the state remains a powerful hierarchical actor but one that operates by jockeying for position and authority in an often thick set of changing negotiations.[4] These negotiations are set alongside other forms of state power, for instance in relation to patronage and voting calculations, or moral claims from community groups made to particular officials.[5]

In the case of sanitation in Mumbai, the politics of attending is a provisional and in-the-moment politics, involving a set of distinct local actors, pressured urban densities, and social infrastructures that operate in relation to groups like CORO. We find this kind of contingent politics of attending to fragments regularly across the economic margins of the urban world.[6] It is a politics, following Elizabeth Grosz, that notwithstanding the occasional use of checklists and monitoring routines, is not so much "mapped out in advance" as it is "linked to invention, directed more at experimentation" than "step-by-step directed change."[7] It is not that the results don't matter, of course, but that the politics needs to be adaptive to whatever the work of attending calls for in the moment, to the small and large changes that reconfigure the textures of locales and lives. This is a politics that not only emerges from the incomplete and multiple city, but which actively works with its limits and possibilities.

The politics of attending is composed through open human and material agencies that are variously expanding and narrowing. As distinct actions "happen upon each other," attending entails monitoring and intervening in how events, actors, and materials entangle with one another or are pulled apart.[8] Pursuing a politics of this form means learning which kinds of actors or events to "listen to" or ignore, and this learning is all the more intense and demanding in the context of the changing and dense "throwntogetherness" of marginalized urbanisms.[9] The challenge of attending is, as Ignacio Farías and Anders Blok suggest in a different context, one of learning "how to inter-articulate, compose and make co-exist, however precariously, the multiplicity of urban assemblages, entities, relationships, circulations, and sensations that make up the city."[10] While it can be unpredictable, and lack guarantees, it is an important part of how residents and activists, as Achile Mbembe and Sarah Nuttall put it, "negotiate conditions of turbulence" and bring "order and predictability into their lives."[11]

This politics of attending can also operate to fit with a more dominant global script of shifting responsibility from the state onto already heavily pressed communities. It resonates with a wider turn toward "best practice" in international development, from global actors like the World Bank to local NGOs, where a discourse of "community empowerment" or "participatory citizenship" sometimes positions residents and their social infrastructures, and not states, as responsible for the often deeply laborious work of attending to infrastructures.[12] Social infrastructure ought not to be seen in oversimplified terms as a resource to be promoted instead of state support. Indeed, it is sometimes the case that it exists in the form that it does as a result of a lack of state provisioning. A crucial political question then becomes how to augment or, where necessary—for example, when residents are having to expose themselves to risky practices of attending to waste systems—replace social infrastructures with adequate state-based systems.

In her research on waste infrastructures in Dakar, Senegal, Rosalind Fredericks shows how urban governments and NGOs subjected residents, and especially women, to "dirty-labor burdens" in the name of building "community"- and "neighborhood"-based waste systems that tap into local knowledge and rhythms, and to ostensibly develop "gender empowerment."[13] She describes one NGO project, for example, in which women were enrolled to use "traditional" sanitation systems like horse-drawn carts to collect garbage from their neighbors, working several times a week for a small fee. Not only did this project reinforce local ethnic power relations by working with one group over others, it entrenched gendered discourses of women as responsible for cleanliness and led to tensions over fees between collectors and residents.[14]

Infrastructures are, then, "peopled" through women's bodies and labor, in ways that exploit the energies of residents and expose them to risk and illness, while at the same time further entrenching the fragmentation of urban infrastructure. A discourse of community empowerment and control is used in different ways: by local states to offload budgetary cuts and austerity onto communities, and by NGOs to sustain their role and funding. Women were left, argues Fredericks, "to literally pick up the pieces of a degrading infrastructure as the neighbourhood's new 'housekeepers'," and told it was "empowerment."[15] The politics of attending to, then, can operate in all kinds of ways. It is both fundamental to the reproduction of provision on the margins of cities across the urban world, but can also be insufficient, exhausting—especially for women—and exploitative. As I show later, it is for these reasons that residents and activists often reject being condemned to having to attend to fragment urbanism.

IN-BETWEEN

When we met in the spring of 2016, Monis, a Syrian refugee, had been living in Berlin for two and a half years. He explained the work he'd been doing in the city to bring together knowledge across Berlin, between old and new Berliners, in order to support refugees in the city.

In Damascus, Monis had managed a publishing company and a design studio, and was a freelance journalist. "It was the journalism that got me out of Syria." He had been working with the *Los Angeles Times* in 2008, when he was accused by the Syrian state of spying for the Americans. By the summer of 2011 he was placed on the government wanted list, went into hiding, and eventually made his way to Lebanon and later Jordan. There he established an NGO—Syrian Charter—to support democratic change in Syria but faced constant questioning from authorities. He was contemplating a return to Syria when he received a phone call from the German foreign office, who were looking to set up a radio station for Syrian refugees. He quickly struck up an affinity with Berlin, albeit a precarious one: "I would love to stay here. But as a refugee honestly I have no plan, it is not my decision. When I came I had no plan to stay—I never spent one day thinking how my life would be here . . . I can't see five or ten years from now."

Monis was living in the in-between—between here and there, invitation and application, stability and uncertainty, risk and possibility—and it is the in-between that was to become the focus of his work in the city. Monis wasn't linked to any particular organization, but was able to use his history of skills and experiences to build reciprocal connections, and became part of work that helped to network more than 120,000 Syrians in Germany. Forming and organizing connections is what Monis did in Syria, and when he arrived in Berlin it didn't seem like anyone else was doing it. No one was doing what he called "the in-between work": "If you are a governmental foundation and you are investing money, what is the point in building beautiful things if there is no connection to the refugees? The private sector says in the media that they want to help and they plan, but again they never talk to any refugees when they do it. So, they don't understand the needs."

This in-between work is, too, a politics of attending, but of a very different kind from CORO's inspection activities in Mumbai. Here, the attending is less to material fragments, and more to knowledge fragments, connecting the bits and pieces of knowledge that different individuals and groups possess and trying to find a way not to make them more "complete" but more connected for social and economic ends. Which is not to say the in-between work did not require a material geography. Over time, Monis—working with other refugees and volunteers—managed to get temporary access to an office donated by a private company. What he called the "Integration Hub" now had a physical space. "The Hub in my mind is a place where you can connect people without controlling anything." The primary aim was to connect knowledge distributed across the city, knowledge "out there" but not visible, limited in its ability to act in support of additional learning, networking, and opportunity. For refugees looking to find out how to get by and get on in the city, the Hub offered access to the internet, to office tools, to small rooms to work in separately or together or to hold meetings or workshops, and at the same time the ability to meet other initiatives.

Monis didn't do all this on his own, but through the connections he was able to make or become enrolled within, which depend often on a social economy of hospitality. Internet access was donated by volunteers who helped to share costs, electricity by the owner, drinks by students, furniture by the digital festival organization Re:publica, and the work of cleaning was shared. An improvised social infrastructure for connection and shaping offline and online densities developed, an infrastructure in which Monis was a kind of connecting device. As is so often the case on the margins of the urban world, a new kind of social infrastructures became the lifeline that enabled and sustained a response to fragment urbanism.

Monis focused a lot of his work on developing a database of projects and contacts designed to coordinate across different groups. "I could connect people," he says. Building on existing data on refugees in the city collected by civil society organizations, the database was designed to connect local people to refugees looking to learn more about specific parts of the city or urban life. "[Let's say] an initiative wants a website to match refugees and donors. You are a barber arrived from Syria and have done this for ten years. You don't know how to do this here—the situation, the law, the language, are all different. This website will find you a local person who has the same experience. They meet, and the local person becomes a mentor." Or, take the case of an initiative that offered housing services to refugees. Berliners volunteer to host refugees while they are being registered and have yet to be allocated accommodation. But these same Berliners may have no idea about the refugee's background and culture, and opportunities could be put in place to begin to address that. It helps, he added, that social media was a big part of life in Syria before the war, and many Syrians arriving in the city were using it intuitively to find out what's going on: "Now there is a Facebook page to exchange this information. The group became a newsfeed. People may say: 'I just met seventeen refugees needing accommodation for one or two nights,' and others respond."[16]

This bringing into relation of people and knowledge fragments is often strategic, frequently temporary and purpose-based rather than deep or ongoing. But in this context, this is all the politics of attending seeks to achieve. If this is about network-building, it is also about forming a density of connections and possibilities. As Bruno Latour has put it, "one does not reside in a network, but rather moves to other points through the edges."[17] The densities of connection Monis helped locate and generate form not so much a fixed network as a revisable, expanding, and multiple social infrastructure linking people, knowledge, and the geographies of the city. While the particular form of dense connectionism briefly described here mobilizes digital technologies, we are quite some distance from the hyped promises and corporate boosterism of "smart cities." Digital technology here is a vehicle for redistributing urban data and connecting urban "meanwhiles" into new opportunities and relationships.[18] Monis was acting as a "connectionist." For William Connolly, to be a connectionist is to view the world as always in becoming, which is to attune perception and action to the potentials of the heterogeneous trajectories of the city moving in different directions.[19]

Filip De Boeck uses the term "knotting," where forms and practices of connection produce amalgamations, cultural weaving, and intertwining. Knots are moments or spaces of entangled densification formed among sometimes disparate actors. De Boeck describes this in his discussion of knotting and cultural practice in urban central Africa:

> The often disjointed infrastructural figments and fragments that make up the urban landscape are embedded in other rhythms and temporalities, in totally different layers of socially networked infrastructures, punctuated by varying spatial, temporal and affective oscillations between connectedness and disconnection, situated in the waxing and waning movements between foreground and back- or under-ground, between surface, fold and gap, between the visible and the invisible, darkness and light, movement and motionlessness, continuity and discontinuity, flow and blockage, opening and closure.[20]

Connections are not just good to have, they can be critical in enabling people to cope and get on. Another refugee from Syria, who arrived in the summer of 2015, told me of feeling abandoned by the state. Upon arrival, Saman had been told "go to LeGoSa," the state office in Moabit for registering refugees. He had no idea what or where it was, and the response—"get the U-bahn"—wasn't much help. When an official at LeGoSa lost Saman's Syrian ID, he found himself in a limbo in which he couldn't access services. How, in this context, to learn the city in a context of—despite Berlin's often multicultural atmosphere—occasional racism, in a place where you don't speak the language, following a long struggle to get out of Syria and arrive safely, where the coordinates of urban life have been thrown in the air, and where the authorities are woefully unprepared? Saman started volunteering with an NGO in the city supporting refugees, helping with translation and getting basic everyday supplies together. His connections at the NGO became vital for meeting daily needs and getting by in the city, especially through new social infrastructures that bring people together.

The politics of attending that Monis and others like him pursue operates in at least three ways. First, it draws on and helps shape dense, heterogeneous collections of trajectories in the city—it helps form knots, openings, connections, and potentials into social infrastructure. Second, it seeks to improve conditions for people on the economic margins, and in doing so to help people cope with the material fragments that refugees in Berlin often arrived to and which the state was initially poorly prepared to address (and which I will return to later). And third, it seeks to contribute to the archive of the city itself, shaping in a small way the city's socialities and identities.[21]

I've focused here on Monis's story, but there is a world of this kind of attending to knowledge fragments going on in Berlin, densifying and knotting, forming connections and social infrastructures. For example, groups like Zusammenskunft (ZKU) or Campus Cosmopolis bring together activists, artists, and refugees to promote multicultural dialogue and low-cost community interventions. ZUsammenKUNFT is a play on words: Zukunft means "future," while zusammenkunft means "gathering" or "assembly," so ZUsammenKUNFT refers to making the future through gathering, a kind of prefiguration of the future city. Harry Sachs, a ZKU activist, described the ways in which they bring different groups together—activists, artists, refugees, and more—as a "field of experimentation." This is in part about creating encounters between "old" and "new" Berliners, and in all kinds of ways—art, drama, dance, music, gardening, and so on—in an effort to change perceptions, foster mutual learning and reflections, and generate new understandings of identities and the city. In the center of Berlin, just a short walk from Potsdamer Platz, ZKU was involved in the conversion of a multistory hotel to temporary accommodation for refugees. On the two top floors, including the former penthouse rooms, activists and artists worked with refugees and asylum seekers on a host of small cultural projects. Like many residents in the city, the activists had been energized by the arrival of thousands of refugees, particularly in 2015.

There are lots of other examples we might point to in Berlin of attending to knowledge fragments through connections, dialogue, and learning, and which reflect the multiple forms of expression, experience, and politics through which refugees encounter the city. For instance, the Exile Ensemble is a platform for professional artists who have been forced to live in exile, based at the Maxim Gorki Theatre. Since November 2016 seven actors from Syria, Palestine, and Afghanistan have been working as part of the theatre. The Gorki identifies itself as a space of coming together for artistic expression among cultural diversity and amidst different forms of crises. When I spoke to Ayham Majid Agha, the Syrian artist director at the Exile Ensemble, in 2017, he was "dreaming of a laboratory," a concentration of creative workers who could produce a larger program. In contrast to what he saw as short-termist refugee projects, he was looking to build a larger long-term collective.

As Ayham and Monis are well aware, knowledge fragments are not always simply accessible or legible; there are mistranslations, losses, stories that never travel, ways of knowing that cannot be straightforwardly captured in exchange. Ayham pointed out, for example, that Berliners are often too quick to see him as a refugee with a story of war and flight to tell, a set of expectations that can delimit the kinds of understandings that emerge. Being expected to perform the role of the refugee, with the attendant stories of war, displacement, and suffering, is for Ayham itself a form of marginalization: "I don't want to have to prove I'm part of the resistance. I'm a person. I've been all over the world touring, even before the war ... I love to break the expectation." Like Monis, Ayham was seeking out connections across the city, within and beyond refugee groups, hoping to create a density of people and things that allows new forms of expression, reflection, and livelihood, setting out as a Berliner with a stake in reinventing the city. As Tariq Jazeel has argued of knowledge production, the results of Ayham's efforts to "break the expectation" are not always clear or apprehensible, and sometimes they may not be—or even have to be—particularly deep and ongoing, yet they might nonetheless be generative of new kinds of knowledge, seeing, and action even in their uncertainties and failures.[22]

Generative Translation

Is there any infrastructure more incomplete than a toilet without walls? Some may have joked that it was the "loo with the view," but it was no laughing matter.[23] In 2011, in the leadup to the municipal elections, the City of Cape Town (CCT) provided communities in the poorer parts of the city with open-air toilets, i.e., toilets with no walls. Infrastructures and services are often provided as fragments—provided as already incomplete and/or disconnected rather than broken or breaking up—but the open-air toilet was a dramatic material and symbolic insult.

While the CCT claimed to have conducted consultations with residents on how to spend the budget for sanitation, such an affront to dignity infuriated many residents and became a flashpoint in what some called the "toilet wars."[24] The open toilets were "improved" by the CCT using walls of corrugated iron, which African National Congress Youth League (ANCYL) activists tore down amidst claims of insults to the dignity of the predominantly Black poor, demanding concrete instead.[25] "It would seem," Steve Robins has written, "that the historical processes of racial capitalism were condensed and congealed into the spectacular image of the open porcelain toilet."[26]

An important victory for sanitation campaigners came in 2011 with a Western Cape High Court judgment. In September 2010, Mrs. Beja, a 76-year-old woman who had been attacked and stabbed on her way to an unenclosed toilet in Makhaza, filed an application against the city. In April 2011, Judge Erasmus of the High Court handed down judgment against CCT and the province. He ordered the CCT to enclose 1,316 toilets in the Silvertown Project, which includes Makhaza.[27] The judgment stated that by building 225 unenclosed toilets in Makhaza in 2009, the CCT had violated the constitutional rights of the citizens living there, and highlighted too the absence of provisions for disabled people. Here, a legal judgment effectively stated that, whatever the Constitution says about "progressive realisation," whereby infrastructures, services, and housing are gradually improved over time, *some forms* of urban fragments are not acceptable.

Cape Town is a deeply fragmented city, particularly through historical inequalities at the intersection of race, class, land, and labor.[28] While there is evidence of racial mobility in the labor market in South Africa, there is also evidence of growing unemployment among poor Black groups, and 61 percent of all Black citizens live below the poverty line.[29] As Jean and John Comaroff have starkly put it, the economic liberalization that accompanied the transition to democracy was to "hollow out bodies, property, and institutions, and to leave behind only their facades," a process intensified by the concentration of wealth and corporate power alongside both the casualization of labor and the extension of "cost-free labor" left toiling "ceaselessly without pay."[30]

Residents of low-income neighborhoods in Cape Town—both informal settlements and townships—are forced to live with an inherited set of partial provisions of sanitation in the form of broken or poorly maintained toilets, inadequate in number for the densities to which they serve, often lacking sufficient water and electricity, meaning that they sometimes have to share urban space with their own individual and collective human wastes. There are over 200 low-income informal settlements in Cape Town, many of which had rarely experienced state investment before the end of apartheid.[31] If the transition to democracy in the 1990s was accompanied by considerable state investment across the country, including the delivery of hundreds of thousands of housing units and utility connections to cities, an estimated 500,000 (out of 3.74 million) residents in Cape Town experience inadequate sanitation services.[32]

The relations among race, disgust, oppression, and protest have a long history in South Africa. Mongane Wally Serote's 1972 protest poem, "What's in This Black Shit?," examines the relationships among race, inequality, dignity, and shit during apartheid. The poem begins with the "toilet bucket" and how the profoundly embodied struggle with inadequate sanitation, especially for women and girls, connects to a larger experience of racism and poverty. It is about how the human waste that is not collected becomes a force not just for sickness but for all kinds of action, frustration, violence, inequality, and politics, and concludes:

> I'm learning to pronounce this "Shit" well
> Since the other day
> At the pass office
> When I went to get employment,
> The officer there endorsed me to Middleburg,
> So I said, hard and with all my might, "Shit!"
> I felt a little better;
> But what's good, is, I said it in his face,
> A thing my father wouldn't dare do.
> That's what's in this Black "Shit."

The poem tracks a shift in a kind of self-disgust linked to the material and symbolic geography of human waste in the city, toward a radical recasting of waste in Black consciousness against the forms of power that perpetuate racialized, classed, and gendered inequalities in the city.[33] The themes of disgust, anguish, and condemnation are, as David Attwell argues, recurring themes in Serote's poetry, as was a radical and liberatory politics. The poem connects the experience of residents in townships and informal settlements—who were forced to leave waste outside their doors for collection every night—to the inequalities in how the wealthy live and are serviced by those same marginalized residents, and reflects on how poverty and violence are lived in poor neighborhoods.

But, as the lines from the poem above suggest, it is also about the liberation of turning waste against power in the city and specifically against the white "face" of the pass office, where permission was required to work in white-only areas (the individual in the poem ends up being sent to Middleburg, an area of the Eastern Cape with relatively few jobs on offer).[34] Instead of venting frustration at home—embodied in the poem in the figure of the father—anger is directed toward the apartheid government;[35] "flinging the disgust back to its point of origin."[36] Disgust and time are thrown here into a new relation, and a break is introduced to the historical humiliation of waste in the city, as waste is expressed as a potential symbolic political weapon. The narrative here echoes Julia Kristeva's description of abjection in *The Powers of Horror:* "The time of abjection is double: a time of oblivion and thunder, of veiled infinity and the moment when revelation bursts forth."[37]

In 2014, residents in the informal neighborhood of Barcelona, Cape Town, were in intense discussions about their daily conditions and their political possibilities. City officials, some residents believed, were either ignoring them or paying them lip service. They had protested, requested meeting after meeting, but nothing had changed. For weeks, their toilets had not been cleaned. The private company paid by the city to collect the "buckets" in the standalone "bucket toilets" had gone on strike over a wage cut imposed by the municipality. The buckets were not a broken-off piece, a portion left over, or an incomplete form. Nor were they necessarily breaking up. They stretch, then, the definition of the fragment. But given their sheer inadequacy, in the experience of those who depend on them these buckets are partial, radically insufficient forms, produced as such through the inability of the state to deliver this most fundamental of provisions.

As verbs, fragments are not just things but potentials that can be put to different uses and given distinct meanings, for better or worse. Just as different people and groups—residents, activists, states, and so on— attend to fragments in ways that pull them into different relations, so too are fragments occasionally reinvented as political tools. One of the residents suggested: if they won't come and collect the waste, let's bring the waste to them. A group of activists and residents decided to take uncollected buckets of human waste and emptied them at different sites in the city. They deliberately targeted symbols of sanitized and powerful Cape Town, including the international airport, the steps of the state legislature, and the premier's car. They disrupted major roads into the city. Sithembele, one prominent activist in the protests, said they had targeted the airport "because this is one of the things the government is grandstanding about—as if they don't have any problems." And they targeted the steps of the state legislature, he continued, so that "it would smell like it does in Barcelona." This was a politics that formed a kind of generative coalition among discarded residents, uncollected waste, and limited provisioning. From a politics of neglect emerged not a politics of attending but an active refusal to do the work of attending.

Through a politics of shock and spectacle that might—and did— force a new debate in the city, the activists—dubbed "poo protestors" in the media, but known as Ses'khona or "We are here"—inverted and mobilized material fragments in order to stage a critique of urban development in the city, connecting histories of race, class, and gender to fragments of infrastructure, urban space, political economy and policy.[38] This was a politics of juxtaposition that powerfully entwined partial materials and the larger city, an urbanism that makes its performative mark through what Walter Benjamin called "dialectical images":

the entanglement of distinct spaces that reveal something wider about the nature of the urban condition, while at the same stroke changing the political context.[39] Buckets of waste were expressed in an inventive and powerful political light by being brought into the light of day in contexts where they are usually barely spoken of let alone seen or smelled. In the act of reinventing buckets of waste, the activists brought together *both* fragments and histories of fragmentation.

Benjamin's pedagogy of fragments—textual fragments about material and knowledge fragments—opened spaces of critique and possibility. The task of this pedagogy was the reinvention of the urban experience: to jolt ways of seeing how urban life had become ever more alienated and unequal, to imagine and practice new ways of using objects, commodities, and technologies, other ways of seeing and of experimenting in the city.[40] If Benjamin was, in Stephen Jackson's phrasing, a "broken world thinker" trading—especially in his vast work of textual fragments, *The Arcades Project*—in a "peculiar, fragmentary, archival, and recuperative mode of working," this broken world of things and spaces was also a propagative world.[41]

Benjamin invoked Baudelaire's poetry to allegorically conjure the image of Paris streets as an abyss. In the *Arcades,* he revisits time and again the underground city, the catacombs used for political resistance, or the sewers carrying the "unworthy nature" the city transformed by Haussmannization. What he called the "dream houses of the collective"—"arcades, winter gardens, panoramas, factories, wax museums, casinos, railroad stations"—are repeatedly juxtaposed with images from, for example, Victor Hugo on the putrid sewers of Paris.[42] Just as Benjamin challenged the power of Haussmannization in Paris with images of discarded, displaced, forgotten, and fading Paris—a Paris constructed *as waste*—so too did Ses'khona challenge and juxtapose the powerful and elite spaces of the city with the waste fragments it fails to manage.

Ses'khona reconstituted fragments by disrupting the ways in which they are conventionally storied and spatialized, and expressing them in a new context. No longer just the products of capitalist urbanization and racial cultures, they became repoliticized. Expression here is a kind of urban fabrication, a process of translating fragments into new social and political relations.[43] The re-expression of discarded urban things is more than just a form of coping or moving on; it is an effort to "reformat"[44] current conditions through politicizing the "condensation and knotting of histories."[45] In the process, materials and wastes become political agents, dramatically emplaced, as Rosalind Fredericks puts it in relation to trash strikes in Dakar, in a new "political terrain of refusal."[46]

Here, the political economy of the city—investing in elite (and hyper-sanitary) spaces like the airport over underserviced neighborhoods—was called into question not so much through political debate or electoral choices but through the realm of the senses, especially smell and visuality. The "insanitary slum" bemoaned by urban elites is turned in and against a particular imaginary of the city through a political claim that combines political economy, affect, shock, and the senses. Ses'khona dramatized the relations between the geographies of provisioning, race, and urban historical reproduction through the urban sensorium, and as such the movement is part of a wider history of activism and critical thought in South Africa that radically connects fragments and the whole. This too is a kind of pedagogy of fragments, wherein the themes of disgust, anguish, and condemnation, as David Attwell has written of critical South African poets such as Serote, become the ground—even if only for a moment—of a disruptive politics.[47] There is a long tradition of critical thinking on race here that has charted these politics.[48]

The spectacular and stark critique of the city in this case is a relatively rare form of politics. There are examples like it, more often with solid waste than human waste, for instance in the trash strikes over workers' conditions from Oaxaca to Dakar and Beirut.[49] Yet, rare as these kinds of acts may be, there is an important insight here into the nature of the urban political more generally. In particular, there are two points about the political to make. One is that here politics surprises. It is not easily scripted in advance. It responds to conditions and searches out possibilities, daring to invent new and even shocking action. The politics of fragment urbanism can jolt us, and by doing so it can remind us that the urban political cannot always be anticipated. Its actors, connections, and alliances emerge contingently, sometimes laden with uncertainties as they unfold. The second implication for understanding the urban political here has to do with the ontological coalitions at work. Ses'khona formed a loose coalition not just with activists, residents, and long-entrenched political formations like the ANC Youth League but with material fragments and human waste. In the emergent politics at work here is a particular political ontology of coalition building. The ontologies of fragment urbanism can generate particular kinds of politics and urban questions; politics may shape the material conditions of fragment urbanism, but fragment urbanism can also shape politics.[50]

Reformation

The 1965 Watts protests in Los Angeles began when a white highway patrol police officer impounded the car of a Black man for drunk driving. The incident drew a large crowd from which unfolded what is often described as the "Watts riots," taking place over six days in which thirty-four people were killed, thousands injured and arrested, and millions of dollars of damage done to property. Across those six days, African Americans responded to decades of mistreatment, racism, and marginalization with "an outpouring of grief and rage."[51] The moment of the police encounter was the spark to a long, deep history of oppression. A combination of systematic disinvestment in Watts, along with rising unemployment, police supervision and violence, and sociospatial discrimination that intensified in the post–World War II period, fed not only those six days of turmoil but the wider civil rights movement and the Black Panther Party, the politics of school busing and housing segregation, the formation of community development corporations and "community unions," and more.[52] That politics is still with us today, such as in the death of George Floyd and the protests it precipitated linked to the Black Lives Matters movement.

In the Los Angeles of the early 1960s, Watts was one of the densest parts of the city, a Black neighborhood that sat in contrast to some of the more spacious lower densities of white neighborhoods in the city.

Split densities in LA were the result of sociospatial fragmentation under-pinned by law, infrastructure, economic exploitation, political neglect, hyper-policing and criminalization, and racism. As Marcus Anthony Hunter and Zandria Robinson note, "the web of post–World War II freeways and racial discrimination made Los Angeles difficult to navi-gate physically, socially, politically, and economically for Black resi-dents," enforced too by "police supervision and brutality."[53] Here, the history of making urban densities—high and low—as in so many cities across the global North and South, was a deeply political and geograph-ical project of fragmentation, one that entwined dominance in the social with control over the spatial. Martin Luther King, in the months after the riots, argued that the unrest could hardly come as a surprise "when its [the city's] officials [had] tied up federal aid in political manipula-tion"; when "unemployment soared above the depression levels of the 1930s; when the population density of Watts became the worst in the nation . . . . [and when] California in 1964 repealed its law forbidding racial discrimination in housing."[54]

From the debris of those six days, a group of artists—Noah Purifoy, Judson Powell, Debby Brewer, Ruth Saturensky, Max Neufeldt, and Arthur Secunda—made art: "Sculptures crafted out of burned wood, rusty fumigation cans, old piano pedals and piles of blackened nails, sculptures that played as much with art history as they did with the charged nature of the materials, which still reeked of smoke."[55] Purifoy and colleagues gathered objects from 103rd Street, which had been referred to as "Charcoal Alley," and put the objects they found there on display. Purifoy "felt drawn to the lingering traces of what remained after the violence had ceased," artist Chandra Frank has written, and he described how "while the debris was still smouldering, we ventured into the rubble like other junkers of the community," left contemplating the "smell of the debris" and the violence and possibilities that "had began to haunt our dreams."[56]

They called their collection, which pulled together a dense three tons of fire-damaged urban detritus, *66 Signs of Neon,* and exhibited it alongside a catalogue, *Junk Art.* The following spring they put the works on display at Markham Junior High School in Watts, then later at the University of California, Los Angeles student union, and then to universities across the United States before an exhibition in Washing-ton, DC. Across his career, Purifoy's work included high-profile instal-lations that explored themes of social change, poverty, waste, and con-sumerism through the relations among Dada assemblage practices,

African sculptural histories, and Black folk art.[57] His form of assemblage sculpture, which brought a political intent to the repurposing of fragmented things, was to become influential for a generation of critical artists.[58] Purifoy's work was resolutely oriented toward art's potential to provoke social change. Collecting bits and pieces from the street was not itself new for Purifoy. In the early 1960s, working at the Watts Tower Arts Center he helped to found and was to become the first director of, Purifoy participated in community arts programs in which he and local children produced collages from whatever was at hand in the neighborhood. When the protests began, he was making his own collages as drawings or sculptures from plexiglass.[59]

The collages he and his collaborators produced from the material fragments of an urban uprising resonated with the larger social struggle: *that from destruction, something new can be made.* As we saw in Cape Town, these are both received fragments—remainders—and created fragments. The emphasis on reformation is distinct from forms of art that perform destruction or point to decay, such as Michelangelo Pistoletto's self-destructing newspaper balls two years later in Turin, which, as Richard Williams notes, were used to critique commodification and the new trends in throwaway consumption.[60] Instead, Purifoy's fragments endured through their transformed relations, becoming something new that at the same time held the continuities of the long history of racial violence and poverty.[61] If there is an allegorical power at work here that mirrors the capitalist imperative to turn potentially anything into commodities, and to give new meanings to those commodities through display,[62] this case radically disrupts that logic by transforming the racialized detritus of fragmentation to provoke other ways of imagining the possible.

It is instructive to reflect on what the "possible" stands for here. The collection produced through the debris of violent histories and geographies, in new kinds of arrangements, is in itself a forceful provocation. The musician Judson Powell, who accompanied Purifoy on walks rummaging through the carnage, piling stuff into a wagon, reflected simply that "we had no idea exactly what we were looking for and didn't know what we would do with it," yet for Purifoy there was a deeper politics at work in the process of retrieving bits and pieces of debris and displaying them.[63] This was about claiming what he saw as the *human right to creativity.* The *Junk Art* catalogue that accompanied the exhibition opened with a statement on the potential of creativity to communicate nonverbally. Purifoy argued that "creativity ranks alongside food and shelter as absolute necessities . . . [art education] stimulates the whole process of learning . . . [everyone] should be given the potential to express."[64] And, he went on, art can go beyond the creative act to be a medium of communication to effect change. As Cameron Shaw has argued, Purifoy and his collaborators believed that artistic creativity could be a tool for transforming consciousness and provoking social change, and so *66 Signs* was always "more than a restructuring of physical materials"; it was a "restructuring of values."[65]

Purifoy's focus on creativity and social change extended beyond collage to poetry. In his 1966 poem, "A Book Flown," written to promote *66 Signs of Neon,* Purifoy explicitly positions fragments as more than just the wastes of historical racialized violence. Assembled in new relations and new contexts, fragments are now—forced along by "the first strong winds"—sites of the possible, not so much telling a story but acting as a defiant placeholder for the multiple stories that might be told from the discarded streets and neighborhoods of LA and elsewhere:

> These fragmentations may only mean that
> I am fragmented,
> That as I symbolize what you say and agree
> Can I then leave you
> To set these lines in order,
> Assemble them into a book
> And by the first strong winds,
> Permit its leaves to be torn from its cover.
> Let them fly high and, like leaves,
> Light into the lap of the Universe
> Separate of and by themselves
> Within without complete
> Yet incomplete.[66]

Reflecting on Purifoy's work, Rosie Lee Hooks, director of the Watts Tower Arts Center, points out that if Purifoy recasts urban waste—all sorts of things, from burned-out wood, metal pieces, melted neon signs, shredded newspapers, old cans, discarded hairbrushes, broken drinking fountains—such recasting always has a cultural and economic politics: "It looks like junk. It's stuff that has been thrown away. But he has made it into something beautiful. It teaches us about how we regard people, disadvantaged people who don't have a lot, who are cast aside because of their race and because they are poor."[67] Watts here emerges not just as a poor and dense neighborhood on the economic and social margins of LA, but as a neighborhood of creative densities of people

and things able—notwithstanding the vast challenges of historical fragmentation, marginalization, and violence—to write different kinds of
futures. Purifoy was engaged not just with fragmented things but with
a form of fragment urbanism as a *process* to promote creativity, expression, and value.

Purifoy and his collaborators were saying something about Watts that
speaks to what Hunter and Robinson refer to as the struggle in Black
neighborhood spaces for a political reimagining and "for a place to
be."[68] It is a history, of course, that maintains into the present. As Kath-
erine McKittrick has argued in relation to plantation geographies, the
plantation is a "conceptual palimpsest to contemporary cityscapes that
continue to harbor the lives of the most marginalized."[69] Ananya Roy
has shown in her work in Los Angeles and Chicago on the demolition of
public housing, tenant eviction, and the foreclosure of homes that sometimes end up remaining empty, that urban transformation in the United
States persists as a process not just of gentrification but of "racial banishment."[70] Groups like the Chicago Anti-Eviction Campaign and the LA
Community Action Network that Roy examines pursue an urban knowledge and politics that critique displacement, banishment, and racial
power, and seeks community empowerment, voice, and rights.

As a space of reflection, the encounter with Purifoy's art is a provocation to audiences to ask how urbanism could end up as fragments, but
it also asks the viewer to consider the potential of reformation, of making something else even amidst the historical moment of wreckage. Ted
Michel, writing in the *66 Signs of Neon* catalogue, described the exhibition as "an evolving system of philosophy" in which fragments had
become "objects of art" that "jabbed the viewer low in the abdomen,
squeezed his heart, pricked his mind."[71] If the city is always pulling
together even as it falls apart—and in this case fragmentation and densification are firmly about the intersections of race, class, and capitalist
urbanization—it is at the same time a space of multiplicity and possibility. As with Cape Town's Ses'khona movement, the process at work
here involves a form of generative translation, prompting alternative
ways of thinking and seeing by juxtaposing fragments into different
relations in a new context, but one that positions material reformation
as central to its politics. Dale Davis, an artist who visited the exhibition
at the time, reflected: "It was sophisticated, but it had that raw edge.
This is a period of upheaval. It's the Vietnam War period. It's Watts. It
was all very unsettling. And the show captured the period. . . . By the
time I got to it, I was like, *this* is it."[72]

There is a long historical and global association of fragments and art, whether of antiquity—parchments, sculptures, paintings, and so on— assembled in museums, or remnants of partially forgotten poems, songs, myths, stories, or folklore. Indeed, a dominant imaginary of the fragment derives from its deep historical association with antiquity, in the form of the relic or ruin.[73] Art in all its urban spatialities—on the street and in public spaces, as graffiti or in museums, and more—has been vital to how cities are understood, made, and contested.[74] While there is a body of critical research exploring how art can be used to support forces of exclusion in the city, for example in the use of contemporary public art in gentrification and urban "blandscapes," art can also act in all kinds of other ways that open different political directions.[75]

Art can be a powerful medium through which to investigate how, as Ash Amin and Nigel Thrift have put it, urban worlds "are continually cast asunder as they move into new formations."[76] It can disrupt dominant understandings of the city, its spaces, and its inhabitants, can create a voice for marginal groups, and can contest how urban space is produced and cities are run.[77] Perhaps most importantly, art can provide a way of "narrating differently" urban spaces, groups, and issues, and open out new questions, stories, debates, and a sense of the possible.[78] Artistic experimentation with fragments can forge different registers of narration—in visual, tactile, and written encounters—that provocatively or playfully suggest alternative urban archives. These archives force a kind of "stepping back" and reflection on the city and on living together now and into the future, but very often do so in relation to a kind of moving toward, an immersion in the bits and pieces, the ruins of violence and glimpses of lives so often hidden from mainstream view.

RELOCATING

Artistic experiments in formation and reformation can provoke all kinds of politics, from provocations and destabilizations, to contestations and spaces of reflection. We see this, for instance, in the wider tradition of recovering wasted things to tell a critical story of the city through damage and transformation. Architect Dennis Maher, for example, a former demolition worker in Buffalo, New York, addresses the material, social, and psychological impacts of urban demolition, or what he calls the "intense unmaking" of the city.[79] Some of Maher's work examines precisely the interrelation between the city falling apart and then pulling together, densifying and de-/re-densifying through histories of capitalist accumulation and social valuation.

As with Purifoy, although in a quite different urban political context, Maher repositions fragments in new relations. His sculpture *Aggregate Lost* assembles discarded materials to provoke a reimagining of things. This extends to Maher's home in Buffalo, which is itself a dense collection of the detritus of urban life, partially sorted and sifted into new combinations and uses. In what Maher calls the "Wardrobe Room" of his house, writes *New York Times* journalist Penelope Green, "there are closet parts, deconstructed bureaus, valets and screens," a few suitcoats, pipes from an old organ on the wall, and "a teetering sculpture made from a chair base, model airplane fuselages, a drawer, and a model train station."[80]

If there are echoes here of artists like Robert Rauschenberg, who also worked with urban decay and ruin in the rubble, broken pieces, and discarded objects of New York in the 1950s and 1960s, Maher describes his work not just as art but as civic activism. This includes repurposing "wastes" into new configurations for housing or vacant spaces, a particular politics of densifying urban space. He founded ASSEMBLY HOUSE 150, a nonprofit space for experimental art/architectural projects. Using drawing, photography, collage, and constructions, Maher experiments with a social urbanism that operates in the relations between the city that is "undone" and the city that might be.

There is a global history around how artists explore urban conditions and possibilities through creatively assembling waste in the city. Senegalese artist Viyé Diba, for example, connects art, fragments, and the city in provocative ways. Diba produces abstract and colorful work, ranging across painting, sculpture, performance, and installation. Much of his work consists of local materials such as cloth, paper, wood, string, rope, wire mesh, plastic, and sand—what he calls "remnants of human activity."[81] Diba comes from a poor, rural family in Senegal. He won a competition to attend art school in Dakar, later received a PhD in urban geography in Nice, and is a professor of Visual Arts at the National School of Arts in Dakar. He describes how he came to art with a particular sensitivity to the details and properties of materials and their interrelationship. He grew especially interested in recycled materials from everyday objects in the local economy.

His art involves closely working with materials, creating what he calls a kind of tactile "dialogue" and "intimacy." He approaches the materials not as passive things but as historical agents with life and force, or what he calls "a sociological discourse" or "socialised objects."[82] Textiles, for instance, can carry the history of fabric weaving, while a wall might reflect histories of the city, in the graffiti, images, damage, and erosion that it displays. We see this too in key themes in his work, such as how identity becomes refracted through the mixture of translocal influences in the production and transformation of everyday things.

Some of Diba's practice examines how bits and pieces are lived in urban space, in streets and markets and neighborhoods, where they are appropriated in all kinds of ways, and this is where identity, for Diba, is worked out. He partners with local carpenters and textile workers, paying attention to how they interact with materials and the environment, the practices they use working with their hands—what he calls "the intelligent hand," the prehensile know-how of embodied labor—that have been passed across and translated through generations.[83] Here again, then, fragments take on new life and meaning, forms of inhabitation, tacit knowledge, and translocal flows.

As with Maher, the making and unmaking of urban densities plays a role in Diba's work. He has argued, for instance, that pressures on urban space and the densities that result are central to both everyday conflict and political upheaval in different urban African contexts. For Joanna Grabski, Diba's work explores how human activity "transforms the street into an economic and social arena," where the densification of urban space through informal and formal production and consumption economies demands engagement with and navigation through people and things.[84] Diba's installation spaces, Grabski goes on, are populated "liberally with materials that evoke the littered streetscape."[85] Diba, she argues, explores "the aesthetic possibilities of materials sourced from urban life," ranging from fashion, the buzz of the street, the sound of sewing machines, and the craft of production, to globalization's various impacts on the local economy.[86] The fragments of things that are put to work are about space and time in the city, and how craft, culture, economy, and identity mesh, fade, translate and act as sociomaterial forces in everyday densities.

There are resonances between Diba's approach and other artists, such as Ghanaian artist El Anatsui, who uses discarded bottle tops, wood, cloth, metal, and all manner of other materials, from driftwood and nails to milk tins. Anatsui too assembles materials to tell abstract stories about the historical mixture of urban culture in constant motion and transformation. One high-profile example is his aluminum bottle-top assemblages sewn together by copper wire, which provoke questions around translocality, waste, and urban cultures of consumption. Like Diba, Antsui simultaneously explores how specific locations transcend space to prompt reflection around contemporary living, whether through themes of weaving and mixture, waste and creativity, or the fusions and tensions of culture, power, and economy. "The amazing thing about working with these metallic 'fabrics'," writes Antsui, "is that the poverty of the materials used in no way precludes the telling of rich and wonderful stories."[87]

Other artists pursue similar relations among fragments of things, collage, and storytelling. We see this, for example, in the collage paintings of Nigerian artist Njideka Akunyili Crosby, who weaves fabrics, acrylics, photographs, prints, and drawing to create multilayered artwork of domestic interiors and moments, often of families and couples. Crosby describes her way of collecting fragments of things and images without a clear sense of purpose, until eventually the work is distilled through a printmaking technique that reflects movement among different cultural spaces:

> As a way of staying connected to home [while living in the United States], I collected images from the web, looking at Nigerian social pages, at musicians and designers I liked. Every time I went home I'd take photographs and bring back society magazines. I knew that those photos were important to me, but I didn't know what to do with them. Every time I had a studio visit, instead of talking about my oil paintings, I ended up talking about these pictures that were scattered all over . . . And then I remembered transferring, a printmaking technique that I had done at the Pennsylvania Academy . . . I liked how transfer reduces the visual sharpness of the photograph. It seemed symbolic of how information is lost as people move between cultural spaces.[88]

As with Purifoy and others described above, Crosby describes here collecting fragments without a clear sense of specific purpose. Later, their potential falls into place and they are instantiated and put to work, becoming not just things but processes, both nouns and verbs. There is a sense here that the different fragments in the collages create juxtapositions that reflect the experience of "making jumps in worlds," and Crosby talks about her work as trying to make sense of Nigeria as "something that's constantly changing," not in spite of the discontinuities but through the jumps in space and in time:

> For me, switching between transfers and collage is synonymous with traversing different worlds . . . As your eyes move from one place to the other, you're making jumps in worlds. You could be looking at a photograph of my oldest sister as a little girl in Nigeria in 1992, but next to it is a painting of a

chair from my Brooklyn apartment. So there are shifts in time and location, but there are also shifts in painting language. You might find a flat and geometric area, but when you move your eyes, suddenly, perhaps you're seeing something that looks like Northern Renaissance painting. I'm always trying to keep the composition active.

We see this effort to connect fragments, movement, and identity too in other art, such as that of Betty Acquah, who paints extraordinary, swirling pictures of women in movement in Ghana. Acquah is herself a dancer, and builds a feminist politics of movement, energy, joy, and purpose into her art, often using pointillism, a form of painting that builds an image from dots of color.[89] But less visible in Diba and Crosby's work, and more prominent in the earlier discussion of Purifoy, is the violence and destruction of histories of fragmentation that have played their part in the shaping of Diba's "intelligent hand." Other artists have shown how the material fragments of economy and culture enter into the making of urban lives. Vivan Sunderam's exhibition, *Trash,* for example, explored the relationship among waste, life and the city in India, including the materialities of demolition and waste. Working with wastepickers, Sunderam pulled together fragments often found in urban waste grounds—"bricks, cans, wire, bottles, tins, tape, cardboard, glass, bottle-caps, batteries, and transistors"— and explored how "global artifacts" become, as Tania Roy has put it, remade through "zones of degradation, rescue and re-evaluation."[90]

Sunderam's exhibition uses wastes to assemble miniature urbanisms—bulldozed homes, landfill sites, swaths of landscape, master plans, sparse living quarters, moments of recuperation and escape amidst the laboring of waste, and more—to produce an "alternate urban ecology" that provokes reflection around the conditions, nature, and lives of urban waste.[91] As with Purifoy and Maher, Sunderam's art generates a space of reflection in which we see anew the violence of fragmentation—the unmaking of urban densities and the repurposing of urban fragments—and asks us to imagine how cities might otherwise be arranged. Sunderam's objects, such as the soles of shoes salvaged from waste grounds, provokes ideas of things that have undergone both "subtraction" and reuse, and of the labor and lives of people as both present and removed in the city.[92] This is an urbanism that is at once dismantled and fabricated, where time and space collapse into an often brutal, excessive landscape. When the exhibition opened, the Chemould Prescott Road gallery in Mumbai wrote: "The rubbished fragments of a day-time city rise and fall, collapse, and swirl. Towers blow over and topple in the wind and smoke one by one, structures big and small sway and whistle and turn askew."[93] There is, after all, a deeply powerful connection between the densities of waste, fragments, and garbage a city generates on the one hand, and the densities it privileges as it builds to satiate its real estate speculative economy on the other—and there are few cities with a more violent and intensified real estate economy than Mumbai.[94]

The cases discussed here are inevitably selective, given the long global history of artists who have experimented with the city as—to use Esther Leslie's phrase—a "rubbish tip of ephemera, degradation and the thrownaway, in which artist-ragpickers might profitably rummage."[95] Artists have long rummaged around in and recontextualized waste as a critique of modernity, technology, and the city, and put art to work to suggest other ways of imaging, knowing, being, and shaping the city beyond the relentless discarding and circulating of commodity capital. Leslie points to movements and individuals like Dada and Surrealism, Marcel Duchamp and Charles Baudelaire to Kurt Schwitters, Joseph Cornell, and Tony Cragg, but also to thinker-collectors like Walter Benjamin, who was heavily influenced by artists and whom she describes as "montaging a pile-up of disparate industrially produced fragments, trash and parodies of the natural form to be found inside the junk shops of the arcades."[96] The cases discussed here reflect a much longer history of artists using wastes to narrate the material and human consequences of destruction and reformation, despair and hope.[97]

The historical fixation with the idea of the fragment across all kinds of epistemologies—art history, archaeology, the classics, as well with the critical theories of modernity produced by thinkers like Benjamin or Adorno—reflects both the significance attached to the fragment in different historical contexts and the disillusionment with ideas of progress, wholes, and integration connected to the Enlightenment and modernity. The fragment is both a figure of the destruction of history and a statement of endurance—of finding a way of living with the devastation and somehow going on with things anyway, perhaps generating new openings and possibilities.

The artist Eduardo Paolozzi worked with this sense of fragmenting. Paolozzi used all manner of wastes in his sculptures from industrial remnants to the consumerist present, from toys, twisted forks, electric parts, and pieces from factory tips to shards from car wrecking yards or the bark of trees. Paolozzi saw this as more than collage, in that his sculptural work sought to capture the very process of ruin and wasting—less collage and more "damage, erase, destroy, deface and transform."[98] His aim was to "keep faith," as Hal Foster has put it, "with the fact of historical destruction."[99] Paolozzi's work assembled the traces of the world *onto* the sculptures in order to show how the world can leave figures shattered, damaged, and cracked, the body and psyche "under strain, of literal impressions from a broken world."[100] And yet at the same time, Foster argues, the figure protects itself, or finds a means of survival, precisely by absorbing the imprints of historical violence and fragmentation as a kind of shield in the world—"as if, in a perverse troping of Christ, what is dead cannot die or, rather, in a paradoxical updating of Nietzsche, what kills me makes me strong."[101]

Artists and activists can translate and even radically reform fragments in displaced formations in order to provoke political, social, and ecological questions. The examples discussed here reveal the potential of telling stories with fragments, or of opening spaces in which others might forward their own stories, imaginaries, and possibilities. The fragment politics described in relation to generative translation and reformation comment distinctively on the urban condition and the possible, from Ses'khona's powerful displacement of waste and the fragments that carry it to Maher's focus on the "intense unmaking" wrought by housing demolition in deindustrializing cities, Diba's emphasis on the "socialized objects" that contain histories, cultural practices, and transformations, or Purifoy's dual emphasis on destruction and creativity to spark debate about social change.

In each case, something suggestive—an opening or new angle on conditions—is generated from translation, disturbance, or destruction, even as these examples remain with the violence, oppression, and inequalities of history. These experiments hold the potential for expression, creativity, and transformation—whether as urban identities in Diba's work, or, more boldly, the "restructuring of values" in Purifoy's terms. Density is important in all kinds of ways: in the *destroyed* densities of lives and homes, as a concentrated *collection* of fragments from which to convert the debris of fragmentation into something else, as a *context* in which to understand how life is and might be organized, as a *condition* for the urban imagination, or as a *massing* of activists staging a spectacle in the city of the profound inadequacy of waste fragments.

Surveying Wholes

If the political framings discussed so far in this section *stay with* the fragments—by attending to them, or translating them in new relations and contexts—other interventions seek to address poverty and marginalization by *shifting away* from the fragments. For these activists, the locus of struggle is not the fragment per se, but the legal, economic, and political processes that shape fragment urbanism. "Surveying wholes" turns to a form of politics that revolves around data, accountability, and citizenship rights, and which is typically slower moving than the shock politics of the Cape Town case described earlier. It is a politics not of spectacle or artistic reformation but of number, entitlements, and state responsibilities, and of density as the numerical imbalance between the number and quality of provisions and number and everyday lives of people.

We see this in rights-based movements focused on citizenship entitlements for water, sanitation, or housing. One example is Mumbai's "Right to Pee" movement. Right to Pee builds databases of sanitation provision, and lobbies the local state to invest in adequate sanitation throughout the city as a constitutional citizenship right, particularly in dense areas where the need is most pressing, especially for women and girls, from informal neighborhoods and railway platforms to busy public spaces across the city. Here, the political logic is that localized fragments can only be addressed through transformation at the scale of the city as a "whole." If Ses'khona's "poo protests" are a spectacle politics emerging from the city in the wild—both a critique of and an expression of the failures of the liberal city to see poverty—Right to Pee turns its attention directly toward the traditions of the liberal city of data, budgets, and planning.

When Right to Pee was formed in 2011 through CORO for Literacy, its first priority was accurate data on sanitation provisions in the city. Right to Pee began by surveying 129 city toilet blocks. This data was then compared with the municipality's own data, which had been made available through a Right to Information request, and which revealed the relative budgetary neglect of sanitation, especially sanitation for women and girls. In 2012, the activists launched a public signature campaign on the railway stations. The signatures called for an improvement in provisions, typically woefully inadequate and usually broken or poorly functioning. Given that Mumbai's rail network is one of the busiest in the world, the provisions that do exist fall far short of need in often extremely crowded stations trains, especially at rush hour. From the start, then, the campaign was not only about low-income neighborhoods but about sanitation experiences *across the city*—in town, in transit, near home, and for everyone from low-income vegetable vendors to middle-class commuters. One Right to Pee activist remarked: "Today, the Right to Pee is everyone's campaign—from women fruit vendors to doctors and educationists, to town planners and gender experts."[102]

In 2013, Right to Pee petitioned the state minister for women and child development to provide public toilets for women free of charge. The group delivered a list of 50,000 names, gathered mainly from the city's railway platforms. The minister helped introduce the *Maharashtra Policy for Women* in 2013, which mandates the construction of a women's toilet block every 20 kilometers (12.4 miles)—still, to be sure, a considerable distance between facilities and nowhere near providing for the densities in question and how they change over a day or week or season, but the fact that this constituted an improvement in provisions is itself a powerful reflection of what women and girls, and poor women and girls in particular, can access around the city.

If this deeply gendered urbanism is to be tackled, then writing change into the planning process itself is one vital step. Right to Pee has been arguing that toilets need to be better identified as public amenities for planning in relation to any public place, including schools, markets, and transport stations. For example, in late 2015, the Mumbai High Court responded to a Public Interest Litigation filed by activist groups around health and the rights of women in relation to public toilets. The petitioners invoked Article 226 of the Constitution, which empowers High Courts to interpret the Constitution, and argued that the poor condition of public toilets led to safety concerns, nonaccessibility or unhygienic conditions, and medical consequences for women and girls. The High Court agreed, insisted that toilets must have trained maintenance staff and reasonable charges, and concluded: "[Women] need these facilities at public places like Railway Stations, Bus Stands, Banks, Public Offices like State Government Offices/Municipal Offices . . . it is the duty of the State and the Corporations to ensure that public latrines, urinals and similar conveniences are constructed, maintained and kept in a hygienic condition."[103] Welcome words, but there is a long way to go. On March 8, 2016, on the occasion of International Women's Day, Right to Pee returned an award that the city's mayor, Snehal Ambeka, had presented to them for their work on sanitation and gender. Supriya, a Right to Pee activist, told the *Times of India:* "Nothing has changed on the ground. The BMC budget has no provisions for women's toilets in the city and focuses only on household and community toilets."[104]

Right to Pee's work is a politics of sustained pressure and accountability that can be measured and anticipated in targets and steps, documents and budgets. Through surveys of toilets, they have been compiling a case that speaks in traditions of the liberal state through data, rights, policy proposals, and provisions. In the process they focus less on the fragments per se and more on rights in the city as a whole. As Sonia Faleiro writes of the movement, "the unprecedented acknowledgement of a woman's right to a public toilet [at senior policy levels] was seen as a victory not just for the fight for better sanitation, but for the women's movement."[105] The question of toilets here is a question of equality, of protecting women from violence and promoting empowerment, and of actively producing and being part of the planning and life of the city. As Shilpa Phadke, Sameera Khan, and Shilpa Ranade have put it, "if we had to pick one tangible symbol of male privilege in the city . . . the winner hands-down would be the public toilet."[106] Supriya, a Right to Pee activist, argued that "it's discrimination based on gender . . . it's not about facilities, it's a political statement."

Supriya argued that the campaign had "evolved" from "right to pee to right to city," while Sujata—another Right to Pee activist—talked about the "freedom" to participate in the city, to move around and not be stuck indoors, and repeatedly asserted that the struggle was about "citizenship." If there are no provisions, Sujata argued, then the city is saying to people: "Shut up and stay home." Instead, added Supriya, they are asking: "How do you claim your city as a citizen?" Mumtaz, another activist, talked about the need to address the wider system and to deepen democracy: "I'm looking for my place in the city. My own safe place, with dignity."

Political Becoming

The question of whether to pursue one or more of the politics described so far—attending to fragments, generative translation, reformation, surveying wholes—depends on the objectives at hand. There is, though, a challenge here for activists who seek to maintain more than one of these politics at a time. As Lisa Björkman has shown in her work on Mumbai, a politics that shifts register to a whole, such as in the form of rights, can also entail "a conceptual disentanglement of things from their actual sociomaterial contexts."[107] Some of the best guides through these questions are urban activists themselves. Right to Pee emerged from CORO for Literacy, and as such the larger politics of the group combines a politics of attending—through the inspection work of community toilets—and a politics of surveying wholes in their focus on planning, policy, and city budgeting. This has opened out a simultaneous focus on fragments and fragmentation, in which urban maintenance emerges as a connective device between fragments and wholes, in that it involves the inspection and negotiating activities around repairing local toilet blocks, and informs the campaign for city budgeting and planning. As a connective device, urban maintenance is also a calculation of density, both in relation to in-situ local monitoring of toilet blocks in dense neighborhoods, and in relation to the number of toilets provided at different points across the city as a whole (I will return to the idea of "connective devices" in the book's conclusion).

Activists pursue forms of fragment politics that seem most relevant to their context and objectives, and may indeed move between different forms over time or operate more than one simultaneously. Without a view on context, there is little to be gained by suggesting that one or other of these forms of politics is more strategically useful or important. Nonetheless, while there are challenges in operating different politics simultaneously, there are also risks in pursuing just one tactic over time. For instance, a politics of attending involves, as the name suggests, an effort of attention to the issues most immediately at hand, and can then divert focus away from a critique of the drivers of fragmentation processes. On the other hand, focusing exclusively on the latter may undermine not just an understanding of the issues on the ground, but the potential to support those struggling with fragments on an everyday basis.

The simultaneous hold on different forms of politics—attending and surveying wholes—in CORO and Right to Pee's work resonates with Elizabeth Grosz's elaboration of a politics of *becoming*.[108] Writing not about cities but about bodies, Grosz positions becoming in relation to both recognition (e.g., rights) *and* the contingencies of practice. Grosz finds in Deleuze's thought, for example, not a rejection of rights and identity politics—Deleuze and Guattari recognize in *A Thousand Plateaus,* for instance, that such a politics remains vital—but an insistent pressure to push beyond rights to break into new ways of being and relating that do not fix and freeze categories like "woman."[109] If left to a politics of rights and recognition alone, the category of woman can become a fixed knot that, even as it mobilizes people and informs claim-making, closes off difference and new possibilities.[110] If we think about the inspection activities of CORO, for example, the kinds of issues that surface through a politics of attending—working through assemblages of landlordism, political power-brokers, caste relations, and particular material conditions—cannot always be anticipated, nor captured in a politics of rights aimed at city planning. From this position, rights are both utterly indispensable and practically insufficient for generating more progressive urban conditions, particularly so in large, diverse, and changing cities like Mumbai.

A politics of becoming that works with and beyond rights and recognition is not without its challenges, as Grosz recognizes. There is always a risk of losing sight of either rights campaigning or local contextual struggles and differences. A politics of attending can narrow the political terrain just at the same time as a politics of surveying can expand it. A politics of wholes is not necessarily "larger" or "wider" than a politics of attending.[111] Other critical political traditions have shown this too. In queer theory, for example, there is at once an embracing of a diversity of identities and a close attention to "the messy, fleshy indeterminate stuff of everyday life," stuff that is often "fragmented and fleeting," pushing at the boundaries of what politics is in the city and who and what gets to be included within it.[112]

From this position, a politics of becoming addresses the transformation of wholes that produce fragments as such—for instance through planning, legal and regulatory frameworks, and policy change—while recognizing that the excessive, relational, and generative nature of fragment urbanisms in conditions of high densities requires attending to particular contexts and struggles.[113] While there are certain political demands that remain central to projects seeking a more just city—decent housing, basic rights to adequate infrastructure and services, the right to work and move, and so on—there is no simple model or blueprint to change. Cities and their political conditions do not stand still, and—like their inhabitants—they can surprise, exceed, improvise, and disclose new ways of doing and seeing things.

Grosz's focus on a politics of becoming is one route for working through the classic tensions of political action in relation to structure and agency. It does so by bypassing the fixed and clunky baggage of those terms, shifting from an often reductive reading of "agency" as local action to a focus on changing and expanding relations over time. In their very different ways, CORO, Right to Pee, and Grosz insist that the political struggle cannot be resolved through attention to the whole alone, because urban life continues to unfold and surprise, forcing new struggles to the fore. A politics of becoming is not one that privileges this or that approach over another, then, but which recognizes the value of different routes to change while also demanding attention to the multiplicities of the city-in-the-making, and the possibilities that emerge through those. It is a view of politics that works not just with fragments as nouns but with fragments as verbs, pulled into different kinds of relations over time and space across the city.

Occupation

On a bright spring morning, Ali walked me around Oranienplatz, in Kreuzberg, Berlin. There were seventy men from ten different countries living in the camp, said Ali—he arrived from Libya via Italy—although others estimated the number at closer to two hundred.[114] The camp was set up in 2013 as a protest space, disseminating information about the struggles of refugees applying for asylum and trying to find a livelihood in Germany, and for a time became a "heartland" of the refugee movement in the country.[115] The refugees had been there for eighteen months, in the middle of the square, in houses that were wooden in the main, some sackcloth. In winter, local people and charities brought heating and water, and food was donated by civil society organizations that also helped to set up a kitchen.

The camp was embellished with a series of political messages, emblazoned on many of the homes: "they spend money on war but won't feed the poor," "no one is illegal," "the right to asylum is not a privilege—it is a human right," "break isolation, stop deportation," "deportation is murder," and more. Some were simple demands for recognition of the people there: *"we are here,"* read one sign. The refugees had a set of demands that they publicized and sent to the Berlin Senate, including abolishing the *Residenzphflicht* ("mandatory residence") law that forbids free movement within the country (regional states have the power to overturn this—Hessen, for example, did so), putting an end to isolating and inhumane conditions in refugee camps, changing the rules so that asylum seekers can work, and stopping deportations of asylum seekers.[116]

The area was dotted with benches and a couple of tables in an open space at the center of the site, a few bicycles, and makeshift provisions. A barber was operating outside one of the tents. For a while some of the refugees occupied a nearby abandoned school, along with squatters and housing activists, and moved between the school and the camp. The wives and children of many of the men were living nearby in hostels or in the school. While women played a role in leading the protest camp in the platz, most of the leaders were men. Some women claimed a wing on the second floor of the school as an "International Women's Space." Men were not allowed, and issues ranging from access to toilets and showers—toilets were often shared with men, and the few showers that existed often didn't have a door—to health care and coping with life in the city were discussed.[117] The lack of showers became a trigger point among some of the refugees, and sometimes there was conflict in the queues. On one occasion a man was killed.[118] One refugee, Alnour Ahmad-Hassan, from Sudan, who had been living at the school described the relationship between sanitation, conflict, and the public authorities: "After the death, we took to the streets again and demanded the showers not only in official letters sent to the city council but also at the demonstrations in front of the railway station. Authorities were to blame for the death. They knew what the situation was and didn't want to do anything about it. Instead of showers we received an eviction notice."[119]

Sometimes the refugees received threats from neo-Nazis. Local residents, said Ali, always came in numbers to support them. On one occasion, a public toilet on the site was burned to the ground. Ali speculated that neo-Nazis had committed the act, likely both to disrupt basic everyday life, as well as to turn residents against refugees by forcing refugees to use space in and around the square as a toilet. The police took photos, but nothing followed. A charity later provided a temporary toilet block nearby, a small structure that was locked at night until someone broke the lock. At the time, signs on the refugee camp's "infopoint"— a tent that provided information about refugees and their struggles, as well as activism supporting refugees—explained that they were raising money for a new toilet, but Ali thought it was unlikely enough funds would be gathered.

The camp became a small, politicized occupation focused at once on everyday fragments of showers, toilets, and other provisions, on basic rights, on the right to occupy the square, on collaborations with residents in the neighborhood, lobbying the city and the state, and so on. The struggle grew into a controversial and high-profile presence in media debates in the city and beyond. There was support from activists, residents, and some political figures—including the mayor of Kreuzberg—support that was expressed vocally and through provisions, such as individuals and civil society groups helping with services like garbage collection. But there was opposition too. Some Senate politicians, for example, claimed that many of the refugees had already had their applications rejected by another regional state in Germany, and therefore should be deported.

As Judith Butler has argued, political occupations can take on all kinds of forms: a blockage to capital, a shared silence, a defiant refusal, a communal insistence simply to be seen and heard, and so on.[120] Occupation can be a means of asserting basic claims to survival and to being heard. If the other political framings discussed earlier are often defined by an explicit effort to address the fragmented nature of urban life on the margins, the occupation is much more about asserting a fundamental claim to presence, to being heard and subsisting, than it is about fragments. Nonetheless, in the growing numbers of struggles faced by more and more internally and externally displaced refugees across the urban world, fragments play an important role in survival, living, and politics. We see this, for example, in the construction of makeshift camps and staging of protests with sometimes shoddy materials, the inadequate provisions of housing, infrastructure, and services that are often precarious and demand ongoing attention, and the politics of demolition and displacement in which occupation is turned into fragments.

The individual and collective body, in densification and disassembly, forces attention to its own needs: decent shelter, employment, health care, food, a secure future, the possibilities of the city so often denied.[121] At the same time, occupation is highly vulnerable and can end up being reduced to fragments, sometimes violently so. A few weeks after the conversation with Ali, the camp was demolished by city bulldozers and police. While many of the residents had agreed to move to a hostel and other nearby accommodation offered by the Berlin Senate—with assurances that their asylum applications would be dealt with and that they would receive 100 euros in cash at the hostels—riot police were met by protestors who sat on the ground in front of them. A Sudanese refugee, Napuli Langa, a human rights activist who became an influential leader at the site, climbed a tree in the square and went on a hunger strike in the week before the police arrived.[122] Police prevented supporters from providing her with food and blankets.[123] At the nearby school, from which they were also evicted, around forty refugees occupied the roof of the building for over a week, and the school was surrounded by police, after which the women received financial support from a local organization to continue the work of the International Women's Space in a nearby building.[124] By August 2014, almost 20 percent of the refugees at the camp were ordered to leave the city and return to either the German state or EU country they had stayed in before arriving to Berlin.[125] It was rumored that some of the refugees did not receive promised housing and ended up homeless.[126]

The struggle at Oranienplatz was at once bodily, gendered, racial, infrastructural, public, legal, and translocal. A politicized temporary occupation—located precariously between the city's hospitality and different forms of legal and political violence, between assembly and disassembly—the struggle for urban life here was expressed across multiple concerns: toilets, showers, food, construction and deconstruction of housing and services, national labor regulations and policy positions, and city party politics. The occupation was both site-based and translocal, both collectivized density—"we are here"—and differentiated by nationality, gender, and political predispositions, and always uncertain about its future, with an ever-present threat of demolition, displacement, and deportation. This is a politics of fragment urbanism that connects fragments to rights, where bodies are sites of struggle for basic provisions and political tools in the form of barricades, occupation, and hunger strikers.[127] In echoes of the discussion of Right to Pee, this is a form of political struggle that moves between fragments (showers and toilets, for instance) and wholes (rights and regulations), although it is distinct too, in part because it is less about surveying data and more about staging moral claims to human and legal rights.

The occupation at Oranienplatz was both a seizing of urban space by those on the economic margins of the city and an enactment of a particular kind of experimental urbanism of being together. The occupation posed the cosmopolitical question of living together across difference not just to the platz but to the city itself, to what kind of city Berlin is and might become. It expressed both a different image of the city and a hope for the basic provisions enjoyed by much of the rest of the city. For Alex Vasudevan, the occupation was not only about the right to the city but the right to be in the city, and as such is part of a longer set of histories in Berlin of occupation that includes squatters and housing activists who, in their assemblies, disclose "tactics for how we might still come to know and live the city differently."[128]

The occupation at Oranienplatz was part of a series of acts of political pulling together (and falling apart) around refugees in Berlin that put bodies on the line, and was itself formed from another protest camp (in Heinrichplatz), which emerged in turn from a set of protests and marches in Germany that followed the suicide of a refugee in 2012.[129] The relations between fragments and rights can become barometers of the city of refuge. The year after the Oranienplatz struggle, in 2015, the number of refugees arriving in the city significantly increased, and residents, activists, and refugees found ways of working together in the face of an ill-prepared state apparatus. At stake here was not just a struggle around particular sites but over Berlin as a progressive and multicultural cosmopolis. The challenge of urban cosmopolitics, of the making of "urban common worlds" composed through a cosmos of open and often unknown agencies in the city,[130] is not simply a territorial struggle but a spatial relation of heterogeneous, intersecting threads, and a making visible of matters of concern around living with and beyond fragments.[131] This, ultimately, is the test of the historical idea of the city as a space of refuge.

PROVISIONING

Cities are at once sites of expulsion, violence, and destruction, and of refuge, sanctuary, and care. The resonances of this double movement throughout history, and the lives and struggles caught up in it, have been fundamental both to the idea of the city and to expressions of justice and equality. We can draw an historical line, as many narratives have done, from the Biblical injunction to cities of refuge in the Old Testament through to the City Sanctuary movement and its afterlives, taking in thinkers from Kant to Derrida on cosmopolitanism, hospitality, and refuge.[132] Histories of racism, segregation, class prejudice, and gendered power continue to inform the articulation of the urban cosmopolis. The struggle for refuge is also fundamentally place-based and contingent, and worked out and fought over in ways that seem to be constantly shifting through world events. Think, for instance, of how the ideas of refuge or sanctuary in the United States were differently attacked, politicized, and remade in what Ananya Roy calls "the city in the age of Trumpism," or in the lurch to the political Right in India and Brazil, or amidst Brexit in the UK.[133]

In Europe, an important moment in the struggle over the city of refuge, and in which we can see a politics of fragment urbanism at work, is the response to the displacement of millions of refugees due to the war in Syria. Berlin received approximately 79,000 refugees in 2015, mainly from Syria, 54,000 of whom stayed on.[134] In 2015, Germany suspended the European Union's Dublin regulations in order to speed up processing refugees from Syria. Ninety percent of Syrians who applied for asylum in the European Union (EU) in 2015 and 2016 applied to Germany.[135] The year 2015 was described as "the summer of solidarity," a celebration of German *Willkommenskultur*—a welcoming disposition from across society (politicians, businesses, institutions, residents) toward arrivals—but it was not an unequivocal solidarity. The open welcome to Syrians was not matched with a similar commitment to refugees from Afghanistan, Iraq, or the Balkan states, to name a few.[136] In the same year, the federal government passed the Integration Bill, requiring refugees to participate in language training while waiting for decisions on their asylum application, and lowering barriers to the job market by abolishing preferences for German and EU job applicants.[137]

Moreover, set against the promotion of a *Willkommenskultur* was a growing disquiet and in some cases explicit xenophobia directed against newcomers in Germany. Amnesty International claimed that over a thousand homes of refugees and asylum seekers were attacked in 2015, and the far Right Alternative für Deutschland (AfD) made worrying gains in elections.[138] In September 2016, AfD took 14 percent of the vote in the Berlin state election, and polled over 20 percent even in some of the more progressive and multicultural districts such as Neukölln and Prenzlauer Berg. The far Right Pegida movement attracted thousands of people to its rallies. A terrorist attack in late 2016 at a Christmas market in Berlin exacerbated the tensions and changing mood. In response, the government committed itself to speeding up deportations, and a controversial 2016 pact with Turkey ensured migrants who had entered through Turkey to Germany would be returned in exchange for financial concessions. In the three years following 2015, there was an estimated four thousand attacks on asylum hostels and foreigners, and in 2016 an average of ten hate crimes per day were registered against migrants.[139]

City administrations have been caught between *Willkommenskultur* and a growing atmosphere of refusal and hostility. They were expected to register arrivals, identify short-term housing, integrate children into schools, facilitate language and employment training, and ensure health provisions, security, and access to services. Depending on their route into Germany, most asylum seekers are barred from working for the first three months, during which time they can participate in vocational training or internships. They receive asylum welfare for fifteen months and, following that, slightly higher social welfare. Provisions for accommodation varies: those in designated refugee centers receive €135 per month, while those renting privately can claim €354.[140] While Berlin is a relatively cheap German city, this money quickly disappears, and most asylum seekers struggle to get by.

A federal quota system distributes refugees across the country, based on population and tax revenues across German states. This means that more densely populated areas receive proportionately more refugees, with the consequence that Berlin had significantly more refugees per square kilometer than any other German city.[141] On the face of it Berlin is in a good position to manage large numbers of arrivals—housing is relatively cheap compared to other major German cities, and there has been a good number of unused buildings in the decades since the Wall fell. On the other hand, the city has spent most of the post-Wall years in debt. The housing and land markets are transforming: between 2004 and 2014 Berlin witnessed a 45 percent increase in housing rent, it has one of the fastest-growing housing costs in Europe, it has pursued neoliberal public sector cuts, and the subsidies from federal government for refugee housing costs do not come close to the actual municipal costs.[142]

Berlin's encounter with refugees has been a multiple and sometimes contradictory politics. Alongside extraordinary commitment by so many residents in support of the provisions, rights, and opportunities for refugees, there have been acts of intolerance, destruction, state failures, and partial support. Just as the forms and politics of fragment urbanism in cities are multiple, so too are refugee struggles in the city. As Jonathan Darling has argued, the experience and politics of refugees within and between cities is plural, and takes the form of different kinds of presencing, claim-making, organization, and struggle.[143] He examines how refugees in the city inhabit what Oren Yiftachel has called a "gray space" between the formal and informal, the legal and illegal, a status of precarity and uncertainty along with other marginalized groups, including residents of informal neighborhoods and those who are homeless.[144] If the city is a space of encounter—an accumulation of things, objects, people, and situations that are co-present and diverse—that encounter can also become a test of the historical promise of the "city" as an idea.[145] Progressive cities require not just a *Willkommen-skultur* but a set of decent provisions, not just a respect for difference but adequate housing, infrastructure, and services.[146]

As Darling shows, local and national states approach refugees in very different ways, from systems of managed marginality that locate refugees in camps to more dispersed systems within the existing housing fabric, or from the Sanctuary City movement that provides support to refugees accessing services, housing, and infrastructure, and often cultural programs, to efforts to repackage central government policies on, for instance, labor regulations.[147] Darling describes a "politics of presence": of not just rights, legalities, and procedures, but refugees and longer-term residents working together in the city, changing urban configurations and producing new spaces and possibilities, even amidst the often sharp limits and constraints of culture, economy, and law. Occupation, such as that in Oranienplatz, is one politics of presence in the city, and what was to emerge in Moabit, a district in Mitte, central Berlin, was a different case of presencing.

Moabit is a largely working-class and student area with a history of migration from Turkey, the Middle East, and North Africa. The area is often described as one of relatively high unemployment but cheaper housing than some of the trendier parts of central Berlin.[148] In the public debate about refugees in the city, Moabit was to become one of the key reference points, specifically around the question of whether and how the Berlin Senate, in the form of the State Office for Health and Social Services (LaGeSo), was willing and able to support the tens of thousands of mainly Syrian refugees arriving to the city (Figure 7).[149]

In 2015, a group of local residents in Moabit who wanted to help refugees sleeping rough outside the LaGeSo offices formed a new collective, Moabit Hilft (Moabit Helps), a group that was to quickly become one of the most high-profile and politicized refugee organizations in the city.[150] Refugees, including children and pregnant women, were living homeless at or next to the site at the LaGeSo buildings, where they were expected to register their arrival. They slept on vacant land, sometimes for days, sometimes for weeks. There were no provisions for toilets, food, blankets, or shelter—just one water tap, and that of dubious quality—and parents were forced to wash diapers and reuse them. "You should have been here six months ago, because this was a slum," said Christiane Beckman, one of Moabit Hilft's leading activists.

This was a quite different kind of occupation from Oranienplatz—not a politicized collective, albeit a group whose very presence is politi-

FIGURE 7. Moabit, near the LaGeSo building, with the Moabit Hilft building in the lower image (Photos by author)

cal, but people waiting to have their applications processed and hoping for secure housing. And yet the occupations have concerns in common: in both, people seek out basic recognition and provisions, and in both, being *there,* occupying the space, was key to expressing those hopes. The Senate, and the LeGeSo building in particular, became the site of political struggle, supported by groups like Moabit Hilft. As Christiane put it: "We became a massive pain in the ass for them!"

The Senate was taking weeks to process people's registration, and while LaGeSo staff insisted that they were understaffed and that the numbers of refugees arriving were far beyond what could be managed, the people who were waiting did so often after horrendous journeys. Some were infirm, ill, injured, pregnant, or very young. Moabit Hilft pushed these individual cases with LaGeSo and got many sped up. Still, Christiane believes at least two pregnant women lost their babies because of the conditions of being homeless. The Senate, Christiane argued, was "lucky" that Berlin had a mild winter in 2015–16, and fortunate too, she added, that there hadn't been more illness outbreaks in camps and gyms across the city—one case of measles, she reflected, could spread rapidly, and many children were not inoculated.

Eventually toilets appeared, tents were provided for people to sit in, and doctors were provided on-site to treat people. Moabit Hilft was given space on the ground floor of a building across from the LaGeSo offices to support refugees. LaGeSo's job is to register refugees, which in turn entitles refugees to receive a small allowance as well as vouchers for clothes and food, and to receive help into accommodation and health care. LaGeSo does not decide on applications for asylum, which is a central government responsibility. Once people are granted asylum, their status is held with the job center, but until that time, refugees must report to LaGeSo for support. The sheer number of asylum applications, often not met with an adequate rise in staff, meant that applications were taking longer and longer to process. In 2013, according to the Federal Agency for Migration and Refugees, most refugees were from the Middle East, Afghanistan, and Chechnya.[151] In 2014, there were 9,500 asylum seekers in Berlin,[152] and by the following year that number had increased fivefold.[153] In the summer of 2015, with winter approaching, the situation at LaGeSo was spiraling out of control, with families living outside near the offices and in the surrounding areas without shelter and basic provisions. The site became the focus of national media attention, especially with the tragic news that a four-year-old boy from Bosnia had been kidnapped and killed.

For all that Berlin is rightly thought of as a multicultural city, there is certainly evidence that its policy positions, for example around "integration," have not only often ignored the social realities of immigrants but in some cases exacerbated the challenges immigrants face.[154] In the leadup to 2015, however, there was a quantitative and qualitative shift for which the Berlin Senate was poorly prepared. While the number of refugees arriving in Berlin increased by more than ten times in the three years between 2012 and 2015, the number of staff at LaGeSo, claims Silvia Kostner, who works in the Moabit office's press relations, did not grow.

"Until October 2012, refugees were only about 5% of my work," said Silvia, "but then that changed. In August that year we had an upgrade of the financial report and more funding was provided for the refugees. Then there is the Syrian war, and the situation in Afghanistan, Iraq and Iran getting worse." The office was overwhelmed. The situation, Silvia argued, was a "catastrophe"—a category that requires an emergency plan under German law, just as, say, a nuclear accident would—but the central government refused to characterize it in this way. Instead, she continued, "everyone said we were responsible for everything."

"The refugees were in front of the Haus [building]," recalled Silvia. "They needed food, somewhere to sleep, medical services." The staff decided that rather than continuing to wait to register refugees, they would open emergency rooms to provide beds and food prior to registration:

> But for that alone you need hundreds of persons. We didn't have the staff. The President of LaGeSo asked from 2013 for more staff and was told we don't have the money—Berlin is "poor but sexy" . . . 2013 passed and 2014 came and nothing changed. Then we got ten people more in the asylum department—ten people! We needed one hundred! So everyone said, the LaGeSo is bad and don't register and let people starve and I don't know what. But it was not possible with the staff we had.

As a result, staff cut corners, including sending refugees to shelters that hadn't been inspected. As a result of the pressure, including from the mayor who had joined the voices calling for a change in leadership, LaGeSo's president—Franz Allert—was forced to resign. Silvia's role was to defend LaGeSo staff, and she argued that critical voices in the media or in organizations like Moabit Hilft were never prepared to see the challenges from their perspective:

> There were times we had no beds to give to refugees. The organizations say we are not doing what we should. But if the state is not recruiting buildings what can we do? . . . they did not see the situation of our staff, working twelve hours, going to bed, falling asleep, not seeing their families . . . Every week we did new things—a tent with two thousand meals, another week a tent with medical support, next week vaccination support, the following week we did x-rays, the following week we opened a house for Moabit Hilft for clothes. Every week improvements, but of course it was never enough.

Christiane and Silvia sought to address the same fragments of housing and infrastructure, but with sharply contradictory interpretations. The "crisis" of the summer of 2015, Silvia argued, was what changed circumstances—the situation in Moabit was gaining sustained media

attention, and the political parties were focusing on it. Things got eas-
ier: "The Senate opened the fifty sports halls, all the other empty houses
we have in Berlin, they opened Tempelhof airport, and the situation
became better." From late 2015 the number of staff at LaGeSo working
on asylum increased by around two hundred, many of whom were sec-
onded temporarily from other departments. The labor, she added, was
better organized through work groups and a "Competence Team" that
monitors how the service is operating. By 2016, there were 140 shelters
in the city, and close inspections were underway.

The extra support was vital, but anger toward the Senate for what
were often seen as violations of basic responsibilities and provisions ran
deep, and not just among civil society activists such as Moabit Hilft. For
example, at the end of 2015, over forty lawyers filed a criminal com-
plaint against the former head of LaGeSo—Franz Allert—and the city's
social affairs senator Mario Czaja (from the Christian Democrats
Union), alleging that the institutional neglect was "causing bodily
harm": "In no other state are politicians and administrators failing as
systematically as here," said lawyer Christina Clemm, claiming the
results were injuries, illnesses, hunger, and homelessness.[155]

The struggle over basic provisions and rights in Moabit emerges as a
result of the contradictions in the German state's approach to the Syrian
refugee crisis. While the central state, and Chancellor Angela Merkel in
particular, espoused, in 2015 at least, an open progressive policy, a few
miles from Merkel's office the Berlin Senate was underprepared and
historically underresourced. But this scalar contradiction plays out not
just within the state but between state and civil society, for example in
the ways in which activists both come to perform essential state responsibilities while vehemently criticizing the state publicly. These contradictions became, then, the intersections through which the struggle to
be in the city proceeds as a form of fragment urbanism that connects the
body to infrastructure, housing, and legalities.

It was left to groups like Moabit Hilft to address the gaps. In 2016,
the *Hauss* where Moabit Hilft was based had a small lobby area, with
refugees sitting in seats along the walls. Refugees came to Moabit Hilft
for supplies—everything from diapers and sanitary products to clothes
and something to eat—and as many as a thousand people passed
through every day, people from Syria, Iran, Iraq, Afghanistan, Ukraine,
Turkey, and other places. At a desk sat a volunteer. She or he took the
person's identification, and then asked other volunteers in an adjacent
room to get some supplies, mainly toiletries. If they need clothes, the

refugees went through to a long corridor at the rear lined with adults and mainly children's clothing on racks. There was often a lack of certain kinds of supplies, such as sanitary towels, diapers, and strollers. Outside, refugees and volunteers busied around with supplies or stood and talked, occasionally giving advice to people arriving. The atmosphere was welcoming and upbeat, with kids bumbling around and a warm, friendly chatter. Nearby, heated tents, provided by the Senate as winter approached in 2015, were used by refugees who sat, talked, or played. Like other voluntary and activist groups in the city, the NGO became an important space and actor around which social infrastructures could be formed.

"This is not just about providing some clothes and services," said Christiane. "This is about solidarity." For Christiane, the organization is political. This takes a variety of forms: struggling with the Berlin Senate authorities for basic services for refugees, including their registration so that they can get access to the small amount of money and provisions they are given, or for access to accommodation, or treating refugees not just as refugees but as people—not just saying, "Here's your jumper, if you don't want it because of the size then tough," but saying, "Come and have a look, if you want this, fine, if you don't, that's also fine, because clothes affect how people feel." But if there was a politics of solidarity, that didn't mean there wasn't occasional tension. People might complain that they needed more provisions, or argue with one another, sometimes due to national or religious differences or sometimes simply due to the myriad challenges of life as a refugee. On rare occasions Christiane had people thrown out who exhibited prejudice toward others.

Moabit Hilft entered into a pseudo-state role in providing or facilitating urban life—including food, clothes, shelter, language training, a sense of belonging, while at the same time actively pressuring the state for greater resources and attention to detail. It is not enough to know refugee needs *collectively*—housing, infrastructure, services, and so on—there also needs to be the flexibility to meet *individual* needs. Volunteers know, for example, that some people may have disabled children who may need more diapers, so they give more than the allocated amount. Fragment urbanism here is not one thing; it is a process composed of heterogenous needs and groups, a cosmopolitical challenge of providing for and living together.

The area in and around the Moabit offices became a space of refuge and solidarity, a kind of temporary neighborhood that had gone from desperate conditions of squatting to more established and organized forms of provision. As with Oranienplatz, it reflected to no small extent the often contradictory relationship both city and national authorities have toward refugee provisioning.[156] As the months went by and refugees were increasingly moved indoors, the struggle over fragment urbanism changed. If the densities on Oranienplatz and outside the LaGeSo offices in Moabit were political partly because of their visibility—or, rather, if visibility was a vital element of what made those densities differently political—the fact that collectives became increasingly distributed and hidden across the city altered the politics of refuge. In late 2016, Christiane reflected that while struggles were "now more hidden, the fact that people sleep inside doesn't take away challenges." She went on:

> There are 20,000 people who have gone past the six-months status as asylum seekers but who haven't been transferred to the new status. This means they continue to receive the small amount of 135 euros per week. Thirty goes immediately for the weekly metro and that leaves 100 for everything else, and that they have to take food cooked in canteens and not cook their own food . . . The government is breaking its own laws.

Part of the city state's solution was to build container homes for refugees, which could be occupied for up to three years at a time, and which one official at the new LaGeSo—Landesamt fur Fluchtlingsungelegenheiten (LAF)—acknowledged was a product of "a lack of imagination" by the state on housing for refugees. These new "villages" were built through a legal loophole—Article 76 of the Building Code—which allowed for construction without consent from the authority in the local borough, and are composed of modular housing in areas such as Lichterfelde-Zehlendorf, with six locations of 2,400 units having been identified in the city in the first instance, built using containers and supplemented with glass fiber to improve their appearance, and often with gyms built on-site.[157] Alongside this, Moabit Hilft continued to perform state functions by providing basic provisions. Christiane again:

> Just last week a family—mother, father, five-year old, one-year old—came to us. They hadn't been paid the [government] money into the account. Eight days they waited. If you are on this budget, with a family, you can't survive. Someone at LAF gave them a note saying come to Moabit Hilft, and a leaflet with soup kitchens! This is not rare—every day something like this happens.

Investigating the city of refuge through the equation between fragments and rights reveals not only how the lives of refugees are policed and limited in the resources granted by the state, but the multiple ways in which refugees and activists get by, get on, and contest urban conditions.[158] From political occupation and claim-making or basic provisioning, to forms of connection and cultural expression, the city of refuge is one of poverty and sometimes violence, and at the same time one of solidarity and social infrastructure. To see like a city, David Kishik argues, is in part about recognizing the city as a space of refuge made and remade through different gatherings and undoings, and where the cosmopolitical challenge is posed anew again and again.[159]

Value

How does the city produce value? We are by now familiar with the ways in which the city is increasingly turned into a speculative and extractive space through real estate markets. In this process, global in scope, value takes on a particular economic character, expressed as either a number or investment potential. The relentless focus on generating economic value from urban land has given rise to a more general territorial logic, in which city governance—itself increasingly shaped by corporate power—focuses less on the needs of its residents and more on the speculative potential of the land.[160] In India, for instance, Michael Goldman reports on a "speculative urbanism" seeking to intensify the global commodification and tradability of land, infrastructure, and other public goods, a process accompanied by the fracturing of space into "spaces of exception"—Special Economic Zones and other "premium spaces," for instance; an activist judiciary actively pursuing the aesthetics of the "world class city"; and the narrowing of democratic control and voice for ordinary urbanites.[161] Increasing numbers of residents, old and new, are forced into different kinds of often dense, informal neighborhoods, spaces frequently composed of all kinds of material fragments of infrastructure, housing, and services.[162] This is a form of valuation that drives particular logics of densification and sociospatial fragmentation.

Against this highly particular form of value, in which the city is cast less as a crucible of human life and possibility and more as an economic investment vehicle, Andy Merrifield identifies actors seeking to produce a quite different vision of value in the city. He connects Occupy, Greek protestors, and activists in Palestine as pitted against this predatory power and attempting to counter and reconstitute the city, fighting "the *same* civil war, fighting as territorial foot soldiers, as relative surplus populations sharing a common language and, significantly, a common enemy."[163] Here, as Merrifield points out, is another kind of densification, one in which people gather together to demand that their social and ecological concerns about, and alternatives to, inequality, marketization, and destruction are positioned centrally in the production of the city.

It is time, as Brian Massumi has argued, to take back value. Value, after all, has never been entirely colonized by capitalist measures.[164] There has always been more at work in talk of value, a social residue that persists and which can be nourished. As we saw in relation to artistic experiments in a politics of reformation, or in the "in-between" work of attending to knowledge fragments in Berlin, responses to fragment urbanism can support a conception of people and places as human, creative, and full of potential. Given the plurality of the city and of urban life, *urban* value needs to be opened out to reflect the different ways in which "urban" and "value" might come together. The "urban" might feature in all kinds of forms of generating value: a gathering that operates in productive and often inventive ways, a political terrain of contesting state spending decisions, a material resource for political activism or creative expression, and so on.[165]

This does not mean rejecting the economic. There are plenty of cases in cities across the urban world of formulating the economic and social in ways that generate an alternative urban value. We might think here of the postcapitalist economy that Gibson Graham describes, including economies of self-provisioning, gifting, caring, savings collectives, worker cooperation, feudal enterprises, and reciprocal informal markets, that bubble around as a loose ecology of practices and experiments, and which are often under the radar.[166] Here, value is often refracted through ideas of community, the commons, becoming subjects, ethics, hope, diversity, and so on. We see this, for instance, in the social infrastructures of care and consolidation in Kampala described earlier in the book that do not draw dividing lines between the social and the economic, but instead around vectors of reciprocity or kin or friendship. The economic and the social elements of value collapse. At the same time there is also a reminder here in valuing certain forms of social and reproductive labor that often aren't economically valued.

Care—domestic, friendship, neighborly, or among informal traders, and so forth—is an important example. The question of urban value demands both working with how people or places are viewed and situated within dominant relations of power in economy, culture, and polity, and creating spaces and possibilities to shape the city and its futures. It is also about recognizing that the resources people put together on the margins of the city—the social infrastructures, forms of connection and attention, artistic experiments, activist interventions and occupations, and more—are forms of value that have a crucial part to play in a different kind of city and urban world.[167]

EXHIBITING STORIES

The flyer in Figure 8 was produced for an exhibition, *Celebrating Namuwongo,* at the Uganda Museum of snapshots from six people's lives in Namuwongo, Kampala. The exhibition sought to bring ordinary everyday experiences on the economic margins of the city into a larger story in one exhibition space at the country's national museum (it was organized by Jonathan Silver, Joel Ongwec, Helen Friars, Josephine Namukisa, and myself). In explicit contrast to conservative constructions of "slum" lives as *wasteful* and the "slum" neighborhood as a place of waste, the exhibition very deliberately set out to celebrate the neighborhood and its residents. Namuwongo, like many informal neighborhoods globally, is often portrayed less as a lively, diverse set of communities, and more as "wasted space" living under the threat of "planned obsolescence," better off used in some other way best decided by people other than those who live there.[168]

In Kampala, Namuwongo's reputation is often a deeply negative one. As resident and filmmaker Joel Ongwec, who co-designed the exhibition, has put it, residents of nearby middle-class neighborhoods often "claim that the people are lazy, thieves, and possess just about any negative attitude you can imagine."[169] Claims that the area is violent, crime-ridden, and populated by unemployed drug-taking and potentially explosive young men are not uncommon.[170] The central challenge of the exhibition was to tell a different story, one that reflected at least something of the multiplicities and possibilities of the neighborhood, and in so doing to provoke a space of reflection. The hope was that this could provide a basis for contesting, albeit in a small, temporary way, the often negative characterization of the neighborhood by more mainstream discourses and

CELEBRATING NAMUWONGO

ABOUT THE EXHIBITION

WHAT IS EVERYDAY LIFE LIKE FOR THE PEOPLE LIVING IN NAMUWONGO? THIS EXHIBITION EXPLORES THE LIFE EXPERIENCES OF SIX PEOPLE FROM NAMUWONGO, INVESTIGATING THE WAYS IN WHICH THEY MOVE AROUND THE CITY, COPE WITH CHALLENGES, IDENTIFY AND DEVELOP OPPORTUNITIES AND ENCOUNTER THE PEOPLE AND PLACES AROUND THEM.

NAMUWONGO IS VERY POORLY UNDERSTOOD NEIGHBOURHOOD IN KAMPALA. BUT RUTHER THAN REPEAT NEGATIVE STEREOTYPES OF THE NEIGHBOURHOOD, THIS EXHIBITION CELEBRATE LIFE IN NAMUWONGO.

- Venue: Uganda National Museum
- Starting: 30 / 05 / 2015
- Ending: 28 / 06 / 2015

Contact Organisers:

(+256) 784 798 518, (+256) 773 002 218
(+256) 779 180 984

FIGURE 8. Flyer for the *Celebrating Namuwongo* exhibition, May 2015 (Compiled by Colin McFarlane and Jonathan Silver)

actors in Kampala, and provoking other stories and imaginaries of the place.

How might urbanists use fragments of stories to provoke conversations about the life and potentials of devalued places, feed into new urban imaginaries and possibilities, and promote alternative forms of social and spatial value? By bringing knowledge fragments together, the exhibition paid attention both to the specificity of each individual story and the larger story produced. The question of how to live together with density, and the role of the state and other actors in helping to address the fragmented provisions of the neighborhood, was at the center of the space of reflection the exhibition produced. While, as Bruno Latour writes, "an exhibition cannot do much," what it can do is "explore new possibilities with a much greater degree of freedom because it is so good at thought-experiments . . . visitors or readers can compare the different types of representation."[171]

The exhibition allowed a staging of different expressions of urban life, an opportunity to hear about and compare stories, and a provocation to reflect on what's already going on, or to identify ways of doing things differently. The exhibition can be a tool for (un)learning and (un)seeing space and possibilities. It can create, among the urban public, what Jane M. Jacobs describes as "the conditions to see multiplicity," a space of reflection that works against "the dissimulation of singular, overcoded, explanatory frameworks."[172] Richard Sennett points to the value of thinking "about collage and assemblage . . . about fragments that are important to people" as another way of developing socially improved urban conditions.[173] The exhibition drew upon a set of individual stories often forced to the geographical and discursive margins of how the city is understood, and produced a story and map of the city from the repertoire of people's everyday lives. The project was a small one and worked with just the six people's stories we encountered in the discussion of social infrastructure in the *Pulling together, falling apart* section of the book—Jennifer, Josephine, Ali, Isamael, Masengere, and Amiri.

Putting together an exhibition is itself an exercise in arranging and rearranging fragments in a process of generative translation: parts of photos, sections of maps, amalgamated images, sections of text, mixing paints, all of which are pieced together from conjoined tables, posters, and cards (Figure 9). At the entrance to the exhibition, local residents painted images from the neighborhood with "Celebrating Namu-

FIGURE 9. Assembling the exhibition (Photos by author)

FIGURE 10. Opening day (Photo by author)

wongo" emblazoned across it. As the preparations came to an end, there was a sense of fragments made into a "whole," but a whole that is of course unfinished and incomplete, and which tells a situated story of a place that is multiple, changing. Before anyone arrived, the exhibition space is a kind of void, an anticipatory space imbued both with expectation and anxiety and the hopes of a team that has been able to work together to produce an exhibition within a tight time frame.

On opening day, the void becomes a dense cacophony of all kinds of interactions and voices. Over a hundred residents from the neighborhood attended on the day, and a short article was released (Figure 10).[174] People's initial response was big: smiles, laughing, pointing at themselves and each other in images, making jokes about how people and places have been presented. As the atmosphere quietened and people read and talked about the exhibits, some reflected on how shocking it was to see their neighborhood, a poor place largely ignored by more economically elite Kampala, thrust into the light of a formal exhibition space at the country's national museum. Some of the conversation was serious and focused on the challenges of life in Namuwongo, but the atmosphere was generally light, with kids excitedly running around.

The six residents expressed surprise that the Uganda Museum, and indeed the larger Kampala public, would be interested at all in how they spend their time. Masengere commented that "most of the time people don't think of us." Josephine hoped that the exhibition would expose her story to different people across the city, and perhaps encourage them to think twice about their perceptions of the neighborhood. For Amiri, the exhibition created a space for discussing ideas about conditions and how to change them, and about how to organize young people, even if it fell short on ideas around how to find work, develop skills, or build a more independent, consolidated life. Discussions at times focused on material fragments of housing and infrastructure, but journeyed far beyond those issues to all kinds of concerns, hopes, fears, and potentials. It was an energized and lively set of people, debates and reflections.

The exhibition remained open for over a month and attracted visitors from across the city and beyond. As part of this, we organized discussions among different people on the exhibition, including one on a rain-soaked afternoon in which a group from across the city gathered in the old library at the Uganda Museum. We huddled around a large oval wooden table in the middle of the library, flanked by an impressive range of texts from contemporary anthologies of Ugandan poetry to aging colonial tomes. The group consisted of the residents from Namuwongo who had featured in the exhibition, staff from nongovernmental organizations, and academics (and a few vacant seats for those who, we later learned, had turned back in the face of the worsening traffic as the rain fell). A participant from an NGO that works on housing and infrastructure in low-income neighborhoods—ACTogether—was one of the first to speak:

> I take so many things for granted. I concentrate on the big things. Housing, land, water. You don't give times to the simple things—like how does someone spend the day, how do they get through the day? Namuwongo is alive—that statement means there is a lot of energy, a lot of enthusiasm, and the interconnectivity and how they work needs a hand. So, I need to nurture some of the efforts that I see there.

The exhibition, for him, encouraged a way of seeing beyond material fragments per se—in "housing, land, water"—to the "energy" and "interconnectivity" that gives shape to neighborhood life. He was pointing here to the everyday flow and force of urban relations, and to how an organization like his might nurture what is already there. There was a sense, in his reflections, of working not only with the fragments, but doing so by seeking to understand and support the range of goings-ons across people's lives. For example, other NGOs at the meeting reflected on how they could offer specific training that might enhance existing relations, for instance around setting community issue groups, or helping to draw attention to local conditions and activities among policymakers.

A long conversation followed about Namuwongo and its future. About the difficulty of investing in an area where habitation is always at risk because demolition is a constant threat, but the need nonetheless to invest in urban fragments, from drainage and sanitation to roads and energy, in order to deal with the challenges of daily life. There was a consensus that there needed to be more dialogue with the Kampala Capital City Authority (KCCA), that nothing would be achieved unless there was a spirit of collaboration at some level. Some of the NGOs pointed out that while the KCCA as a whole might not be officially supportive, there are individual departments and people there who are prepared to work with residents and this is where change needs to strategically start. Others shifted the conversation onto difference itself. Jennifer talked about widows, the difficulties they find in integrating into other women's groups, and the need to form groups focused on the issues they face (the toll of HIV/AIDS affects a high proportion of widows in Namuwongo, who struggle to find livelihoods and security in an often patriarchal society). Amiri talked about the need to focus on the skills and energy of young people. Josephine wanted to focus on the struggles of children, reflecting on her own experience: "I came to Kampala in 2000. I did not go to school, I have no job and I have four children and I am a widow. I sell fruit, since 2000 . . . to raise money for the kids. I am also taking care of my sister's kids. If I spend a day without selling fruit I have nothing. School fees, renting, medication are all big issues."

Discussion flowed across a range of subjects: collaboration between groups old and new and yet to be formed, visions of the future of Namuwongo, community organization, planning, networking, raising awareness about the range of struggles going on, security and peace, and more. The exhibition and discussion were spaces of reflection on both key strategic challenges—negotiating with the state, for instance—and on the diversity of urban life, struggles, and opportunities (youth, widows, work, security, schools, medicine . . .). Here, the city was not only a space fragmented but a space of potential, where people working together and across different actors might be mobilized to foster improved urban conditions. Set against the stereotypes of Namuwongo that often circulate the city, the exhibition and the discussions around it opened out an alternative set of conversations, a politics of value not only celebrating but underlining the needs and aspirations of the diversity of lives in the neighborhood.

None of these discussions were naïve or romantic. Everyone was keenly aware of the contradictions of the state, and in particular the plans of the KCCA, alongside the wetland and railway authorities, to evict and demolish many parts of Namuwongo, partly in view of stuttering redevelopment plans that extend to Lake Victoria and Port Belle. Yet the municipality, some added, has also been responsible for providing some essential services such as waste collection and road improvements. One urban planner at KCCA we spoke to on another occasion embodied the state's contradictions. The state, she insisted—both the central state and the KCCA—has a responsibility to ensure that all of its citizens have housing, adding that beyond the question of state responsibility it was anyway a "human right." But, she went on in the same breath, "If people choose to locate housing on land without permission, then they have to accept that demolition is a possibility and that the state cannot be expected to provide compensation." These are the kinds of "gray spaces" that so many residents in low-income neighborhoods globally are forced to live with, and it is in these sometimes violent and often uncertain contexts that an alternative politics of value struggles to develop.[175] In Kampala, the local state, while far from holding a progressive commitment to learning from and with the connections, collaborations, and practices of residents in low-income neighborhoods like Namuwongo, has at least not closed the door on collaboration. If an alternative politics of value is to be built, it is not likely to happen overnight through a catalytic event, but through—as NGOs in Kampala like ACTogether have argued—a slow, patient, incremental process of relationship-building with supportive individuals.[176]

There are, of course, limits to what can be communicated through an exhibition. Josephine reflected that some issues had been left underrepresented in the exhibition: there wasn't enough, for example, about homelessness, or about children who dropped out or could never get to school due to fees. Given that, as she saw it, the question of children and education is not a focus of NGO action in the city, it may have helped to have given it greater attention in the exhibition. While she was pleased about the conversations that had gone on around the exhibition, she also felt there had to be more direct focus on issues like income generation, an issue Jennifer also felt was missing, and whether there is anything that can be learned from other places. Jennifer also talked about how the important issue of drainage hadn't featured in the discussions, and—like Josephine—felt NGOs could talk persuasively about their own plans but rarely turned up in the neighborhood to ask residents what their priorities were. For Amiri, the exhibition had revealed something of daily life in Namuwongo, but there was so much that hadn't been captured—about what people did in their spare time, with friends or family, or about the struggles some people had with unemployment and especially those who could not work because of physical reasons.

These and other concerns not voiced are critical reminders of what we do and do not see when we foreground an alternative politics of value in the city. There will, of course, always be excesses, exclusions, trajectories, and relations going on far beyond what is made visible in any one intervention, particularly in dense heterogenous neighborhoods like Namuwongo, but even in those mistranslations and failures there can be politically progressive knowledge, ideas, and atmospheres generated. This goes to the heart of the question of knowledge fragments in the city: not just a question of what researchers and collaborators see, but how they see from their specific position and context. Experiments such as putting together an exhibition can force people out of their comfort zones to form new alliances, learn other ways of seeing the city, and produce new stakes in provoking urban conversations and possibilities—but they can also serve as reminders of the fragments unseen or on the edges, and which might tell other stories about the city and its futures.[177]

Walking Cities

Not to find one's way around a city does not mean much. But to lose one's way in a city, as one loses one's way in a forest, requires some schooling. Street names must speak to the urban wonderer like the snapping of dry twigs, and little streets in the heart of the city must reflect the times of day . . .

—Walter Benjamin, *Berlin Childhood around 1900* (2006), 53–54

Encountering the City

One of the most important ways in which we learn about cities is by moving through them. When I was growing up in Glasgow, some of the most formative experiences I had of the city were on foot. Like all kids, I developed my own routes through our neighborhood in the south of the city. I knew where to be and when, and when not to. I knew enough about the rhythms and main protagonists, and felt part of the place. The city center, however, was daunting and unfathomable. I found its Victorian buildings and grid structure grand and imposing, and its busy streets unnerving. Worried about getting lost, I would look down at my feet and stick close to the grown-ups. The city center seemed to be for other people—people with more money, clearer purpose, greater skill in handling the confusion. Later, and in particular as a student, I grew to love long walks through the city center, and especially the ways in which the same walk might feel very different on a quiet Sunday morning compared to a busy Friday night. The hum of the city had changed, the atmosphere had shifted, and the built urban form registered more directly. I came to value the grid structure that I'd once found intimidating (and realized that it made getting lost actually quite difficult!).

Throughout the period of writing this book, I became increasingly aware that walking was playing an important role in how I understood fragment urbanism. Walking generates a particular, situated knowledge of the city, a knowledge that is not fixed but which is often provisional, changing over time, often uncertain. In this part of the book, I explore how walking reveals fragments through particular routes in three quite distinct cities: Berlin, Hong Kong, and New York. My aim is to explore how walking might provoke, or indeed withhold, a particular reading of fragment urbanism. All three cities are important in their world-regional contexts in different ways, and have distinctions in culture, polity, economy, and environment. But this is not a formal comparative study.

The reports on walking these cities emerge from being there while researching other issues, rather than through a research methodology that set out to compare walking in each. Most of the walks were one-offs or conducted only a few times, and they all took place during the day and on weekdays, so they are very particular snapshots.[1] I examine some of the possibilities and limits of walking, from my own situated encounters and perspective, reflecting on the insights and knowledge walking might generate as well as the unknowability that accompanies it. What follows, then, is very much a discussion of my own sense of an immersive and embodied experiment of walking, and my interpretation of the limited sensorial field that I absorbed at particular times and places in three large, complex cities, and in doing so I reflect on the importance of supplementing walking with other methods in order to dig deeper into fragment urbanism.[2]

Walking operationalizes a fleeting appreciation of how fragments variously act in the city, for instance by getting in the way and changing urban flows, or by being repurposed. It reveals occasional experiments with fragments, from everyday improvisations to forms of urban art. The fact that some areas in the city are more fragmented than others suggests some of the priorities of urban development and political economic (dis)investment. Walking creates a feel, too, for how fragments surface in relation to urban rhythms and atmospheres within and between neighborhoods. It gives a sense of the mundane ways in which urban mobility, flows, and density shift in relation to fragments as the built environment is altered and renovated, the city reproduced, and the expectations of everyday urban living met or not. Walking the city offers an entry point into knowing fragment urbanism that differs from interview, documentary research, or ethnography, and allows an alternative perspective for reflecting on the limits of how we see and know. Out there, walking, the city surfaces in different ways: a space of repetition, habit, routine, and familiar architectural or commercial forms; an emergent, incomplete accumulation of diverse relations that pull together even as they fall apart; a set of entangled trajectories that throw up occasional surprises and moments of uncertainty and indeterminacy; a space that hides far more than it reveals, and more.

Walking these cities entailed three elements. First, each walk was at once immersive and fleeting, a snapshot and often speculative exposure. This kind of walking constantly reproduces the limits of making sense of the sites, forms, and relations in front of you, which left me often wondering not only what those things might be, but about the drivers—political, cultural, economic—that are either entirely absent or hidden from view. Second, each walk was both abstract and embodied. Abstract because, as an effort to "read" urban space through fragments, it entails a recurring imperative to draw out analytical reflections, and embodied because the city repeatedly presses in on the senses and body, shaping (or disrupting) analytic work.

As a white, able-bodied male, walking carries with it a history of sovereign action and legibility. The white, male body is often able to move with an ease that bodies of different intersections of race, ethnicity, gender, and age cannot. This manifests in all kinds of ways, from the level of confidence with which I took this route and not that, or the length of time I spent in this or that place at certain times of day or night, to the ways in which passersby or security guards or shopkeepers might interact with me. Urban walking—even sometimes the very possibility of being able to do it at all—is an expression of socioeconomic privilege, intersectional power-geometries, and the design of the city by the powerful to better enable this and not that body. At the same time, the act of walking pushes against the illusion of autonomous cohesive experience and perception. The intersections of spatial organization, collective atmospheres, and affective and emotional relations enter into and shape experience and perception in ways that cannot always be predicted or controlled.

Third, and finally, each walk was both attuned to place, in that I sought to make sense of the here and now moment by moment, and in dialogue with similarities and differences to other parts of the city as well as to different cities. Comparison was always pressing in, jockeying for position with the immediate surroundings, taking the form, for example, of repeated speculations about whether a particular form or practice in one city may or may not be found in, or understood through, another city. This meant that as I walked through New York, for example, Berlin sometimes sprang to mind, shaping in small ways the sense I was making of encounters with fragments.

Intersecting Writings

The phrase "walking the city" immediately conjures, for many urbanists, Michel De Certeau's chapter of that title in his influential text, *The Practice of Everyday Life*.[3] He considers Manhattan from atop a skyscraper, where the city becomes a "universe that is constantly exploding," of architectural and historical textures that are continually reinvented as if striving to avoid being trapped by the histories of the city.[4] At the same time, he insists, such a view of the city is a fiction, a God-trick, a totalizing vision than is in practice just a picture "whose condition of possibility is an oblivion and misunderstanding of practices."[5] Down below are the walkers who write the stories of the city, forming and reforming "networks" of "intersecting writings" that have no author or spectator, and which are "shaped out of fragments of trajectories and alterations of spaces" and which exceed the grasp of totalizing representation.[6] This sense of walking as a form of "writing" shaped from fragments of trajectories and alterations is useful. Walking here makes a mark in the flows of the city, however fleeting and insignificant, a kind of urban inscription that is also subject to the differences, adjustments, and disruptions generated by urban life.

Walter Benjamin's thought owed a great deal to walking, and to writing about walking—particularly through the image of the *flaneur*. For Benjamin, the flaneur emerged as an urban type as part of the modernity that Paris in the nineteenth century so powerfully revealed.[7] Benjamin didn't explicitly define the flaneur, but the idea has been historically conjoined to the image of the strolling man, detached and observing, drawn to crowds and display. In Benjamin's discussions of the flaneur in *The Arcades Project,* walking was an encounter with the restless densities of people and things in the city. In Paris, the flaneur was a figure moving through crowds, including accumulations of commodities set in dazzling displays and orchestrated spaces in arcades, streets, and stores. Benjamin's thinking was in part motivated by becoming lost in the crowd, searching faces and streets, walking until exhausted, trying to interpret the parade of urban spaces and activities, sometimes with the help of hashish. The flaneur is the quintessential image of the solitary urban male explorer, adopting, as Benjamin wrote, a "laissez-faire" view, moving from street corner to street corner, being drawn to that which aims to attract attention—department stores, exhibition halls, railway stations, cafes, and so on.[8]

Benjamin was well aware that the built form mattered for these experiences. Walking was shaped not just by densities of people and things but by growing road traffic, including the road macadamization that made it possible "to have a conversation on the terrace of a café without shouting in the other person's ear," and the street gas lamps that allowed walking at night.[9] The flaneur was drawn into new urban spaces and atmospheres, such as the gas light dazzling in mirrors of taverns or cafes: "Paris is the city of mirrors. The asphalt of its roadways smooth as glass, and at the entrance to all bistros glass partitions."[10] These were the infrastructures of walking, opening out new kinds of experiences and encounters, allowing densities to form and dissipate in new rhythms.[11] The potential of walking here lies in its capacity to provide an immersive, sensorial experience of the city as a "pluriversal experiment," to use a phrase from Ash Amin and Nigel Thrift writing in a different context.[12]

There is a sense in Benjamin's writing that the flaneur is both a product of the urban modern—a capitalist male consumer indulging a commodified urban space—and a figure disrupted by walking. The emergence of the flaneur depended to some extent on the removal of fragments from the pre-Haussmann urbanism of Paris, with its garbage heaps, ruins, and congested narrow lanes—from an urban "wild" that was cut down to make way for a spatially mastered liberal modernism: "The damp, intimate, claustrophobic, secretive, narrow, curving streets with their cobblestones sinuous like the scales of a snake had given way," writes Rebecca Solnit, "to ceremonial public space, space full of light, air, business and reason."[13] If the flaneur, Solnit argues, is an urban type that has existed far more as an imaginary—this idea of the detached detective-like male reading the landscape—than in practice, many urbanites nonetheless recognize flaneury as a practice that has been intimately, and often politically, connected to life in the city.[14]

For Benjamin, walking could be more than an act of consumption. It might also be contemplative, perhaps productive of new ways of thinking and seeing, even political—"a demonstration against the division of labor," for example.[15] Walking can be a cue to imagining other conditions and possibilities for the city. Through walking, we are sometimes provoked to ask why places and situations are as they are, and whether they might be otherwise. A commitment to walking the street, AbdouMaliq Simone and Edgar Pieterse argue, is a vital means for getting to know cities, to attuning oneself to what's going on and how it might change, of developing ways to "re-describe the affective dynamics of everyday urbanism and the kinds of horizon lines to which they may be pointing," and for developing "an anticipatory politics and research ethic for the city."[16] Walking, for Benjamin, could become a route to a new way of seeing the city: "Not to find one's way around a city does not mean much. But to lose one's way in a city, as one loses one's way in a forest, requires some schooling. Street names must speak to the urban wanderer like the snapping of dry twigs, and little streets in the heart of the city must reflect the times of day, for him, as clearly as a mountain valley."[17]

When Benjamin writes of losing one's way in the city, he is getting not at a sense of being physically lost but at a kind of relinquishing to the existing and potential connections between self and other, here and there, and past and present that make and remake the urban experience. "One does not get lost but loses oneself," writes Solnit; "it is a conscious choice, chosen surrender, a psychic state achievable through geography."[18] As Solnit intimates, this sense of lost is at once spatial and temporal. Being lost is to both remember the past and experience the present, to find that which had been lost or left unexplored.[19] As Benjamin and Solnit suggest, being lost in this sense is also a choice, not only as a method but through what Solnit calls a "psychic state." The South Korean artist Kyung Hwa Shon offers one example of what this kind of walking might generate. Shon's art is a psychogeography of the city, woven through image, text, sculpture, sound, and photography. Her work explores the "interplay between imagination and accidental experiences of the psychological shocks in the context of the city," generated by walking all kinds of cities—Seoul, Chicago, London, Paris.[20] In those walks, she looks to attend to the fleeting relations that differently foreground the urban experience and that influence how we perceive and see the world around us. She brought some of this practice together in her 2015 exhibition, *City of Fragments:*

> The myriad ambiguous signs and letters in the street and fragmented specular images on shop-window displays are, for me, crucial elements in creating peculiar relationships with the world of things, implying the emergence of the imagination. Through these elements, the infinite boundary of the imagination unleashes the city as unaccustomed, disoriented, and reencountered. My work implies the opening of the urban landscape to a distinct poetics of the city in which mythology, sign, symbol, voice, text, and trace occur.

Shon's work is also concerned with the routes through which people live the city, how the city generates again and again—even in the same sites—"peculiar relationships with the world of things"—and how urban routes express inequalities. Her work *Chicago City Maze,* for instance, maps the navigations homeless people make among the city of skyscrapers. Her work connects the fragmentation of the city—its divisions and inequalities—to the sensorial disorientation of fleeting encounters, and the combinations of people, things, and places that provoke the imagination. The phrase she uses below—"ruffles of the imagination"—she takes from Benjamin, and uses in connection not to material or knowledge fragments but to a sensorial fragmentation that is as much about disorientation and the unknown as it is about knowledge and learning, including surprising forms that might spring out in the city to interrupt the familiar:

> To me, wandering the city means without beginning or end, entry into an opaque labyrinthine expedition. . . . A number of unanticipated situations and experiences in the city unfold into extensions of imagination that oscillate between virtuality and actuality. Ruffles of the imagination heighten the sense of unpredictability, instantaneity, excitability, simultaneity, and disorientation. It opens out a space for the possibility of experiencing a rapid transition of both spatiality and temporality, as well as sensory experiences of fragmentation. It results in the moments of awakening out of familiarity and habit in banal daily life, creating peculiar relationships with the world of things and multiple perspectives about the urban circumstances.

As Benjamin, Solnit, and Shon suggest, there are different ways in which we might think about urban walking. Filipa Matos Wunderlich distinguishes between "purposive walking" as getting to a particular destination, "discursive walking" as reflecting on the experience of the journey, and "conceptual walking," which is less about the journey and more about the practice of walking as a means of getting to know the city.[21] There is a history of experimenting with walking as a route to different ways of reading, being in, knowing, and politicizing the city, with much of the canonical thinkers reflecting the dominance of the roaming white male as an urban subject, walking European and North American cities, especially Paris and London: Charles Baudelaire's unreserved poetic immersion, Charles Dickens's search for difference and texture, Benjamin's dream-like wandering, André Breton's surrealist surrender to the "startling juxtapositions" and "poetic possibilities" of walking,[22] the free-flowing seduction of Guy Debord's drifting (*dérive*), Iain Sinclair's planned routes and attentiveness to the "occult and the political . . . the hidden and the neglected," and so on.[23] Increasingly, walking the city is mediated by digital technology, and in particular by smartphones that can adjust routes in real time, provide information about particular places or activities (cafes, restaurants, parks, and so on)—sifting and sorting the city through densities of e-data—forging distinct and often fleeting encounters, trajectories, experiences, and perceptions of urban space.

At the same time, walking is profoundly embodied, and fragments that are seen and experienced in the city—and how they are seen and experienced—is a politics of gender, race, ethnicity, class, sexuality, and the body. As scholars in disability studies have shown, the long romance with walking the city is one that almost always assumes an able-bodied male, in control of his senses and direction even as he chooses to "lose" himself.[24] As Lauren Elkin argues in *Flâneuse,* accounts of walking the city often have little to say about the pervasive anxieties and risks that so routinely accompany the experience women and girls all over the world have of urban walking.[25] For Elkin, the "flaneuse" is more than just a "female version" of a male subjectivity; it is a category yet-to-be written. Elfriede Dreyer and Estelle McDowall, in their discussion of the flaneur as a woman, argue that whatever the flaneuse might be able to be, there is a continual struggle in evading the connection between consumerism and women in urban space, both through male gaze and objectification and through the stubborn positioning of women with acts of consumerism. Their conclusions are not hopeful: "Women's presence on the street is equated with pleasure—whether to be consumed or be the consumer . . . women's disempowerment in the public space of the city streets entails a continuation of the figure of the prostitute."[26]

Indeed, when women feature in Benjamin's walks, it is often as urban types: beggars, prostitutes, or Parisian shoppers, for instance. In Paris, the flaneur abandoned himself—almost always a he—to the urban marketplace, immersing himself in both the glow of urban commodities and the public performance of seeing and being seen, as Benjamin wrote: "The 'city of arcades' is a dream that will charm the fancy of Parisians well into the second half of the century . . . the city assumes a structure that makes it—with its shops and apartments—the ideal backdrop for the flaneur."[27] The flaneur is a voracious male consumer of the city, compressing, as Benjamin put it, "centuries-long movement of streets, boulevards, arcades and squares into the space of half an hour."[28] This flaneur was not just male but most often a wealthy male, a figure looking onto the densities of the city with a detached curiosity: "For the flaneur," wrote Benjamin, "the 'crowd' is a veil hiding the 'masses'."[29] As Solnit argues, the city is cast here as female, elusive, and labyrinthine but always penetrable by a more powerful male.[30]

Solnit argues that the gendering of walking relates not just to power in urban space but to ideologies of the city and mobility.[31] The very terms caught up with walking reflect this—for every "man about town" or "public man," there is a quite different construction of the "woman of the street," of "streetwalkers," or women said to have "gone astray." Being "respectable," particularly for Black women, is caught up with histories of domestication, discrimination, sexualization, visibility, control, and violence. The possibility to roam and be in urban space is fragmented: gendered, raced, and embodied. The experience of urban space, and the ideologies which shape that space, close off some parts of the city, often at particular times. The act of being able to walk and roam freely, reserved more for white, able-bodied, and heterosexual men than any other subject-position, is perhaps the most intense expression of historical cultural power to shape the relations between "public" and "city." Solnit describes her own experience of the threats, fear, and anxiety that women walking in cities, especially at night, are subjected to:

> It was the most devastating discovery of my life that I had no real right to life, liberty and pursuit of happiness out-of-doors, that the world was full of strangers that seemed to hate me for no reason other than my gender, that sex so readily became violence, and that hardly anyone else considered it a public issue rather than a private problem. I was advised to stay indoors at night, to wear baggy clothes, to cover or cut my hair, to try to look like a man, to move to someplace more expensive, to take taxis, to buy a car, to move in groups, to get a man to escort me—all modern versions of Greek walls and Assyrian veils, all asserting it was my responsibility to control my own and men's behavior rather than society's to ensure my freedom.[32]

Solnit narrates a series of shocking instances of everyday harassment and abuse, violence, rape, and murder of people who were simply walking in the city, people marked because they were women or Black or gay. Little surprise, then, that so many people find relative safety in strolling not the streets of the city but, to use Olivia Laing's phrase, "the lit boulevards of the internet."[33] In *The Lonely City,* Laing describes how, having found herself living alone in New York, she sought connection online, only to find an "explosion of hostility in the larger war enacted on the internet against women."[34]

There is a growing body of work examining how different forms of subject-position and embodiment encounter and move through urban space, including in critical disability studies and mobility studies, and here there are quite distinct entry-points to the fragment. In her study of mobility through a wheelchair in New York and Montreal, Laurence Parent argues that while walking has been "naturalized" as a valid and valued means of knowing urban space, the lack of work on wheeling reflects a broader neglect and devaluation of how different bodies and subjects move in and know the city (see, for one example, Judith Butler's walk with disability researcher artist Sunaura Taylor in San Francisco in the 2008 film *Examined Life,* which Parent discusses).[35]

Parent describes her journeys through Montreal and New York with people with disabilities, and presents a powerful analysis of how she, a wheelchair user, and her research participants negotiated the city as they moved through it together. She reflects on the different ways in which she and a blind participant crossed a busy road, or how another blind man she worked with negotiated narrow and uneven sidewalks, as Parent named the obstacles and attempted to harmonize movements and progression. In this collaborative, multiple encounter with urban space, all kinds of material fragments, objects, obstacles, and possible navigations emerge and come to matter. Reflecting on the work, she writes: "I have navigated multiple intersections, including street intersections, narrative intersections, identity intersections, and body and technology intersections."[36] Parent insists that these methods destabilize the apparent neutrality and naturalization of walking the city. They also, she goes on, remind us of the unevenness and diversity of mobility and the forms of power that shape it.

The possibility of roaming, and indeed of writing, the city is fundamentally built upon the historical and ongoing constitution of the city and urban space as power, control, exclusion, violence, and threat. Walking is always already and inescapably political, both scripted and a form of scripting, both historically shaped and caught up in the disruptive and unpredictable nature of urban life. For all that the flaneur was masculinized in embodiment and gaze, and for all that he consumes urban space as if it was there just for his pleasure, Benjamin's flaneur was certainly not all-knowing. Benjamin stays in his writing with the complexities and uncertainties, with the city as "labyrinth."[37] Walking here is also often a kind of puzzling over the city, a constant questioning around the limits of knowing the complex and changing relations around processes like fragment urbanism.[38]

Routes and Their Limits

Berlin is one of the most powerful symbols of the fragmented city in Europe, given its history of division, violence, and destruction. A city bombed into rubble, divided and walled, and rebuilt on a vast scale—a city "always in the middle of becoming something else," as Franz Hessel put it in 1929 before the violent convulsions of the rest of the twentieth century in *Walking in Berlin,* a book Walter Benjamin described as "a walking remembrance."[39] Walk around contemporary Berlin and these histories of fragmentation are everywhere, from the hill at Teufelsberg built mainly by women using the city's wartime rubble, or the remnants of the Berlin Wall, to the still very large—but nonetheless rapidly disappearing—areas of empty or in-construction land across the city.

In the early years following World War II, urban life for Berliners proceeded among shock and demolition. The photographer Walter Shulze walked the city with his camera and produced a remarkable body of work on Berlin in those difficult years, documenting everyday life amidst the debris, political division, and poverty.[40] His images are striking depictions of life in ruin, and assemble a careful story of fragments. They include women returning to survey homes of rubble, or collecting firewood, or removing heaps of debris from roads. Others are of men and women paving broken-up pavements and roads. Several include children playing surrounded by rubble. In many of the images, buildings and walls are barely standing. The devastation led to the occasional oddity: a broken statue discarded in a back garden, washing dry-ing above it; a damaged shop mannequin sat incongruously on a burned-out roof.

In his essay at the end of the book, the writer Rolf Schneider discusses Shulze's attention to the state of housing and infrastructure, from the stovepipes that stare out at boarded windows or the impact of massive energy shortages, to the just-about-working-packed-to-bursting buses and trains—provisions that were at best make-do, falling far short of adequate, particularly during the cold Berlin winters. The violence that the urban fabric endured echoed the violence Berliners themselves continued to suffer, from the rape of women by the Red Army to the hunger of young children and the shattered selves emerging from tremendous loss. The images capture a city that is entirely exhausted, barely continuing, and on minimal life support, yet still having to labor on with all but nothing. Schneider describes an urban world that is "broken," "shattered," and "divided," carved up both materially and—by the British, French, American, and Russian Allies—geopolitically, but which had to find the energy to keep going, reconstructing and building, surviving and protesting.[41]

The legacies of wartime destruction were not felt equally within the city, nor were they separate from the longer histories of urban change and inequality in Berlin. The same is true of other cities fragmented through war. For Peter Jukes, the bombing of poor communities in the war needs to be read alongside the destruction to places that cities and states have themselves unleashed on those same communities. Jukes notes that the East End of London was particularly badly bombed, but that this bombing had followed decades of demolition and displacement of the urban poor. Dropping bombs on housing is clearly of a different moral order than misconceived or outright prejudiced demolition or "redevelopment" plans, but Jukes's insistence on connecting these events is not wrong. He writes, in 1991, "If today parts of it [London's East End] still look like bomb-sites—its streets shattered, its communities smashed—it is as likely to be the result of the impact of planning decisions as of V2s. Given the catastrophic violence of London's development, is it any wonder whole populations appear shell-shocked, and turn to some version of their past to escape an unrecognizable present."[42]

The histories of different rounds of fragmentation, then, remain in the cities around us, and Berlin carries those histories in its built and social geographies. Walking Berlin is an encounter with both those histories and an increasingly multicultural and unequal present. Walking the streets from the city center to Moabit, for example, reveals a trajectory

188 | Walking Cities

of changing fragments. From Postdamer Platz north to Moabit, through Tiergarten and the government district, and along Alt-Moabit Strasse and into Siemensstrasse, there are sharp changes in urban space driven by different forms of authority, regulation, and spatial use: the corporate, towering glass of Potsdamer Platz and its public-private spaces; the relatively low-density openness and porosity of the large public garden, Tiergarten; the more policed, ordered, and gated government buildings of the government district; and the lower-income, denser, and more multicultural neighborhoods along Alt-Moabit. Around Potsdamer Platz are fragments of the Berlin Wall left standing for endless parades of tourists and photographs, next to a piece of a damaged hotel set behind glass next to the Sony Center. Move north, away from Postdamer Platz and the government district, and here there are faded and often no longer readable graffiti, the lampposts adorned with worn posters and stickers jockeying for space over other posters in a palimpsest of urban culture, amidst broken shards of stone on the pavement that become more frequent as the surface turns increasingly uneven and less well maintained outside the main tourist thoroughfares. Then, closer to Moabit, all manner of other things, from fragments of tiles used to decorate a children's playground to discarded bits of furniture. The walk journeys from tourists and shoppers around Potsdamer Platz to lower-income and multicultural neighborhoods where the fragments become the strewn discards of everyday living (Figure 11).

Shift location to a different part of Berlin—the main routes through Kreuzberg and Neukölln, for example—Prinzessenstrasse, Oranienstrasse, Adalberstrasse, and Hermanstrasse—and the city becomes denser and more socially and materially heterogeneous. These neighborhoods contain some of the most multicultural areas of the city, and some of its poorest residents. They are also becoming increasingly unequal as gentrification moves into new pockets, creating urban pitched battles that challenge emerging geographies of fragmentation.[43] Amidst the tempting scent of sweets, bakeries, and falafel are fragments of all sorts: old shops closed and fallen into disrepair, discarded broken chairs, street signs so covered in spray paint and stickers they are no longer legible, doorways that have become canvases for layers and layers of public art, odd bits of furniture in various states, streets and pavements broken up in sections and occasionally being repaired, old bricks and stones now servicing as stands for plants, salvaged sheets of metal used to add extra privacy to gates and fences, construction debris waiting to be collected, and so on. Occasionally, too, works of public art:

FIGURE 11. Berlin fragments (Upper photo by author; lower photo, Creative Commons: https://commons.wikimedia.org/wiki/File:Berlin_wall_at_Potsdamer_Platz_March_2009.jpg)

FIGURE 12. Spoke and wheel sculpture (Photo by author)

Figure 12, for instance, shows a sculpture of metal poles and bicycle wheels, with echoes of Marcel Duchamp's 1913 *Bicycle Wheel*—"the first found-object sculpture," as Esther Leslie put it—shaped into what looks like sprawling antenna, on the edge of the Prinzesseninnengarten community gardens in Kreuzberg.[44]

A walk like this can only reveal a surface geography, but the fact that poorer neighborhoods are more visibly fragmented reflects, of course, some of the priorities of urban development and political economic (dis)investment. The occasional experiments, ranging from small improvisations to more elaborate urban art, remind us that fragments are not exhausted by previous use, but can be fabricated into all kinds of other ends. There is much we don't see, and which demand other forms of investigation beyond the limit points set by walking. We don't see, for example, how disinvestment impacts lower-income homes, or overcrowded and poorly maintained buildings housing the city's refugees, in which people struggle with insufficient clothing, unreliable infrastructures, or fractured healthcare provisions.

Given the histories of Cold War division and war damage, Berlin has been a city of fragmentation, abandoned areas, and "voids."[45] Hong Kong is an entirely different geography. Not only is Hong Kong one of the densest cities in the world, it is spectacularly volumetric, from the horizontal densities of the informal urban markets around Sham Shui Po where over a thousand people per hectare are often sifted into intricate streets, to the dizzying verticalities of apartment and office blocks regularly extending over thirty stories, and the corridors that connect them in a three-dimensional exposition of volumetric urbanism. The city has limited land and strict restrictions to prevent building on green spaces, and high vertical densities regularly exceeding 110,000 people per square kilometer (almost double the 59,000 sometimes found in Manhattan). As an urban form, it could scarcely be more different from Berlin.

Hong Kong is, as Barrie Shelton and co-authors describe it in their discussion of the city's "intenCities," "the quintessential high-density small-footprint city," alongside cities like Mumbai and Dhaka, two other great staging posts of urban modernity in Asia.[46] They use the term "intensity," via physics, to refer to a "quality of force" composing the interplay, organized complexity, movement, and "liveliness" of a place.[47] Intensity here is a name not just for high density but for how high densities of people and things interact and become connected, and in Hong Kong that is a profoundly three-dimensional bundle of relations. Hong Kong was the first city in the world to develop a 3-D urban guidebook, *Cities without Ground,* based on raised walkways connecting premium accommodation, upmarket shopping malls, and transport systems, and often appropriated for street vending, art exhibitions, and public gatherings. Many Hong Kongers live "in suspension," reformulating the very notion of urban ground.[48] Many residents can leave their home and take an elevator straight onto a metro platform. It's possible to move through large parts of the city without setting foot on a street. Meanwhile, the walkways can become theatres for the city's multiculture. In the walkways and surrounding areas in the Central area, rhythms shift over the course of a week, from people going to and from work, to those walking through shopping malls or to restaurants in the evenings. On Sundays, domestic workers from across Southeast Asia, especially the Philippines and Indonesia, meet in these spaces to socialize or connect with cultural practices from home.[49]

Walking the streets of Hong Kong is an immersion in a diverse relay of textures and intensities. At the same time, it is an experience that hides more than it reveals. Hidden from view, for example, are the vertical poverties in the city's housing blocks or "rooftop slums." If De Certeau found from atop the skyscraper that the lives on the ground were hidden, it's also the case that from the ground in Hong Kong the lives atop the buildings are out of sight. In a city of 7 million people, 1 million live under the poverty line, and Sham Shui Po is among the poorest and densest of the eighteen districts in the city. Around half of the urban poor here are immigrants from mainland China or elsewhere in Asia, many working precarious temporary jobs. An estimated 200,000 people live in cramped, often overcrowded, partitioned homes.[50] Approximately three thousand households live in makeshift housing on rooftops sometimes pejoratively referred to as "penthouse slums." Waiting to be allocated public housing—the average is 4.7 years, although if you are young and single the quota system could mean waiting for twenty years—people live crammed into homes as small as four square meters that are underserviced and vulnerable to rain, heat, cold, and typhoons.[51] As Chick Kui Wai, a community organizer with the Society for Community Organisation (SoCo), put it, people are hemmed in, trapped, unable to stay clean, and it is not uncommon to find cases where sleeping areas are built onto ceilings and stairwells.

Walking south from Sham Shui Po, through the markets of Mong Kok in Kowloon, is an encounter with some of the highest horizontal densities in the world, an urbanism of multiple trajectories and fragments.[52] The markets around Sham Shui Po station sell cheap, everyday household goods, from batteries to kitchen utensils, and are driven much more by residential need than many of those further to the south into Mong Kok, where markets become increasingly diverse and tourist driven. Rhythms shift radically over the course of a day. In Figure 13, for example, Mong Kok's Fa Yuen Street and Temple Street are relatively quiet in the morning as stores are assembled.

FIGURE 13. Assembling markets, Mong Kok (Photos by author)

Walking further south toward the city center, other kinds of construction and maintenance materials come into play, creating modified geographies that reroute workers and tourists as roads and pavements are blocked, and public staircases sometimes become difficult to enter or leave (Figure 14).

In Mong Kok, fragments are put to all kinds of work: here to augment a restaurant exterior, there to turn lanes into covered passages and protect open infrastructure. Discarded materials are placed with different intentions, some in the hope they will be collected for the garbage dump, some with the intention of being used again, others are found objects that provide at least some marginal income to those in the informal waste economy (Figure 15).[53] Walking reveals some of the ways in which fragments feature in the ebbs and flows of urban life and labor over time and space in the city, and the often mundane ways in which urban mobility shifts as the built form is reassembled in daily rhythms, repaired, tinkered with, and maintained. These ordinary shifts may seem humdrum and are easy to miss or trivialize, but they are part of the reproductive life of the city.[54] They also call into question a host of everyday expectations of urban living, including the role of different actors—the municipality, traders, commuters, residents, tourists, and more—in helping to ensure mobility and reliability.

While walking points to something of the city's urban inequalities and changing rhythms, that insight is, of course, highly prescribed and demands additional data, whether as documentary evidence or interview research or another form, to better understand the drivers of these processes, the policies and histories shaping them, and the ways in which they are experienced and perceived.[55] It is worth, though, pausing and reflecting on the potential of walking to capture snapshots of the urban condition and how the city is changing. One example here is the work of the photographer Michael Wolf, who documented a particular version of Hong Kong's fragment urbanism. Wolf, who died in the spring of 2019 at age 64, produced a stunning archive of urban life and change in Hong Kong. He sought to track the quick transformation of the city, and while his work included powerful insights into life in a range of cities—his *Tokyo Compression* photographs of commuters squeezed into the world's busiest metro system, for example—his primary concern was with producing a visual biography of Hong Kong, notably in his *Architecture of Density* collection that stretched across 2003 to 2014.[56]

Wolf committed to Hong Kong, walking and photographing again and again and again. He documented the changing and multiple organ-

FIGURE 14. Altered flows (Photos by author)

ization of busy market streets and large low-income apartment blocks, which often depended on intricate ways of organizing fragments. Things had to be to hand, available for the reproduction of everyday living or for commercial purposes like selling food or crafts, or repurposed, for instance, to create space for cables or pipes or as utensils for different tasks at work in the home. Journalist Sean O'Hagan writes:

> For every epic project like Architecture of Density, there were intimately observed series created during his various trawls through Hong Kong's back alleys. There, he caught telling glimpses of the city's makeshift character: customised chairs, surreal arrangements of kitchen mops and wire coat hangers, twisting gas and water pipes, all the mundane everyday objects that speak of the relentless resourcefulness of its residents, and of Wolf's eye for accidental sculptural beauty amid the seemingly mundane.[57]

Wolf's *Informal Solutions* examined the relation between spatial restriction—workers and residents forced into often tiny interstices in the city—and a particular kind of urban learning, a tacit and felt knowledge from which the city's nooks and crannies and bits of stuff can become resources, affordances in an urbanism that is both writ small and widespread.[58] For Marc Feustel, *Informal Solutions* is a "dizzying array of fragments from the city streets," a diverse, functional, and vernacular urban ecology.[59] Wolf described the collection as "an encyclopedia of improvisations in back alleys": "The rule is you never throw

FIGURE 15. Mundane fragments, left and above (Photos by author)

anything away. If you're opening a box which is wrapped in string, you put it behind a pipe. If you see some rubber bands, you have a place where you keep rubber bands. If there's some plastic, you jam the plastic behind the pipe."[60]

This amounts, argued Wolf, to a privatization of public space, but of a quite different order to the capital-driven or corporatization of public space we see in so many cities, including Hong Kong: "In Hong Kong, there is little space, so people take over public areas as if they were their own private area. I love the inventiveness of that. Look behind any given building and you'll find a strange constellation of mops, hangers, chairs, brushes and old furniture stored in a nifty way. Nothing is ever discarded, which is wonderful. Everything is visible, whereas much of Paris is a façade."[61] In Wolf's photography of Hong Kong's streets, there is an echo of Walter Benjamin and Asja Lacis's 1925 essay on walking Naples.[62] Benjamin and Lacis's attention to *porosity* provides them with a powerful set of snapshots of everyday life in the city.

Porosity here is a name for how the city is and operates. Everything in their short essay has a porosity—from the city's streets and homes, to the architecture and the caves leading to the sea, or the courtyards, arcades, stairways, houses, taverns, and more, which seem to continually spill their activities or contents into one another. Buildings are not just homes or workplaces but "a popular stage" of balconies, courtyards, gateways, and roofs. The living room, they write, "reappears on the street, with chairs, hearth and altar," just as "the street migrates into the living room," especially for the poorest who are forced into tiny houses.[63] The central city is a place where "nothing is concluded."[64] "The stamp of the definitive," they continue, "is avoided."[65] All kinds of practices take their turn to claim space, even the same space simultaneously, including eating, sleeping, working, drinking, celebrating, and worshiping. The effect is a kind of routinized "interpenetration of day and night, noise and peace, outer light and inner darkness, street and home."[66] Porosity is the permeability of things, not a byproduct of spatial production, but actively constitutive in the making of urban space. It is part of the "building and action" of the city, vital in the scope of the city to "become a theater of new, unforeseen constellations."[67]

There is, to be sure, a romance in Benjamin and Lacis's essay, just as there is in Wolf's work on improvisational living. Yet Wolf was not naïve about the poverty and struggle of life in contemporary Hong Kong anymore than Benjamin and Lacis were about Naples in the 1920s. Walking and photographing the city's backstreets and soaring housing, Wolf was acutely aware of how hard it was for many millions of residents in the city to make ends meet, particularly with the exorbitant housing costs. If his images depict improvisations with fragments in dense and porous spaces, they also provoke us to think about spatial fragmentation more generally. This is a city in which the urban poor, whether they were born in the city or migrants from across Asia, are increasingly forced into working with slivers of space and recycling all manner of fragments of things. Wolf reflects on this relationship in his work between an obsessiveness with improvisation and density on the one hand, and the larger spatial fragmentation of Hong Kong—and cities in Asia more generally—here:

> In Asia, everything is in constant flux, everywhere there's something being built or a neighbourhood being torn down and it's very unpredictable because there are different rules here. In the 20 years I've been in Hong Kong it has changed dramatically. A large part of my work is also just documenting these older neighbourhoods, the older architecture, because within ten years it's all gone. So there's an aspect in my work that's not only 'wow,' but it's also 'what are you doing to your cities, and what's the quality of life here, and then do we really want this?'[68]

Wolf walked the city with the aim of provoking reflections on urban change that connected the micro and the macro, the specific arrangement of things in place and the spatial transformation of the city. Like other great port cities of modernity, from New York to Mumbai, the public debate on Hong Kong often revolves around the provisioning of affordable housing, with some remarkably small and questionable developments (including "nano apartments" built from converted drainpipes).[69] It is not just that there is often intense pressure on housing supply in large and highly dense cities like Hong Kong, but that urban real estate markets play powerful roles in inflating prices and rents. We see this, for instance, in the growth of "co-living" and "co-working" spaces globally, from Manila to New York, in which regulations on minimum space for homes are "relaxed" in order to build tiny, shared, cheaper spaces.

Such housing may be more affordable, but, as Leilani Farha, the UN's special rapporteur on the right to housing, argues, it is often woefully inadequate.[70] The solution, as Farha points out, is not to build smaller and smaller homes, but to address the financialization of housing that has so often far outstripped earnings and further fragmented the city spatially, socially, and materially into rich and poor areas, entrenching a particular calculation of urban value.[71] Housing in Hong Kong is shaped by a confluence of the city's intensifying real estate market, the state's underprovision of affordable homes, and cultures of prejudice toward immigrants from other parts of Asia—many of whom end up in poorer neighborhoods like Sham Shui Po. To be sure, critical engagement with these trajectories demands more than walking, more than Wolf's stunning photographic archive of urban change, yet walking provides—like the camera—a lens onto some of the textures of fragment urbanism as it shifts across space and time in the city.

New York shares a lot in common with Hong Kong. Manhattan in particular possesses an intensity of vertical and horizontal densities. Both cities are historic experiments in dense modern urban living. Like Hong Kong, densities have historically "shuffled" in New York, driven by economic processes, political prioritization and disinvestment, and cultural debates about the kinds of densities that are most desirable or fitting. For example, since the nineteenth century, Manhattan has witnessed the destruction of "slums"—parts of the Lower East Side, for example, had some of the highest and most multicultural low-income densities in the country in the nineteenth century—the expansion of the subway, and, in more recent decades, the growing power of real estate speculative economies.[72]

Today, the city has one of the urban world's most intensive and expensive real estate markets, and there is a vital debate around affordable housing.[73] Despite the long history of socially reformist housing movements and activism in New York, patterns of gentrification and exclusion continue apace, and progressive politics at the state level exist largely in name only.[74] At the same time, some of the existing housing is decaying, suffering from generations of inadequate investment and maintenance, partly as a result of the collapse of federal funding. Shannon Mattern, in a compelling piece on urban maintenance as a potential paradigm for the contemporary city, notes how the New York City Housing Authority's own Public Needs Assessment describes buildings usually over sixty years old: increasingly subject to breakdown in the heating and water systems, with "leaky roofs, windows, and pipes" that have caused mold and damage to walls and ceilings.[75] Mattern cites Scott Gabriel Knowles's powerful description of the neglect of maintenance as a "slow motion disaster."[76]

Chinatown, in the Lower East Side, remains one of the city's historic landmarks, and is a high-density low-rise area where often small commercial outlets pay high rents to cater to a large footfall of tourists. Walking through some of the key routes and lanes in Chinatown, fragments emerge in all kinds of ways. Old shops and lanes that are no longer used store residential and commercial bits and pieces while temporary roadworks shape new flows and rhythms. Looming tower blocks built and proposed for the surrounding area, next to Manhattan Bridge, point not just to the changing character of this part of the city but to the threat to residents and small traders of rising rents and taxes. A few blocks north, at the heart of the Lower East Side, Seward Park Library and Park speaks of a different time of public municipalism, sitting, as Eric Klinenberg writes, at "a point of convergence for Chinatown, a mass of public housing projects, and a rapidly developing urban glamour zone for young professionals."[77] At the same time, security barriers on roads leading toward the financial district and One World Trade Center, erected following the September 11 attack, have reshaped flows in and out of Chinatown. Contrast this with walking the Upper East Side. Home to the generally very wealthy and large hotels that jut up against Central Park, this is an area of upmarket apartments in carefully conditioned buildings along well-maintained, often quiet tree-lined streets. Street life here is often thin and dominated by cars and building entrances, with guards at the door. Other than the odd piece of scaffolding for building repair or blocked sidewalks for roadworks, wealth buys fragment-free urbanism. Across the water in Brooklyn, walking through Bushwick is an encounter with a quite different urbanism.

Bushwick is a multicultural and traditionally working-class area that is becoming, in pockets, increasingly expensive, owing in part to its proximity to Williamsburg. The area has inherited, from previous rounds of capitalist urbanization, a set of disused and abandoned fragments, including poorly maintained warehouses and factories propped up by walls and parking lots that are crumbling and deteriorating. Some of these spaces have now become an urban canvas. Street art is extensive in parts of Bushwick, and the neighborhood has a reputation for attracting artists, some of it through the graffiti collection under the banner of the Bushwick Collective. Set up in 2012, the Collective paints and repaints wall murals throughout the year. If the Upper East Side is a smooth, disciplined, and highly regulated space, the streets around Morgan Avenue in Bushwick are in places broken up, its gates and fences more makeshift, some of its buildings empty and in disrepair, others now knocked down for more upmarket apartments or offices, and some acting as canvases for art that celebrates different ways of seeing and being in the city (Figure 16).

Without walking, it is difficult to appreciate the extent or repurposing of fragments in this part of Bushwick, where industrial materials of metal, wood, and brick have been moved, tweaked, broken, and remade in new relations to one another, and turned into multiple sites of creativity and social expression. The new activities that are emerging, of artists and art, cafes, office workers, and apartments, create a sense of an open place of multiple trajectories. At the same time, the uncertainty over this area's future underscores the limit of walking as an entry point to understanding fragment urbanism. In particular, walking does not allow an adequate appreciation of the threats to the current conditions in this part of Bushwick.

FIGURE 16. Fragments and the urban canvas, Bushwick, New York, left and above (Photos by author)

One route to better understanding that threat is through, for example, anti-gentrification groups in Brooklyn. These are groups that campaign against what they see as a growing wave of rent and property-based exclusion, which the city administration is often seen as actively facilitating. Embedded communities living on relatively modest incomes are increasingly being displaced by wealthier groups. The Brooklyn Anti-Gentrification Network (BAN) points to a confluence of "real estate corporations, big business elite, and the New York City political machine," as well as the police, as destroying "the cultural, social, and economic diversity of our communities all in the name of making a profit."[78] Various other groups are active in Bushwick, such as the Bushwick Action Research Network (BARN), which works with young people to resist gentrification to produce positive stories of the area and its inhabitants, including through what they call "sidewalk science."[79] Walking can surely take a role in any "sidewalk science," particularly when it is used to compare conditions in different parts of the city or between cities.

The possibilities for affordability, difference, and the kind of urban art we see in Bushwick are increasingly eroding across the urban world. In the historically more affordable Berlin, for example, property prices rose by 20 percent in 2017, the fastest rise that year of any city in the world.[80] As Kevin Baker writes of New York, the transformations in the city over the past decade have led to the active "sensory deprivation of our neighborhoods, where the complex and varied city has also been wiped out," all to produce new kinds of vertical elite density: "Our leaders seem hopelessly invested in importing a race of supermen for the supercity, living high above the clouds. Jetting about the world so swiftly and silently, they are barely visible. A city of glass houses where no one's ever home. A city of tourists. An empty city."[81] Similarly, Richard Williams describes how developers operating in Manhattan sometimes do not expect their buildings to be fully occupied, or even mostly occupied.[82] From Manhattan to London and Dubai, economic value is tied to emptiness, capital accumulation to absence, a curiously anti-density speculative urbanism amidst, in Manhattan's case, some of the highest densities in the world.

To be sure, New York remains a vibrant and often experimental city, but Baker is right that the space for heterogeneity in the economic, cultural, and political constitution of the city is increasingly restrictive. The real estate trajectories make it more and more difficult to build genuinely inclusive urbanisms in the city, and in large swathes of the city it is impossible, while more and more residents are vulnerable to processes of fragmentation. Understanding these trajectories demands methods that exceed walking, but walking provides a sense of the histories, labors, and diversities of fragment urbanisms, and how they differ within and between neighborhoods. Walking enables a degree of understanding of the stakes of the city, of what could be lost among the sometimes fragile urbanisms that texture different areas, and of what might be needed to support the daily rhythms and expectations of urban living.

Remnants

Many of the fragments encountered in walking not just Berlin, Hong Kong, and New York, but any city, are mundane and their origin and purpose is not always clear. The litany of stuff across cities include the remnants of other times, priorities, and projects. It constitutes a fragmented catalogue of the urban fabric that does not always perform to a script, or that conforms to a script which may be long abandoned, perhaps forgotten altogether. In the 1980s, the Japanese artist Genpei Akasegawa collected examples of ordinary objects and features of city streets that appeared to have no purpose. Not knowing what to call these random and seemingly useless things, he used—rather uncharitably, it has to be said—the name "Thomasson" after the baseball player Gary Thomasson, who played with Tokyo-based Yomiuri Giants and who had become, in Akasegawa's view, a less than useful player. Akasegawa described these lingering bits and pieces of the built environment as unintentional conceptual art, a kind of "hyperart."[83]

The term "Thomasson" or "Tomason" is sometimes used—particularly since Akasegawa's 1985 *Hyperart* was translated into English—to describe these urban oddities, and has taken shape as various categories ranging from useless staircases or doorways to defunct boundaries without obvious purpose. Tomasons may have been designed for temporary use, then left in place for a long while, even decades. Despite seemingly lacking purpose, those forms, as Akasegawa showed, are often maintained, even if in only minimal ways. They may appear to have no function, yet it's often more hassle to remove them, or at least no one quite cares enough to go to the trouble of doing so. Rather than name these urban leftovers using Akasegawa's rather unkind description of the former baseball player, I will use the term "remnant" to describe them instead.

Akasegawa's art was premised on an intriguing process of walking urban Japan in which he sought to read the landscape through all manner of remnants. It's a form of walking that demands, as I've been intimating in relation to Berlin, Hong Kong, and New York, a particular kind of paying attention. Walking itself does not guarantee that remnants will leap out at the walker. Finding them requires a labor of attention during which other parts of the city fall into the background. This "deliberate hunt," as Ivan Vladislavic reflects, itself "begins to foul the workings of chance," even as the "eye becomes attuned to everything that is extraneous, inconspicuous and minor . . . abandoned or derelict."[84] Vladislavic, in his often walking-based reflections on Johannesburg, writes about a pole he notices one day on a route he had regularly taken. "I have walked along this pavement a thousand times, there isn't a detail I could have missed, never mind something so big. And such a peculiar, pointless thing too . . . A metal pole, slightly taller than me, the bottom third painted black, the rest silver."[85] Vladislavic identifies the pole as a Tomason, "a thing detached from its original purpose": "It may be a remnant of a larger fixture that has been taken away, or it may be a thing complete in itself, whose purpose has been forgotten."[86] Later, Vladislavic's walks in the city take on a new education of attention, to use James Gibson's phrase: "I seem to notice it [Tomasons] everywhere. The tilt of my head has been altered and significance flares up in odd places. Every day I trawl along my habitual routes ready to be startled by something else I have missed until now . . . Every time I go walking, I stumble right out of the present."[87]

These urban remnants exist on a spectrum from the entirely forgotten but still around, to the well-remembered but largely ignored and, as Vladislavic writes, they thrive in cities because cities are "spaces that are constantly being remade and redesigned for other purposes."[88] They can be both everyday overlooked objects woven into the textures of urban routines, and things are that stumbled upon and which might elicit a confused passing glance. The city nearest to where I live, Newcastle in northeast England, has its own geography of remnants that you might occasionally come across while walking its small, compact urban center. One example is the half-built network of elevated walkways in the city, largely developed in the 1960s under the notorious city

FIGURE 17. Unfinished walkway, Newcastle (Photo by author)

council leadership of modernist T. Dan Smith, who eventually ended up in prison for corruption (Figure 17). This was a particular kind of urban ideal, separating out motorway traffic below from pedestrians above, building a modern city inspired by modernist postwar planning as well as by cities abroad—Smith, for example, famously spoke of the city becoming "the Brasilia of the North."

Some of the walkways are still accessible, but generally they are not used, partly because they can be disorientating (read, for example, the *Guardian*'s walking tour of central Newcastle with the urbanist Stephen

Graham).[89] In some places, they linger as sections that come to abrupt and incongruous stops in mid-air. The city has been left with a set of walkway fragments that are both material inheritances that hang around, minimally maintained, and ideational remnants of a culture of planning and urban thought that has now largely departed the city. Newcastle is not the only British city to have them. Walking in London also reveals these kinds of remnants. Chris Bevan Lee's 2013 film, *The Pedway: Elevating London,* is a journey into the City of London's abandoned network of elevated walkways.[90] The pedway is both strikingly visible—raised concrete above busy streets in the city's financial center— yet curiously unseen and relatively unknown. The system was a utopian planning ideal developed in the 1950s that promoted walking and movement beyond the noise and bustle of traffic, an integrated network, a kind of "whole" in itself that promised an ease of movement. It was a grand plan that, as the film notes, was both thought and built as a whole but which was also never completed, mainly because the city around it changed and the growth of the pedway failed to keep up.

As the film shows, the idea's utopianism was formed in the wake of the destruction of World War II, which left a third of the financial district in rubble. As the debris gave way to large roads, and the density of traffic exploded, the pedway was designed as a safe space above the fumes and noise. This was to be more than just an infrastructure. It was presented as an urban ideal and aesthetic, inspired by central London's postwar dilemmas, Venice's highly decorative bridges, and the determination to separate traffic and pedestrians in the Bauhaus movement—a kind of inversion of Le Corbusier's vision of elevated roads for fast-moving cars—as well as legacy visions of the urban future from popular film such as Fritz Lang's 1927 *Metropolis.* In practice, the walkways were confusing to navigate, and people anyway had their own routes, their own "intersecting writings" as De Certeau described them, through the city that often privileged the street over climbing stairs to walkways. They were expensive and became difficult to maintain and connect as the geography of buildings changed around the network, leaving what one commentator in the film describes as "a load of fragments," in which here and there you can glimpse in passing, as another comments, a "dead bit of pedway that was never connected up." As planning moved toward pedestrianization, public transport, and the integration of pedestrians with traffic flows, the pedway finally receded into the background of both the city and the urban imagination. It is now largely empty and forgotten.

Outside of particular spots, such as the popular route along London's South Bank, elevated pathways are no longer a part of London's urban agenda. The pedway is a remnant both in material form and as a way of knowing the city, but in other cities, forms of the pedway are alive and kicking, from New York's controversial and tourist-heavy High Line, caught up in debates around gentrification and property speculation, to enclosed elevations in cities with temperature extremes, such as Hong Kong, Singapore, and Montreal, through to highly contested skywalks in cities like Mumbai so often critiqued for damaging the mixed street life of the city.[91] Remnants are inevitable features of the geographies of fragments in the urban world. They are at once familiar and everyday, and curiously unseen and unknown. They are clues to histories of the city, and to urban knowledges and materials that are made, politicized, lived, and unmade. They are a species of material and knowledge fragment, traces half-forgotten, lures to pasts and activities that may no longer be retrievable but which might nonetheless generate insight into the city as a never-complete project. They are stark reminders of the dynamic play of knowing and unknowing, presence and absence, fragment and whole, that fragment urbanism carries with it. And they remind us that conjecture and uncertainty are so often close accompaniments to walking the city.

Space and Time

Walking provides a tangible sense of the histories, labors, and diversities of urban life, and how they change over time and space. It enables a limited, situated appreciation of how fragments—those that can be seen at least—variously act in the city, from those getting in the way and changing urban flows to others caught up in the occasional experiment or artistic expression. It provides some insight into the priorities of the state in terms of where it invests and what it maintains, its contemporary priorities and forgotten remnants, and to the legacies of historical rounds of fragmentation. It enables a degree of understanding of the stakes of the city, of what could be lost among the sometimes fragile arrangements that texture different parts of the city, and of what might be needed to support the daily rhythms and expectations of urban living. This is partly why—in my experience at least—residents are often so keen to show people around their neighborhoods.

Walking is also dialogic, in that it is about what's going on at a given moment and place, but seen in part through elsewheres—and else-whens—within and beyond the city. This comparative experience is as much about how a place feels, looks, sounds, and smells as it is about differences in, say, economic configurations, policy choices, or cultural practice. These moments prompt reflections around, for instance, the extent to which neighborhoods in some parts of Manhattan are able to generate the mixed urban street life we often see in neighborhoods in Hong Kong, or how fragmented provisions to low-income spaces in

Berlin, with its historically strong social democratic civic realm, compare with New York, or whether street densities connected to urban food in Hong Kong might inform urban policy or practice in Berlin, or whether forms of urban appropriation of fragments for art in New York might be politically feasible in Hong Kong, and so on. The comparative emerges as a form of conjecture that operates between immersion in the moment and a provocation or resonance for (or from) elsewhere. The result is a multiplicity of threads and openings, none of which can be answered through walking alone.

At the same time, the relational dialogue between sites within and between the cities that these encounters enable is prescribed by a quite specific, male gaze. The walks I did were both enabled by the relative ease of walking the city that comes with being male and white in cultures and environments with different configurations of patriarchy, race, and able-bodiedness, and limited by the forms of seeing that flow from that subject-position. The relative ease with which I moved both opened up and closed off the universe of urban fragments that I was able to see and experience. The effect of this, as well as the impact on the kinds of random encounters with people—traders, café staff, and so on—that I had, is cumulative, and is a performance of privilege less available to other subject-positions.

But what makes walking the city political is not just the specific moments of access and the relative ease of movement. Walking the city does not only "become" political because of specific encounters, but because of the very constitution of the city. Cites have historically been organized through prevailing forces of social power, and those histories continue into the present in the norms and codes, violence and harassment, territorial controls and exclusions, policing and alienation, and in the distribution of provisions from cultural facilities and shops to the width of pavements and the availability of public toilets. Just being able to roam the city is already political, let alone the question of how that movement unfolds. Partly for that reason, it is important to recognize that while privilege may enable access to and ease of movement, it does not provide a special access to urban fragments. Indeed, it may preclude the ability to see a wider geography of urban fragments. All of which is to underscore the limits, uncertainties, and unknowability of walking the city, even as it operates as an indispensable route to apprehending cities and urban life.

In Completion

Completed works weigh less than fragments.

—Walter Benjamin, "Hashish in Marseilles"

An Exploded View

Cornelia Parker's sculpture *Cold Dark Matter: An Exploded View,* like much of Parker's work, deals with objects that seem familiar and that persist, but which have been transformed and fragmented, their identities altered (Figure 18).[1] As John Scanlan wrote, "Fragments of matter, and indeed, matter transformed—crushed, melted, sketched, or recovered— appear throughout [her] work," resurrecting seemingly "dead" materials into "beguiling forms."[2] Parker's work captures something of the destructive power of the world, of the force of division and violence, but it is also suggestive of how bits and pieces stay with us in a form and set of relations we might not have expected.

The pieces in *Cold Dark Matter* remain frozen, static in space. The fragments may have been, in Scanlon's theological description, "resurrected," but they are nonetheless left hanging there, with seemingly little capacity to act. There is a structure at work, a sculpture fixed and held rigid in space. The sculpture might be said to mirror the histories of fragmentation that carve up the city spatially and socially, shaping a shattered geography. What, though, if Parker's fragments could move, or be put to different kinds of work? What if they were not only the spatial products of fragmentation, but elements caught up in different kinds of instantiations? How might they be represented not as fixed things in space, but as objects that might also become something else, pulled into different kinds of relations and potentials?

FIGURE 18. *Cold Dark Matter: An Exploded View,* 1991. Sculpture by Cornelia Parker (Source: https://commons.wikimedia.org/wiki/File:Cold_Dark_Matter_.jpg; CC BY-SA 4.0)

The histories of urban fragmentation influence and shape the city, but they do not delimit it. If urbanism, as Henri Lefebvre once wrote, is "made manifest as movement," in that movement things fall apart and come together over and over, at different speeds in all kinds of spaces, with different drivers.[3] Like Parker's sculpture, the city is fundamentally fragmented, a sociospatial history of blasting apart while pulling together, densifying and de-densifying in sometimes violent ways, but as the cases explored in this book have, hopefully, suggested, fragment urbanism is also characterized by possibilities, even while fragmentation persists in those possibilities, and amidst the limits and challenges that often prescribe urban living.

I have attempted to gather together fragments from a world archive of cities. This is an archive that is easily overlooked, composed as it is of the labor, encounter, and experimentation with broken down, inadequate, dysfunctional, or discarded everyday things, and snubbed or unheeded knowledges and ways of seeing. The history of fragment urbanism has been largely obscured, sometimes hidden from view, yet together these cases speak to us about the nature of life in the city and about what it means to be urban for increasing numbers of people today. The book, then, is just one iteration of a larger archive of fragment urbanism, seen very much from my own experiences and perceptions, enabled by my own particular geography of encounter and privilege. There are many other voices and stories being told but not recorded here, and which—in their juxtapositions and constellations—would provoke different directions for how we might collectively imagine and build better and more progressive cities.

I have sought to examine how fragments come to matter for people trying to make something of the city, make their way in the city, and develop a politics through the city. These are stories that take place in the changing, multiple, and always incomplete relations among fragments, densities, social infrastructures, knowledge, everyday living, and politicization. They are processes that are, to be sure, often laborious sites of daily struggle just to reproduce some measure of order and predictability to urban life, but they can also force new political questions of the city and the urban condition. I have explored how material fragments, whether they are bits and pieces of sanitation infrastructure or collaged materials for urban art, shift from predefined purposes to different kinds of uses, and examined how different knowledge fragments are brought into partial but generative connection in the work of refugees and asylum seekers in Berlin or an exhibition in Kampala. I have considered the different ways in which we might come to know and express fragment urbanism, from walking and exhibitions to the practice of writing in fragments.

The book has moved across a range of sites and concerns across the urban world: in central neighborhoods in Kampala, on the urban peripheries of Mumbai, in the townships of Cape Town, in the temporary refuge urbanisms of Berlin, in experiments with urban art from Dakar to Los Angeles, walking through Berlin, Hong Kong, and New York, and in the work of the fragment form in different examples of urban writing from Johannesburg and London to São Paulo and Paris. Sure, fragments in the city are oftentimes so many urban remnants, simply *there,* ignored or abandoned or otherwise around. But in many other moments they are animated in all kinds of activities and densities, and can become important to the experience, politics, and expression of urbanism. The city that emerges from a focus on fragment urbanism is not only one of fragmentation, inequality, and hardship—though it certainly is those things—but also one that is propagative, transforming, a city of possibility, even if the scope of those possibilities often seems to be profoundly curtailed by the very fragmentations residents, activists, artists, or writers seek to address, avoid, or contest.

My central contention has been that if we hope to better understand our increasingly urban world, then investigating these relations is one important route forward. Rather than focus on a particular form of fragment—material, knowledge, textual expression, or other instances—I have sought a more expansive engagement with what the figure of the fragment might bring to understanding cities and the urban world, and how they are made and remade. Doing so enables the bringing together of domains that are rarely connected when we think about cities, from sanitation protests in Mumbai or Cape Town to refugee datahubs in Berlin, forms of walking, writing, and photography in London or Hong Kong, and the reconstitution of fragments in the debris of violence in 1960s Los Angeles or in efforts to portray urban life in contemporary Dakar. This approach positioned the fragment as an entry point into the making and remaking of urban worlds—how they are composed, fought over, and represented—and allowed me to constitute a particular and situated reading of fragment urbanism.

Understanding contemporary cities and the urban world demands that we pay attention to the city of fragments and the situated social and political relations that shape them. I have approached the urban world not as a singular process, nor as the relations between the "urban" and the "global," but as different instantiations of being, thinking, and expressing the urban across the world. I have sought to write these relations in the form of juxtapositions and jumps via vignettes of different lengths. Each situation is distinct in its history and context—the social democratic liberalism of Berlin, the racialized apartheid legacies of Cape Town, to mention two—while resonating with one another.[4] The fragments of the city are sometimes caught up in experiments of coming to know and change the city, and at other times they are views onto an often devastated urban world, where life goes on among the pieces.

Experimenting

But hope appears only in fragmented form.

—Theodor Adorno, *A Portrait of Walter Benjamin*

In a time of rising urban inequalities, climate emergency, and health crises, the prospects for the urban world can seem bleak. Millions of urbanites live day to day, struggling for the next meal, living in conditions that lack decent and reliable water, sanitation, or energy, in homes that demand constant work and attention. Their livelihoods are often oppressive and unreliable. And more than the middle classes and the rich, they are exposed to the hazards of climate change and the impacts of pandemics, from flooding to heat and air pollution or illness and disease caused by viruses like COVID-19. The urban world can be a struggle to live amidst destruction. Living with, politicizing, and working with fragments is often, as we've seen, about testing, expressing relations differently, finding ways of keeping things going, putting new relations in place, or disrupting inherited conditions. What does it mean to talk about "experimentation" in a moment that is so often one of despair and austerity? At worst, to talk of experimentation can sound hopelessly romantic, a naïve celebration of the capacity of people to improvise their way through or out of things. The tragic truth is that for too many urban lives, there is little respite, and without support and new opportunities, without radical change to the political economic and cultural settlement in cities across the world, the pain of living in the wreckage of capitalist urbanization will continue.

When I talk of experimenting, it is with this larger context in mind. The cases gathered together here are not experiments in the sense that dominant discourses of urban creativity, innovation, incubation, and laboratory express. This is not experimentation as the bright spark of novelty, even though new arrangements might be at stake or put into place. Nor is it about having a straightforward faith that "collision densities" will lead to better and more effective ideas and outcomes for cities, even though I have tried to show how density matters to the reproduction and politicization of fragment urbanism.[5] Instead, this is experimentation as struggle, whether the struggle to ease poverty, tackle inequality, or give rise to new possibilities. It is experimentation that proceeds not instead of, or by losing sight of, the destruction and violence of division, exploitation, and oppression, but with those histories always woven into the thinking and action of the present. Fragmentation, in short, is constitutive of the experimentation that arises through fragment urbanism. This is where possibility—another keyword that has run through the book—is emergent.

Just as fragments of things come together in different relations with people and places, so too do struggles resonate in overlapping forms of destruction and fragmentation. Bringing these cases together in the book is itself a kind of experimenting. The book is a densification, staging in passing efforts to work with and push at new conditions. The text has moved across migration, policing, clearance systems, and other logics of fragmentation—this coming together is, too, a kind of density work. I have tried throughout the book to hold content and form in relation to one another, and to give an account of the urban world that begins—and ends—with hope in fragments.

Connective Devices

We need a renewed politics of the city. A politics of value that would seek to improve, repair, and reconnect fragmented places and provisions, and that would aim to make space in planning and urban futures for forms of knowledge and ways of knowing historically driven to the margins. A politics focused not on a singular model or framework through which to pursue better conditions, but instead a politics of becoming, open to different political routes depending on context. As many of the residents, activists, and artists encountered in this book know only too well, the state is vital but often insufficient for addressing fragment urbanism. After all, on the margins of the city the state can be profoundly contradictory. Good local councilors in Mumbai, for instance, may help at particular times to improve the quantity and quality of water pipes for one part of a neighborhood, while politicians or municipal officials from a different department remove pipes or toilets built without permission elsewhere in the same neighborhood, often connected to identity politics around religion or ethnicity.[6] In Namuwongo, Kampala, the state is vital in providing the type of support and opportunity that is so difficult, and in many cases impossible, to create through the efforts of residents individually and collectively, however strong social infrastructures might be. Yet the Kampala Capital City Authority (KCCA), alongside the wetland and railway authorities, looks to evict and demolish many parts of Namuwongo, partly in view of a stalled redevelopment plan for the city that extends to Lake

Victoria.[7] At the same time, the municipality has been responsible for providing at least some essential urban services such as waste collection and road improvements.

One key challenge lies in the state's unwillingness to genuinely engage with residents, their experiences and perceptions, partly as a result of the ways in which communities like Namuwongo are stigmatized and marginalized.[8] Residents are often eager to contribute to the development of their neighborhood and to have a voice in urban planning.[9] Part of the challenge for states, and indeed civil society groups and social movements, is to understand how social infrastructures operate and to try to support them. "If states and societies do not recognize social infrastructure and how it works," argues Eric Klinenburg, "they will fail to see a powerful way to promote civic engagement and social interaction, both within communities and across group lines."[10] There are also instances where social infrastructures need not so much enhancing as replacement by functional material systems. In cases where residents are forced to maintain dangerous or unsafe systems, for example by unblocking drains or transporting wastes, or where women and girls are forced to go in groups to makeshift toilet arrangements due to the risk of violence and harassment, the issue becomes not one of augmenting but of making those forms of social infrastructure unnecessary.

Then there is the question of supporting residents with resources and spaces to form new social infrastructures that can enhance everyday life and open out longer-term possibilities. In Namuwongo, for example, Amiri spoke about forming or becoming involved in youth groups, and Jennifer and Josephine spoke about the need for training groups for widows and organizations to support children into schools. Ali spoke about setting up an association that could represent the interests of the market to the KCCA, and which would perhaps generate some security in an area where the rumor of demolition is never far away. There was talk about setting up a forum of some kind that might examine these different issues collectively by bringing together residents, the state, and NGOs. There were questions raised about how the city might be redeveloped with the aspirations of poorer residents, rather than in the interests of the middle and upper classes, more centrally in mind.[11] All plans, big and small, from residents so often squeezed of their time and resources. If the state were to approach residents in a spirit of genuine partnership in many cities across the world, those residents would often respond with a willingness to work together.[12] In Kampala, there are at least some scraps of evidence that parts of the local state are prepared to do this. For example, the KCCA has explored forming collaborations with NGOs, such as ACTogether, based around the role of the urban poor in building housing and infrastructure in secure conditions.[13]

Appealing to citizenship rights will only get progressive politics so far. Sometimes other tactics have more traction, whether the "poo protests" in Cape Town or building alliances between civil society groups and particular state officials in Berlin, or staging a new debate via activist or art interventions. This calls for a revisable politics that expands with difference, reflecting the needs and aspirations of people at the margins of the city and how they might alter according to social relations of gender, religion, caste, race, class, and so on.[14] There is a politics of value at work in these cases, underpinned by solidarity and care. These different tactics open out a range of whole-fragment relations that work with provisional and experimental epistemologies of urban possibility.

Without connecting fragments and wholes, it is difficult to see how poverty on the margins of the city might be addressed and inequalities challenged. We can think of all kinds of "connective devices" here. The forms of urban maintenance, repair, and support exhibited by Right to Pee in Mumbai or Moabit Hilft in Berlin connect political claims, campaigns, city budgeting, and policy frameworks to the often slow, situated, provisional work of improving conditions by negotiating local actors and power relations. With Right to Pee and CORO there is a politics of urban maintenance at work that simultaneously attends to material fragments while campaigning for changes across the city as a whole.[15] We can identify a range of hinges connecting fragments and wholes across the book: activists in Mumbai and Berlin campaigning for new policy frameworks or budgetary commitments, social movements in Cape Town using not data but sensorial shock and affective disjuncture in a politics of spectacle to force new claims, artists remaking fragments to provoke reflection on how to live together in the city. It is, of course, easy enough to idealize or become sentimental about activism. Activism is not immune to exploitative power relations. It can sometimes make false claims on behalf of communities, and can even be downright regressive—indeed, there are plenty of examples of activists protecting their own interests at the costs of urban majorities.[16] Nonetheless, when it comes to connecting fragments and wholes, they are some of our best teachers.

The connective devices between the city of fragments and wholes operate across the liberal city and the "city in the wild." The liberal city has a global resonance, even if it is understood in different ways across world-regions. It is the city of rights, state institutions and processes, planning and policy processing, distributions of land, infrastructure and services, and social contracts. It is difficult to imagine addressing fragmented cities without it. At the same time, the liberal city has been complicit in the histories and geographies of fragmentation we find in increasingly unequal cities today. It has ensured not just the circulation of people, cultures, ideas, and innovations, but—and particularly intensely in its neoliberal incarnation—has actively channeled the circulation of capital into some areas and not others, facilitated the transformation of some sites into spaces of speculation of land and real estate at the cost of existing residents or other neighborhoods, and has left many places suffering from neglect, disinvestment, demolition, and segregation.[17] The liberal city is a profound site of struggle and transformation for the urban commons—the distribution of resources, spaces, and opportunity—and will unquestionably remain so.[18]

But that struggle often takes us beyond the liberal city. The city in the wild is entangled with the liberal city but exceeds it. This is a city of situated everyday negotiating, makeshift political bargaining, forms of protest that might shock and startle, or forms of artistic experimentation and provocation. It is not that the city in the wild "belongs" to marginalized neighborhoods. The city in the wild can be found in city and state planning offices, and not just in low-income neighborhoods.[19] The seemingly disorderly, complex, noncompliant city simultaneously exceeds and yet can also become necessary to how power functions and things get done or contested across cities.[20] The point is not a geographical one but a political one: addressing fragment urbanism requires some form of connection between the liberal city and the city in the wild. Residents, activists, and artists often know this very well. We can learn from how they stitch together—socially, materially, discursively, imaginatively, and politically—the city of fragments and the city of wholes, sometimes through entangling the liberal city and the city in the wild.

I am using the term "connection" rather than "integration" here. Connecting the city in the wild to the liberal city might mean linking residents to preexisting wholes, for instance within urban policy frameworks or particular forms of housing, infrastructural, or service provisioning. There is a politics of connection here, for instance, in relation to providing functional, reliable sanitation systems to economically marginal neighborhoods. But in some cases seeking to integrate fragments into wholes can be a form of violence, subsuming or eviscerating different ways of knowing and inhabiting the city. Knowledge fragments might—*might*—point to different kinds of wholes altogether, perhaps demanding alternative understanding, approaches, and forms of policy or practice oriented to distinct stories and aspirations. The aim cannot surely be to align with efforts to incorporate difference within existing dominant frames, for example in efforts to absorb refugee groups into overriding visions of nationality with their associated codes, sensibilities, and ways of being.[21]

Should, for example, the concerns and knowledges of refugees in Berlin or ethnic and religious minorities in India conform to dominant knowledge frameworks of urban government? Certainly, political parties from the BJP in India to the AfD in Germany might seek that kind of epistemic force. A politics of fragment urbanism entails a different form of connection, not one of subsuming knowledge but of enabling and supporting difference, appreciative of the limits of translation between different forms of knowledge or ways of knowing. And yet an important lesson from subaltern studies here is that we cannot simply step around the problem of incorporation. It lurks always in the background as part of the politics of representation and inclusion, as a delicate line and inescapable dialectical tension between respecting the significance of a fragment and incorporating it within existing frames. To approach knowledge fragments is, inevitably, to continually negotiate this tension and paradox.

Again, there is no singular route or political model that guarantees a route forward here. As David Kishik shows, if Spinoza argued that we do not know what a body can do, then the possibilities are immensely greater with the complexity of the city.[22] For Kishik, this demands less a set of political blueprints and more an immersive and modest pragmatist politics, emerging through the "sheer life" of the city's streets and neighborhoods. I am not arguing against blueprints—my point is that the politics of fragment urbanism I have been exploring here is one that moves between and across blueprints in pragmatic and contextually relevant ways, rather than advocating for this model or plan over others prior to engagement with specific struggles. To develop a more progressive politics of the city and the urban world, we need both the sheer life and the blueprints, and a plural imagination of political change. In exploring these relations, where we might learn to better "see" like a city,[23] we can generate insight into how cities are made and might be remade, whether through supporting social infrastructures, knowledge fragments, and ways of operating with material fragments, or by advocating new systems that ensure improved basic provisions.

As Kishik's pragmatic politics of "sheer life" suggests, density matters for a progressive politics of the margins. Historical processes of fragmentation sift and sort urban densities—indeed, dominant economic and aesthetic valuations of urban density can drive fragmentation. At the same time, density is not a fixed urban store and it can be enacted in all kinds of ways: as a resource for neighbors helping each other out in Kampala or Mumbai, as a way of amassing through occupation in a political protest in Berlin or Cape Town, as a context for reflection and debate provoked by artistic statements, and more. Residents and activists struggle to cope with and politicize the debris of fragmentation in dense contexts, from translating fragments into new uses so that they might work, or peopling fragments through social infrastructures to reproduce urban life, to residents and activists using temporary densities to contest fragmentation. Connective devices can emerge from and put density to work in different ways. Again, there is much to learn here from activists and residents.

In Mumbai, for example, the small urban group URBZ has a rich history of promoting ways of augmenting existing forms of density in poor neighborhoods.[24] As URBZ have shown, rather than argue that residents would benefit from densities being either increased or reduced in order to meet certain social, economic, and environmental goals— usually defined by academic researchers or policymakers and officials— it is often more productive to identify and work with the multiple concerns that different residents themselves attach to density. URBZ looks to improve the material conditions found in poorer neighborhoods and to document and promote the knowledges and ways of knowing shunted to the social margins of the city. This too is a politics of urban value. One of the active political questions here is: how might understanding the different ways in which density is known and comes to matter for residents help to formulate agendas, politics, and plans to address fragment urbanisms? It is unlikely that any one model, whether from the liberal city or from the city in the wild, will be adequate to responding to the challenges of fragment urbanism. Connective devices can and do morph across all kinds of tactics and approaches, and we need the city in the wild as much as we need the liberal city.

Excursions

This book is the result of a range of methodological excursions into fragment urbanism as it is encountered by all kinds of people—residents, activists, artists, writers, urban researchers—through interviews, exhibitions, documentary research, walking, and fragmentary writing. Walking, I argued, by drawing attention to the distribution of fragments across different areas in the city, points to some of the priorities of urban development and political economic (dis)investment. It can enable a particular appreciation of how fragments act in different relations, including changing urban flows, becoming repurposed for everyday improvisations, or altering rhythms, atmospheres, and densities. It gives a sense too of the mundane ways in which the city is reproduced. At the same time, the questions walking prompts of particular spaces and times in the city demand that we bring other methods into the frame, including for instance interviews and documentary data. And the capacity to walk the city is shaped by how privilege—of class, gender, race, and body—is woven into the very production and spatial organization of the city.

Writing in fragments has enabled the juxtaposition of disparate-but-related urban instantiations over time and space as a way of generating knowledge of the urban condition. The movement between a series of cases works with rather than against the heterogeneity of the urban world, identifying a register in-between meta-narrative and local specificities. Writing in fragments can give us insight into the city and urban world by working with distinct instances, encounters, and sights, and

with different voices and sources, while also provoking a wider understanding through resonating conditions. The practice of writing in textual fragments is, like walking, itself a kind of excursion, a particular
and situated portrayal of the damaged urban present and the possibilities that can nonetheless emerge. There are, of course, many ways of
writing in fragments, and the approach I have used—to work with generally longer and more closely integrated narratives than some of the
more strongly broken-up experiments I discussed in the *Writing in fragments* section—has been to express the fragmented and multiple nature
of the urban world while attempting to generate a larger story. The
larger story is one of people struggling to cope with an inadequate
urban fabric, of organizing social infrastructures of support, of embarking on different forms of political claim and contestation, and of developing political or artistic expressions that sometimes look to escape,
and at other times seek to remake, the fragments of the urban
present.

The book is a specific archive of fragment urbanism, and I do not
claim any more for what is assembled here than a modest, partial, and
provisional form of knowing the city and urban world. Indeed, fragment urbanism, as I have approached it, demands a recognition of the
situated, contingent, and limited glimpse that this book provides, and a
position alert to the inescapable power-geometries that come with being
a white, able-bodied male researching and writing. The challenge is to
try to see the urban world from different vantage points of place, living,
knowledge, and aspiration. We have encountered a wide range of ways
in which people have thought with, experimented with, written through,
contested, or remade fragments through different relations. My focus
on fragments derives from my own angle of vision on the cases described
in the book, and has meant bringing a particular interpretation to the
practices and voices of residents, activists, and artists. We are always
pressing against the limits of our own ways of seeing, and the risk of
incorporating different contexts and voices into those ways of seeing is
always present. Moreover, the fact that the discussion has moved across
a wide range of cases means that there is much more to say about each
of them and their specific contexts and histories. It is a form of writing,
at least as I have pursued it here, that often inevitably means sacrificing
depth for breadth. In the end, for all that writing in textual fragments
opens up an experiment in connecting content and form, and in developing resonances across difference, it cannot in itself resolve the challenge of brokering different contexts and forms of expression.

As the world increasingly urbanizes and as cities become increasingly unequal, the fragment will likely become more important to cities, urbanism, and urbanization. There is a disparate archive on the fragment that has always accompanied urban research, expression, and action—from influential interventions produced by critical urbanists and writers, to artistic experiments and activism—but there are few attempts to explore and experiment with the different potentials of the fragment idea to generate understanding of the making and remaking of urban worlds. There is no claim here to completion in this particular excursion into the idea of the fragment, and others would offer very different excursions; indeed, one of my hopes in closing is that others might find their own points of departure in thinking with and through fragments. In the spaces between the fragments and more conventional narratives, very different books might have been written. In this expansive sense, we are always, albeit in different ways and to different extents, only ever writing some version of our own urbanism, and only ever writing in fragments.

Notes

PROLOGUE

Epigraph: Wright, F. L., *The Disappearing City* (New York: William Farquhar Payson, 1932), 44.

1. Michael, C., 'Has Tokyo Reached "Peak City"?', *The Guardian,* June 14, 2019, www.theguardian.com/cities/2019/jun/14/has-tokyo-reached-peak-city, 2019 (accessed June 20, 2019).

2. Lefevre, C., 'The Complete City: Why Density and Amenities Are Essential to Everyday Urban Living,' *Minnpost,* July 16, 2014, www.minnpost.com/the-line/2014/07/complete-city-why-density-and-amenities-are-essential-everyday-urban-living/ (accessed August 19, 2019).

3. Joyce, P., *The Rule of Freedom: Liberalism and the Modern City* (London: Verso, 2002).

4. Vladislavic, I., *Portrait with Keys: Joburg and What-What* (Johannesburg: Umuzi, [2006] 2017), 83–84; my emphasis.

5. Roy, A., 'Who's Afraid of Postcolonial Theory?,' *International Journal of Urban and Regional Research* 40, no. 1 (2016): 200–209.

READING FRAGMENTS

1. Benjamin, W., 'One Way Street,' in *Walter Benjamin: One Way Street and Other Writings,* trans. J. A. Underwood (London: Penguin Books, [1928] 2009), 79–80.

2. Hansen, M. B., 'Benjamin's Gamble with Cinema,' *October* 109 (2004): 3–45, on 9.

3. Marshall, C., 'How David Bowie Used William S. Burrough's Cut-up Method to Write His Unforgettable Lyrics,' *Open Culture,* May 7, 2019, www.openculture.com/2019/05/how-david-bowie-used-william-s-burroughs

-cut-up-method-to-write-his-unforgettable-lyrics.html; Moody, R., 'Swinging Modern Sounds 44: And Another Day,' *The Rumpus,* April 25, 2013, https://therumpus.net/2013/04/swinging-modern-sounds-44-and-another-day/.

4. Berliner, P. F., *Thinking in Jazz: The Infinite Art of Improvisation* (Chicago: University of Chicago Press, 1994).

PURSUING FRAGMENTS

Epigraph: Lefebvre, H., *The Production of Space* (Oxford: Blackwell, [1974] 1991), 355–56.

1. Seabrook, J., and Siddiqui, A., *People without History: India's Muslim Ghettos* (London: Pluto Press, 2011).

2. Chakrabarty, D., 'Radical Histories and Question of Enlightenment Rationalism: Some Recent Critiques of *Subaltern Studies,*' in *Mapping Subaltern Studies and the Postcolonial,* ed. V. Chaturvedi (London: Verso, [2000] 2012), 256–80, at 275; Simone, A., 'The Surfacing of Urban Life,' *City* 15, nos. 3–4 (2011): 355–64, on 356.

3. Pieterse, E., 'Rethinking African Urbanism from the Slum,' *LSE Cities,* 2011, http://lsecities.net/media/objects/articles/rethinking-african-urbanism-from-the-slum/en-gb/ (accessed July 11, 2019).

4. Gidwani, V., 'Six Theses on Waste, Value and Commons,' *Social and Cultural Geography* 14, no. 7 (2013): 773–83.

5. Simone, A., 'Emergency Democracy and the "Governing Composite,"' *Social Text* 95, no. 2 (2008): 13–33, on 13.

6. Gregson, N., Crang, M., Ahamed, F., Akhtar, N., and Ferdous, R., 'Following Things of Rubbish Value: End-of-Life Ships, "Chock-Chocky" Furniture and the Bangladeshi Middle-Class Consumer,' *Geoforum* 41 (2010): 846–54; Gidwani, V., and Maringanti, A., 'The Waste-Value Dialectic: Lumpen Urbanization in Contemporary India,' *Comparative Studies of South Asia, Africa and the Middle East* 36 (2016): 112–33.

7. For different takes on the margins and the city, see Perlman, J., 'The Metamorphosis of Marginality in Rio De Janeiro,' *Latin American Research* (2004); Perlman, J., *Favela: Four Decades of Living on the Edge in Rio* (Oxford: Oxford University Press, 2010); Hickey, S., 'Rethinking Poverty Analysis from the Margins: Insights from Northern Uganda,' *Afriche e Orienti* 11, no. 2 (2009): 119–36; Moser, C., *Ordinary Families, Extraordinary Lives: Assets and Poverty Reduction in Guayaquil, 1978–2004* (Washington, DC: Brookings Institute Press, 2009); Moser, C., and McIlwaine, C., 'Editorial: New Frontiers in Twenty-First-Century Urban Conflict and Violence,' *Environment and Urbanization* 26, no. 2 (2014): 331–44; Dikeç, M., *Urban Rage: The Revolt of the Excluded* (New Haven, CT: Yale University Press, 2018).

8. On the urban margins, especially in Europe, see Michele Lancione's excellent work: Lancione, M., 'Assemblages of Care and the Analysis of Public Policies on Homelessness in Turin, Italy,' *City* 18 (2014): 25–40; Lancione, M., 'Entanglements of Faith: Discourses, Practices of Care and Homeless People in an Italian City of Saints,' *Urban Studies* 51 (2014b): 3062–78; Lancione, M., ed., *Rethinking Life at the Margins: The Assemblage of Contexts, Subjects and*

Politics (London: Routledge, 2016); Lancione, M., 'Revitalising the Uncanny: Challenging Inertia in the Struggle against Forced Evictions,' *Environment and Planning D: Society and Space* 35, no. 6 (2017): 1012–32; Lancione, M., and McFarlane, C., 'Life at the Urban Margins: Sanitation Infra-Making and the Potential of Experimental Comparison,' *Environment and Planning A* 48, no. 12 (2017), https://doi.org/10.1177/0308518X16659772.

9. Hall, S., *City, Street and Citizen: The Measure of the Ordinary* (London: Routledge, 2012).

10. Lancione, M., 'Radical Housing: On the Politics of Dwelling as Difference,' *International Journal of Housing Policy* 20, no. 2 (2019): 273–89.

11. Truelove, Y., '(Re-)Conceptualising Water Inequality in Delhi, India through a Feminist Political Ecology Framework,' *Geoforum* 42 (2011): 143–52.

12. Singh, G., Vithayathil, T., and Pradhan, K.C., 'Recasting Inequality: Residential Segregation by Caste over Time in Urban India,' *Environment and Urbanization* 31, no. 2 (2019): 615–34.

13. Tacoli, C., 'Editorial: The Urbanization of Food Insecurity and Malnutrition,' *Environment and Urbanization* 31, no. 2 (2019): 371–74.

14. See, for example, Bayat, A., 'From "Dangerous Classes" to "Quiet Rebels": Politics of the Urban Subaltern in the Global South,' *International Sociology* 15, no. 3 (2000): 533–55; Gillespie, T., 'From Quiet to Bold Encroachment: Contesting Dispossession in Accra's Informal Sector,' *Urban Geography* 38, no. 7 (2017): 974–92; Kumari, S., and Singh, A.K., 'Working Women in Informal Sector: Geographical Perspective,' *Journal of the Anthropological Survey of India* 65, no. 2 (2016): 185–99.

15. See, for example, Roy, A., 'Dis/possessive Collectivism: Property and Personhood at City's End,' *Geoforum* 80 (2017): A1–11.

16. Merrifield, A. *The New Urban Question* (London: Pluto Press, 2014).

17. Simone, A., and Pieterse, E., *New Urban Worlds: Inhabiting Dissonant Times* (Cambridge: Polity Press, 2017); Fredericks, R., *Garbage Citizenship: Vital Infrastructures of Labor in Dakar, Senegal* (Durham, NC: Duke University Press, 2018).

18. Dawson, A., *Extreme Cities: The Peril and Promise of Urban Life in the Age of Climate Change* (London: Verso, 2017); Bulkeley, H., *Accomplishing Climate Governance* (Cambridge: Cambridge University Press, 2015).

19. Parnell, S., 'Defining a Global Urban Development Agenda,' *World Development* 78 (2016): 538.

20. Amin, A., 'The Urban Condition: A Challenge to Social Science,' *Public Culture* 25, no. 2 (2013): 201–8, on 206.

21. Amin, A., 'The Urban Condition'; Amin, A., and Thrift, N., *Seeing Like a City* (Cambridge: Polity Press, 2017).

22. Simone and Pieterse, *New Urban Worlds*, 187.

23. See, for example, debates ranging across and between accounts of urban worlding (Roy, A., and Ong, A., eds., *Worlding Cities: Asian Experiments and the Art of Being Global* [Oxford: Wiley-Blackwell, 2011]; Simone and Pieterse, *New Urban Worlds*); urban planetarity (e.g., Jazeel, T., 'Urban Theory with an Outside,' *Environment and Planning D: Society and Space* 36, no. 3 [2018]: 405–19); global urbanism (e.g., Sheppard, E., Leitner, H., and Maringanti, A.,

'Provincializing Global Urbanism: A Manifesto,' *Urban Geography* 34 [2015]: 893–900); adaptive assemblages (e.g., Dovey, K., 'Informal Urbanism and Complex Adaptive Assemblages,' *International Development Planning Review* 34, no. 4 [2012]: 349–68; McFarlane, C., *Learning the City: Knowledge and Translocal Assemblage* [Oxford: Wiley-Blackwell, 2011]); urban cosmopolitics (e.g., Blok, A., and Farías, I., eds., *Urban Cosmopolitics: Agencements, Assemblies, Atmospheres* [London: Routledge, 2016]); planetary urbanization (e.g., Brenner, N., and Schmid, C., 'Planetary Urbanization,' in Gandy, M., ed., *Urban Constellations,* 10–13 [Berlin: Jovis, 2012]); peripheral urbanization (Caldeira, T., 'Peripheral Urbanization: Autoconstruction, Transversal Logics, and Politics in Cities of the Global South,' *Environment and Planning D: Society and Space* 35, no. 1 [2017]: 3–20).

24. Sheppard et al., 'Provinicalizing Global Urbanism.' Lancione, M., and McFarlane, C., eds., *Global Urbanism: Knowledge, Power and the City* (London: Routledge, 2021).

25. Jazeel, T., 'Singularity: A Manifesto for Incomparable Geographies,' *Singapore Journal of Tropical Geography* 40, no. 1 (2018): 5–21; Oswin, N., 'Planetary Urbanization: A View from Outside,' *Environment and Planning D: Society and Space* 36, no. 3 (2018); Zeiderman, A., 'Beyond the Enclave of Urban Theory,' *International Journal of Urban and Regional Research* 42, no. 6 (2018): 114–26; Parnell, S., and Robinson, J., '(Re)theorising Cities from the Global South: Looking beyond Neoliberalism,' *Urban Geography,* 33, no. 4 (2012): 593–617.

26. Connolly, W. E., *A World of Becoming* (Durham, NC: Duke University Press, 2011), 173.

27. Caldiera, 'Peripheral Urbanisation.'

28. Sheppard et al., 'Provincialising Global Urbanism.'

29. Amin and Thrift, *New Urban Worlds,* 31.

30. Deleuze, G., and Parnet, C., *Dialogues II,* rev. ed. (New York: Columbia University Press, [1977] 2002); Jacobs, J.M., 'Urban Geography I: Still Thinking Cities Relationally I,' *Progress in Human Geography* 36, no. 3 (2012): 412–22.

31. Massey, D., *For Space* (London: Sage, 2005); Massey, D., *World City* (Cambridge: Polity Press, 2007); Blok and Farías, *Urban Cosmopolitics.*

32. Amin, 'The Urban Condition,' 206.

33. Buckley, M., and Strauss, K., 'With, against and beyond Lefebvre: Planetary Urbanization and Epistemic Plurality,' *Environment and Planning D: Society and Space* 34, no. 4 (2016); McKittrick, K., *Demonic Grounds: Black Women and the Cartographies of Struggle* (Minneapolis: University of Minnesota Press, 2006); Morland, I., and Willox, D., *Queer Theory* (London: Palgrave, 2004).

34. Amin, 'The Urban Condition.'

35. Amin, 'The Urban Condition,' 207, 206.

36. Magnusson, W., *Politics of Urbanism: Seeing Like a City* (New York: Routledge, 2011), 120; Amin and Thrift, *Seeing Like a City;* Simone and Pieterse, *New Urban Worlds;* Söderström, O., *Cities in Relations: Trajectories of Urban Development in Hanoi and Ouagadougo* (Oxford: Wiley-Blackwell, 2014).

37. Comaroff, J., and Comaroff, J., *Theory from the South: Or, How Euro-America Is Evolving toward Africa* (London: Paradigm, 2012), 44.

38. On these conditions across global urban space, see: Hentschel, C., 'Post-colonialising Berlin and the Fabrication of the Urban,' *International Journal of Urban and Regional Research* (2014): 79–91; Vasudevan, A., *Metropolitan Preoccupations: the Spatial Politics of Squatting in Berlin* (Oxford: Wiley-Blackwell, 2015); Vasudevan, A., *The Autonomous City: A History of Squatting* (London: Verso, 2017); Hall, *City, Street and Citizen*; Lancione, *Rethinking Life at the Margins;* Dorling, D., *All That Is Solid: How the Great Housing Disaster Defines Our Times, and What We Can Do about It* (London: Penguin, 2015); Schreker, T., and Bambra, C., *Neoliberal Epidemics: How Politics Makes Us Sick* (London: Palgrave Macmillan, 2015); Garthwaite, K., *Hunger Pains: Life inside Foodbank Britain* (Bristol: Policy Press, 2016); Peck, J., 'Austerity Urbanism,' *City* 16, no. 6 (2012): 626–55; Butler, P., 'More than a Million People Living in Destitution, Study Shows,' *The Guardian,* April 27, 2016, www.theguardian.com/society/2016/apr/27/million-people-uk-living-destitution-joseph-rowntree-foundation?CMP = share_btn_tw (accessed August 15, 2018).

39. Connor, P., 'Nearly 1 in 100 Worldwide Are Now Displaced from Their Homes,' Pew Research Center, August 3, 2016, www.pewresearch.org/fact-tank/2016/08/03/nearly-1-in-100-worldwide-are-now-displaced-from-their-homes/?utm_content = buffer03d18&utm_medium = social&utm_source = twitter.com&utm_campaign = buffer (accessed August 7, 2016); United Nations, 'Nobody Left Outside' Campaign Launched as UN Warns of Dire Shelter Conditions for Refugees,' May 18, 2016, www.un.org/apps/news/story.asp?NewsID = 53964#.V3JIBXidL8t (accessed June 28, 2019).

40. Katz, B., Noring, L., and Garrelts, N., 'Cities and Refugees: The German Experience,' *Brookings,* September 18, 2016, www.brookings.edu/research/cities-and-refugees-the-german-experience/ (accessed March 16, 2019).

41. Shin, H.B., 'Theorising from Where? Reflections on De-centring Global (Southern) Urbanism,' in *Global Urbanism: Knowledge, Power, and the City* (London: Routledge, forthcoming); Yiftachel, O., '"Conceptual Topography" and the City,' *Urban Forum* 31 (2020): 443–51.

42. Schindler, S., 'Towards a Paradigm of Southern Urbanism,' *City* 21, no. 1 (2017): 47–64.

43. See Lawhon, M., and Truelove, Y., 'Disambiguating the Southern Urban Critique: Propositions, Pathways and Possibilities for a More Global Urban Studies,' *Urban Studies* 57, no. 1 (2020); Bhan, G., 'Notes on a Southern Urban Practice,' *Environment & Urbanization* 31, no. 2 (2019): 1–16.

MATERIALIZING THE CITY

Epigraph: Simone and Pieterse, *New Urban Worlds,* 70–71.

1. See, for instance, Kagenda, P., 'KCCA's Night Raiders,' *The Independent,* August 18, 2014, www.independent.co.ug/news/news-analysis/9244-kccas-night-raiders (accessed February 10, 2019); McFarlane, C., and Silver, J., 'Navigating the City: Dialectics of Everyday Urbanism,' *Transactions of the Institute for British*

Geographers 42, no. 3 (2017): 458–71; Raghunath, P., '1000 Evicted Families Rebuild Homes,' *Gulf News India*, June 20, 2015, http://gulfnews.com/news/asia/india/1000-evicted-families-rebuild-homes-1.1537995 (accessed May 10, 2019).

2. Murali, M., Cummings, C., Feyertag, J., Gelb, S., Hart, T., Khan, A., Langdown, I., and Lucci, P., *10 Things to Know about the Impacts of Urbanization* (London: Overseas Development Institute, 2018).

3. "Raksha" is a pseudonym given to protect anonymity.

4. Khan, B. 'BMC Official Holds NGOs Responsible for Mankhurd Toilet Collapse,' *DNA*, 2015, http://54.254.97.154/locality/mumbai-north-east/bmc-official-holds-ngos-responsible-mankhurd-toilet-collapse-54794 (accessed September 10, 2019).

5. Mumbai Human Development Report (HDR), *Mumbai Human Development Report, 2009* (New Delhi: Oxford University Press, 2009); Björkman, L., *Pipe Politics, Contested Waters: Embedded Infrastructures of Millennial Mumbai* (Durham, NC: Duke University Press, 2015); Panjabi, K., 'Report on M-East Ward Reveals the Poor Picture of Mumbai's Unequal Development,' *DNA*, April 30, 2015, www.dnaindia.com/locality/mumbai-north-east/report-meast-ward-reveals-poor-picture-mumbai's-unequal-development-58740 (accessed August 12, 2019).

6. McFarlane, C., Desai, R., and Graham, S., 'Informal Urban Sanitation: Everyday Life, Comparison and Poverty,' *Annals of the Association of American Geographers* 104 (2014): 989–1011.

7. Fernandes, N., *City Adrift: A Short Biography of Bombay* (New Delhi: Adelph, 2013); Dossal, M., *Theatre of Conflict, City of Hope* (New Delhi: Oxford University Press, 2010); Tindall, G., *City of Gold* (New Delhi: Penguin Books, 1992).

8. Pinto, J., and Fernandes, N., eds., *Bombay, Meri Jaan: Writings on Mumbai* (New Delhi: Penguin Books, 2003); Appadurai, A., *Fear of Small Numbers: An Essay of the Geography of Anger* (Durham, NC: Duke University Press, 2006).

9. Roy, A., *Capitalism: A Ghost Story* (London: Verso, 2014).

10. Satterthwaite, D., Mitlin, D., and Bartlett, S., *Key Sanitation Issues: Commitments, Coverage, Choices, Context, Co-production, Costs, Capital, City-wide Coverage*, Environment and Urbanization Brief no. 31 (London: IIED, 2015).

11. Phadke, S., Khan, S., and Ranade, S., *Why Loiter? Women and Risk on Mumbai's Streets* (New Delhi: Penguin, 2011); Truelove, '(Re-)Conceptualising Water Inequality in Delhi, India'; O'Reilly, K., 'Combining Sanitation and Women's Participation in Water Supply: An Example from Rajasthan,' *Development in Practice* 20, no. 1 (2010): 45–56; McFarlane et al., 'Informal Urban Sanitation.'

12. Koppikar, S., 'Death-Trap Toilets: The Hidden Dangers of Mumbai's Poorest Slums,' *The Guardian*, February 27, 2017, www.theguardian.com/global-development-professionals-network/2017/feb/27/death-trap-toilets-mumbai-india-slums (accessed December 11, 2019).

13. See, for example, Sharma, R.N., and Bhide, A., 'World Bank Funded Slum Sanitation Programme in Mumbai: Participatory Approach and Lessons Learnt,' *Economic and Political Weekly* 40, no. 17 (April 23–29, 2005): 1784–89; McFarlane, C., 'Sanitation in Mumbai's Informal Settlements: State, "Slum," and Infrastructure,' *Environment and Planning A* 40 (2008): 88–107;

McFarlane, C., 'The Entrepreneurial Slum: Civil Society, Mobility, and the Co-production of Urban Development,' *Urban Studies* 49 (2012): 2926–47.

14. National Slum Dwellers Federation, Mahila Milan, and Sparc in India, *Toilet Talk,* 1997, https://knowyourcity.info/wp-content/uploads/2018/09/Toilet-Talk-with-photos.pdf (accessed December 11, 2019).

15. Varshney, A., 'People in This Mumbai Slum Barely Make It to Age 40,' *Mongabay,* April 2019, https://india.mongabay.com/2019/04/people-in-this-mumbai-slum-barely-make-it-to-age-40/ (accessed December 3, 2019).

16. Agarwal, S., 'Gleaning the Dumps of Deonar: "I Was Born in Garbage, I Will Die in Garbage",' *Counterpunch,* November 29, 2019, www.counter-punch.org/2019/11/29/gleaning-the-dumps-of-deonar-i-was-born-in-garbage-i-will-die-in-garbage/ (accessed December 3, 2019).

17. Varshney, 'People in This Mumbai Slum Barely Make It to Age 40.' And see Menon, M., 'Maharashtra Faces Growing Urban Malnutrition,' *The Hindu,* April 22, 2020, www.thehindu.com/news/national/article3342953.ece (accessed July 5, 2020); Menon, N., 'Deonar Dumping Ground Is Making Children Sick,' *Mumbai Mirror,* June 2, 2009, 7.

18. Agarwal, 'Gleaning the Dumps of Deonar.'

19. Vince, G., *Adventures in the Anthropocene: A Journey to the Heart of the Planet We Made* (London: Chatto and Windus, 2014).

20. Graham, S., Desai, R., and McFarlane, C., 'Water Wars in Mumbai,' *Public Culture* 25 (2013): 115–41.

21. Björkman, *Pipe Politics, Contested Waters.*

22. Urban Think Tank, *Torre David: Informal Vertical Communities* (Zurich: Lars Muller, 2012).

23. Urban Think Tank, *Torre David,* 209.

24. Urban Think Tank, *Torre David,* 351.

25. Urban Think Tank, *Torre David,* 178.

26. Brillembourg, A., and Klumpner, H., 'Potential,' in Urban Think Tank, *Torre David,* 371.

27. See, for example, Cohen, B., *The Emergence of the Urban Entrepreneur: How the Growth of Cities and the Sharing Economy Are Driving a New Breed of Innovators* (Santa Barbara, CA: Praeger, 2016); Cohen, B., Almirall, E., and Chesbrough, H., 'The City as a Lab: Open Innovation Meets the Collaborative Economy,' *California Management Review* 59, no. 1 (2016): 5–13; Florida, R., *The Rise of the Creative Class Revisited* (New York: Basic Books, 2011).

28. Brillembourg, A., and Klumpner, H., 'Past,' in Urban Think Tank, *Torre David,* 78; see also Caldeira, T., *City of Walls: Crime, Segregation, and Citizenship in São Paulo* (Berkeley: University of California Press, 2000).

29. Massey, *World City;* Davidson, M., and Iveson, K., 'Beyond City Limits: A Conceptual and Political Defense of "the City" as an Anchoring Concept for Critical Urban Theory,' *City* 19, no. 5 (2015).

30. See, for example, Murray, M., *The Urbanism of Exception: The Dynamics of Global City Building in the Twenty-First Century* (Cambridge: Cambridge University Press, 2017); Caldeira, *City of Walls;* Graham, S., and Marvin, S., *Splintering Urbanism: Networked Infrastructures, Technological Mobilities and the Urban Condition* (Oxford: Blackwell, 2001); Harvey, D., *Social Justice*

238 | Notes to Page 40

in the City (Baltimore: Johns Hopkins University Press, 1973); Lees, L., Slater, T., and Wyly, E., *Gentrification* (New York: Routledge, 2008); Smith, N., *The New Urban Frontier: Gentrification and the Revanchist City* (London: Routledge, 1996); Watson, V., 'African Urban Fantasies: Dreams or Nightmares?,' *Environment and Urbanization* 26, no. 1 (2014): 215–31.

31. See, for example, Alsayyad, N., and Roy, A. 'Medieval Modernity: On Citizenship and Urbanism in a Global Era,' *Space and Polity* 10, no. 1 (2006) 1–20; Brickell, K., Arrigoittia, F., and Vasudevan, A., *Geographies of Forced Eviction: Dispossession, Violence, Resistance* (London: Palgrave, 2017); De Boeck, F., and Baloji, S., *Suturing the City: Living Together in Congo's Urban Worlds* (London: Autograph, 2016); Graham, S., *Cities under Siege: The New Military Urbanism* (London: Verso, 2010); Hall, P., *Cities of Tomorrow: An Intellectual History of Urban Planning and Design since 1880*, 4th ed. (Oxford: Wiley Blackwell, 2014); Kooy, M., and Bakker, K.. 'Technologies of Government: Constituting Subjectivities, Spaces, and Infrastructures in Colonial and Contemporary Jakarta,' *International Journal of Urban and Regional Research* 32 (2008): 375–91; Legg, S., *Spaces of Colonialism: Delhi's Urban Governmentalities* (Oxford: Wiley Blackwell, 2007); Lefebvre, *The Production of Space.*

32. See Caldeira, T., *City of Walls: Crime, Segregation, and Citizenship in São Paulo* (Berkeley: University of California Press, 2000), 308; Davis, M., *City of Quartz: Excavating the Future in Los Angeles* (London: Verso, 1999). In *City of Walls,* Caldeira examined the deepening spatial segregation in Los Angeles and São Paulo, driven by a combination of economic restructuring, growing cultures of apprehension and intolerance over multiculturalism, and perceptions of crime, with profound consequences for urban democracy and public space. The urban landscape she described was one increasingly marked by "fortified fragments" of housing, open spaces that were continuously walled and divided, and the creeping private policing, electronic surveillance, and pseudo-public spaces of malls and cultural complexes that Mike Davis had previously described of LA. Fragmentation was a recurring theme in the postmodern turn in the 1980s, from which Ed Soja and others explored LA as increasingly spatiality differentiated by class and race, with growing numbers "barricaded in poverty" and others hidden behind the gates and walls of elite compounds; see Soja, E., *Postmodern Geographies: The Reassertion of Space in Critical Social Theory* (London: Verso, 1989), 242. As a polycentric urban region that seemed increasingly to defy the center-suburb imaginary of the modernist city, Soja investigated LA's globalizing juxtaposition of technology economies, defense complexes, entertainment areas, commercial and residential locales, and more. See Soja, E. 'Taking Los Angeles Apart: Some Fragments of a Critical Human Geography,' *Environment and Planning D: Society and Space* 4, no. 3 (1986): 255–72 at 256; Dear, M., and Flusty, S., 'Postmodern Urbanism', *Annals of the Association of American Geographers* 88, no. 1 (1998): 50–72; Scott, A. J., and Soja, E. W., eds., *The City: Los Angeles and Urban Theory at the End of the Twentieth Century* (Berkeley: University of California Press, 1996).

33. Graham and Marvin showed how infrastructure was increasingly siphoned off from—or bypassed altogether—poorer spaces, leaving certain groups with poorly maintained and inadequate systems, which had an enor-

mous impact on critical urbanism. See Graham, S., and Marvin, S., *Splintering Urbanism: Networked Infrastructures, Technological Mobilities and the Urban Condition* (Blackwell, Oxford, 2001). See also, for example, Anand, N., *Hydraulic City: Water and the Infrastructures of Citizenship in Mumbai* (Durham, NC: Duke University Press, 2017); Coutard, O., and Rutherford, J., eds., *Beyond the Networked City: Infrastructure Reconfigurations and Urban Change in the North and South* (London: Routledge, 2015); Gandy, M., *The Fabric of Space: Water, Modernity, and the Urban Imagination* (Boston: MIT Press, 2014).

34. Lefebvre's writings have been remarkably influential in urban debates in recent years, particularly in relation to urban research; Lefebvre, *The Production of Space,* and Lefebvre, H., *The Urban Revolution (*Minneapolis: University of Minnesota Press, [1970] 2003). See, for example, Buckley and Strauss, 'With, against and beyond Lefebvre'; Pinder, D., 'Reconstituting the Possible: Lefebvre, Utopia and the Urban Question,' *International Journal of Urban and Regional Research* 39, no. 1 (2015): 28–45; Stanek, L., *Henri Lefebvre on Space: Architecture, Urban Research, and the Production of Theory* (Minneapolis: University of Minnesota Press, 2013); Merrifield, *The New Urban Question.* Along with a host of other key voices in the radical urban spatial tradition, Lefebvre argued that if we were concerned with understanding how space is produced, then we need to attend it how it is divided, carved-up, controlled, and commodified. It is a position that has held a commanding influence over how urbanists think and research the city. See, for example, Harvey, *Social Justice in the City;* Smith, *The New Urban Frontier;* Massey, D., *Spatial Divisions of Labour: Social Structures and the Geography of Production* (London: Macmillan, 1984). In *The Production of Space,* for instance, Lefebvre describes space as "homogenous yet at the same time broken up into fragments" (342). Across the text, he describes spatial fragments as the spatial products of capitalist production. This includes a wide variety of physical and imaginative geographies that are divided, carved-up, and controlled, including spaces "subdivided for the purposes of buying and selling," buildings, bodies, subjects, images, practices, and discourses (96–97, 131, 307, 310, 365). Lefebvre argued that to research those fragments on their own terms—to become concerned with "things in space"—would be "deceptive" (37, 96). Instead, critical research must "rip aside appearances," focus on the "production of space," and show how spatial fragments are positioned as part of processes of fragmentation across global capitalist space (92, 37). At the same time, Lefebvre was attentive to how the products of dominant processes might act in the world. Michelle Buckley and Kendra Strauss, for example, engage with what Lefebvre called "the residual": "Far from being the conceptual debris of more important matters, to Lefebvre, the production of residues are of fundamental epistemological, theoretical and political importance" ('With, against and beyond Lefebvre,' 626). For instance, in volume 1 of Lefebvre's *Everyday Life,* the residual is that which is left over, and which can feed into revolutionary potential.

35. Merrifield, *The New Urban Question;* Sassen, S., *Expulsions: Brutality and Complexity in the Global Economy* (Cambridge, MA: Harvard University Press, 2014).

36. Stein, S., *Capital City: Gentrification and the Real Estate State* (London: Verso, 2019).

37. Doshi, S., 'The Politics of the Evicted: Redevelopment, Subjectivity, and Difference in Mumbai's Slum Frontier,' *Antipode* 45, no. 4 (2013): 844–65; Weinstein, L., 'Mumbai's Development Mafias: Globalization, Organized Crime and Land Development,' *International Journal of Urban and Regional Research* 32, no. 1 (2008): 22–39; Weinstein, L., *The Durable Slum: Dharavi and the Right to Stay Put in Globalizing Mumbai* (Minneapolis: University of Minnesota Press, 2013).

38. Merrifield, *The New Urban Question,* 111. See also Gibbs, D., Krueger, R., and MacLeod, G., 'Grappling with Smart City Politics in an Era of Market Triumphalism,' *Urban Studies* 50, no. 11 (2013): 2151–57.

39. Cohen, D.A., 'Seize the Hamptons,' *Jacobin,* November 2014, www.jacobinmag.com/2014/10/seize-the-hamptons/(accessed August 24, 2019).

40. Indorewala, H., 'Indian Cities Have Been Reduced to Just Real Estate," *The Wire,* October 9, 2019, https://thewire.in/urban/our-cities-prior-itise-real-estate-over-ecological-sustain-ability (accessed December 6, 2020).

41. Williams, R., *Why Cities Look the Way They Do* (Cambridge: Polity, 2019), 116.

42. Buckley and Strauss, 'With, against and beyond Lefebvre'; Caldeira, T., 'Peripheral Urbanization'; Parnell, S., and Pieterse, E., 'The "Right to the City": Institutional Imperatives of a Developmental State,' *International Journal of Urban and Regional Research* 34, no. 1 (2010): 146–62; Peake, L., 'The Twenty-First Century Quest for Feminism and the Global Urban,' *International Journal of Urban and Regional Research* 40, no. 1 (2016): 219–27; Perlman, *Favela.*

43. Schindler, 'Towards a Paradigm of Southern Urbanism'; Zeiderman, 'Beyond the Enclave of Urban Theory.'

44. Atlas of Urban Expansion, *Kampala,* 2019, www.atlasofurbanexpansion.org/cities/view/Kampala (accessed July 5, 2019). See also UN-Habitat, *Urban Profile of Kampala* (Nairobi: UN-Habitat, 2011).

45. Branch, A., and Mampilly, Z., *Africa Uprising: Popular Protest and Political Change* (London: Zed Books, 2015); Gore, C.D., and Muwanga, N.K., 'Decentralization Is Dead, Long Live Decentralization! Capital City Reform and Political Rights in Kampala, Uganda,' *International Journal of Urban and Regional Research* 38, no. 8 (2014): 2201–16; Goodfellow, T., 'The Institutionalisation of "Noise" and "Silence" in Urban Politics: Riots and Compliance in Uganda and Rwanda,' *Oxford Development Studies* 41, no. 4 (2013): 436–54.

46. Lindel, I., and Ampaire, C., 'The Untamed Politics of Urban Informality: "Gray Space" and Struggles for Recognition in an African City,' *Theoretical Inquiries in Law* 17 (2016): 257–82; Kimar, W., 'On Raids and Connecting Favela Resistances in Kenya and Brazil,' *LSE,* 2014, http://blogs.lse.ac.uk/favelasatlse/ (accessed August 2, 2019).

47. Branch and Mampilly, *Africa Uprising,* 146

48. Uganda Bureau of Statistics, *ILRI Poverty Report 2007,* www.ubos.org/onlinefiles/uploads/ubos/pdf%20documents/ILRI%20Poverty%20Report%202007.pdf.

49. Kareem, B., and Lwasa, S., 'From Dependency to Interdependencies: The Emergence of a Socially Rooted but Commercial Waste Sector in Kampala City, Uganda,' *African Journal of Environmental Science and Technology* 5, no. 2 (2011): 136–42.

50. Wallman, S., *Kampala Women Getting By: Well-Being in the Time of AIDS* (Athens: Ohio University Press, 1996), 25.

51. Wallman, *Kampala Women Getting By,* 25–26, 27.

52. Wallman, *Kampala Women Getting By,* 98.

53. Branch and Mampilly, *Africa Uprising.*

54. Pfeiffer, J., and Chapman, R., 'Anthropological Perspectives on Structural Adjustment and Public Health,' *Annual Review of Anthropology* 39 (2010): 149–65; Wallman, *Kampala Women Getting By.*

55. Uganda Ministry of Health, *The HIV and AIDS Uganda Country Progress Report, 2014* (Kampala: Government of Uganda, Ministry of Health, 2014).

56. Fredericks, *Garbage Citizenship,* 150.

57. Monteith, W., and Lwasa, S., 'The Participation of Urban Displaced Populations in (In)Formal Markets: Contrasting Experiences in Kampala, Uganda,' *Environment and Urbanization* 29, no. 2 (2016): 383–402 at 392.

58. Angel, S., Blei, A. M., Parent, J., Lamson-Hall, P., and Galarza-Sanchez, N., with Civco, D. L., Qian Lei, R., and Thom, K., *Atlas of Urban Expansion—2016 Edition, Volume 1: Areas and Densities,* 2016, www.atlasofurban-expansion.org (accessed November 15, 2019).

59. Angel, S., Liu, Y., Blei, A. M., Lamson-Hall, P. Galarza-Sanchez, N., and Arango-Franco, S., *The New Urban Peripheries, 1990–2014: Selected Findings from a Global Sample of Cities,* Working Paper 40, June 2018, https://marron-institute.nyu.edu/uploads/content/New_Urban_Peripheries_Working_Paper.pdf (accessed November 15, 2019).

60. United Nations, *Sustainable Development Goals: Goal 11—Sustainable Cities and Communities,* undated, www.un.org/sustainabledevelopment/cities/ (accessed May 1, 2019); Keil, R., *Suburban Planet* (Cambridge: Polity, 2018).

61. Keil, R., 'Extended Urbanization, "Disjunct Fragments" and Global Suburbanisms,' *Environment and Planning D: Society and Space* 36, no. 3 (2018), 494–511.

62. World Resources Institute, *Upward and Outward Growth: Managing Urban Expansion for More Equitable Cities in the Global South* (Washington, DC: World Resources Institute, 2019).

63. See, for example, Brenner, N., and Schmid, C., 'Towards a New Epistemology of the Urban?' *City* 19, nos. 2–3 (2015): 151–82. See also Brenner, N., 'Theses on Urbanization.' *Public Culture* 25, no. 1 (2013): 85–114; Brenner, N., 'Debating Planetary Urbanization: For an Engaged Pluralism,' *Environment and Planning D: Society and Space* 36, no. 3 (2018): 570–90.

64. Murali et al., *10 Things to Know.*

65. Monstadt, J., and Schramm, S., 'Toward the Networked City? Translating Technological Ideals and Planning Models in Water and Sanitation Systems in Dar es Salaam,' *International Journal of Urban and Regional Research* 41, no. 4 (2017): 104–25.

66. Hasan, A., 'Karachi, Informal Settlements and COVID-19,' *International Institute for Environment and Development,* guest blog, May 6, 2020, www.iied.org/karachi-informal-settlements-covid-19 (accessed October 7, 2020); Rahman, P., 'Exploring Urban Resilience: Violence and Infrastructure Provision in Katachi,' master's thesis, Massachusetts Institute of Technology, Boston, 2012.

67. Pacheco-Vega, R., 'Urban Wastewater Governance in Latin America: Panorama and Reflections for a Research Agenda,' in *Water and Cities in Latin America: Challenges for Sustainable Development,* ed. I. Aguilar-Barajas, J. Mahlknecht, J. Kaledin, J. Kjellen, and A. Meija-Betancourt (London: Routledge, 2015), 102–16.

68. Pacheco-Vega, 'Urban Wastewater.'

69. McFarlane, C., Desai, R., and Graham, S., 'Informal Urban Sanitation: Everyday Life, Comparison and Poverty,' *Annals of the Association of American Geographers* 104 (2014): 989–1011; Pacheco-Vega, 'Urban Wastewater.'

70. See Moser, *Ordinary Families, Extraordinary Lives;* Mitlin, D., and Satterthwaite, D., *Urban Poverty in the Global South: Scale and Nature* (London: Routledge, 2013); Mayne, A., *Slums: The History of Global Injustice* (London: Reaktion Books, 2017); Peake, 'The Twenty-First Century Quest for Feminism and the Global Urban.'

71. See, for example, Simone, 'Emergency Democracy and the "Governing Composite"'; Simone, A., 'The Politics of the Possible: Making Urban Life in Phnom Penh,' *Singapore Journal of Tropical Geography* 29, no. 2 (2008): 186–204; Simone, A., *City Life from Jakarta to Dakar: Movements at the Crossroads* (Routledge: London, 2009).

72. Rao, V., 'Infra-City: Speculations on Flux and History in Infrastructure-Making,' in *Infrastructural Lives: Urban Infrastructure in Context,* ed. S. Graham and C. McFarlane (London: Routledge-Earthscan, 2015), 39–58. On water in Mumbai, see Björkman, *Pipe Politics, Contested Waters;* Anand, N., *Hydraulic City: Water and the Infrastructures of Citizenship in Mumbai* (Durham, NC: Duke University Press, 2017).

73. Rao, V., 'Proximate Distances: The Phenomenology of Density in Mumbai,' *Built Environment* 33, no. 2 (2007): 227–48, on 239.

74. Simone, A., *Improvised Lives: Rhythms of Endurance in an Urban South* (Cambridge: Polity Press, 2018).

75. Harris, A., 'Concrete Geographies: Assembling Global Mumbai through Transport Infrastructure,' *City* 17, no. 3 (2013): 343–60; McFarlane, C. 'The Geographies of Urban Density: Topology, Politics and the City,' *Progress in Human Geography,* 40 (2016): 629–48.

76. See Bhan, G., *In the Public's Interest: Eviction, Citizenship and Inequality in Contemporary Delhi* (Athens: University of Georgia Press, 2016); Ghertner, A., 'Rule by Aesthetics: World-Class City Making in Delhi,' in Ray and Ong, *Worlding Cities;* Goldman, M., 'Speculating on the Next World City,' in Ray and Ong, *Worlding Cities.*

77. Amin, A., 'Lively Infrastructure,' *Theory, Culture and Society* 31, nos. 7–8 (2014): 138.

78. Graham and Marvin, *Splintering Urbanism;* Easterling, K., *Extrastate-craft: The Power of Infrastructure Space* (London: Verso, 2016); Marvin, S., Luque-Ayala, A., and McFarlane, C., eds., *Smart Urbanism: Utopian Vision or False Dawn?* (London: Routledge, 2015); Bulkeley, *Accomplishing Climate Governance;* Bulkeley, H., 'Navigating Climate's Human Geographies: Exploring the Whereabouts of Climate Politics,' *Dialogues in Human Geography* 9 no. 3 (2019): 3–17; Gandy, M., *The Fabric of Space: Water, Modernity, and the Urban Imagination* (Cambridge, MA: MIT Press, 2014); Larkin, B., *Signal and Noise: Media, Infrastructure, and Urban Culture in Nigeria* (Durham, NC: Duke University Press, 2008); Larkin, B., 'The Politics and Poetics of Infrastructure,' *Annual Review of Anthropology* 42 (2013): 327–43; Ranganathan, M., 'Storm Drains as Assemblages: The Political Ecology of Flood Risk in Post-Colonial Bangalore,' *Antipode* 47, no. 5 (2015): 1300–1320; Ranganathan, M., 'Beyond "Third World" Comparisons: America's Geography of Water, Race, and Poverty,' *International Journal of Urban and Regional Research,* 2018, www.ijurr.org/spotlight-on-overview/parched-cities-parched-citizens/beyond-third-world-comparisons/.

79. De Boeck, F., 'Divining the City: Rhythm, Amalgamation and Knotting as Forms of Urbanity,' *Social Dynamics* 41, no. 1 (2015): 1–12; McFarlane et al., 'Informal Urban Sanitation'; Silver, 'Incremental Infrastructures.'

80. Simone, *Improvised Lives,* 18.

81. Simone, A., 'People as Infrastructure: Intersecting Fragments in Johannesburg,' *Public Culture* 16, no. 3 (2004): 407–29.

82. Klinenberg, E., *Palaces for the People: How to Build a More Equal and United Society* (London: The Bodley Head, 2018); Putnam, R.D., *Bowling Alone: The Collapse and Revival of American Community* (New York: Simon and Schuster, 2001).

83. Moser, *Ordinary Families;* Bebbington, A., 'Capitals and Capabilities: A Framework for Analysing Peasant Viability, Rural Livelihoods and Poverty,' *World Development* 27, no. 12 (1999): 2021–44; Banks, N., 'Livelihood Limitations: The Political Economy of Urban Poverty in Dhaka, Bangladesh,' *Development and Change* 47, no. 2 (2015): 266–92; Banks, N., and Sulaiman, M., *Problem or Promise? Harnessing Youth Potential in Uganda,* Youthwatch, 2012, www.research.manchester.ac.uk/portal/files/33714156/full_text.pdf (accessed August 1, 2016); Wilke, J., *Understanding the Asset-Based Approach to Community Development,* 2006, working chapter, www.neighboraustin.com/PDF/Understanding%20the%20Asset-based%20Approach%20to%20Community%20%20Development.pdf (accessed August 2, 2019).

84. Lwasa, S., 'Sustainable Urban Development: Managing City Development in Uganda,' *Global Urbanization* (2011): 276–93.

85. Mann, D., and Andabati, D., *The Informal Settlement of Namuwongo: A Baseline Survey for the PECTIS Project,* May 2014, http://suda-africa.org/wp-content/uploads/2014/05/PECTIS_Baseline-Survey-Report_Validation-Draft_reduced.pdf (accessed September 14, 2018); Brown, S.T., 'Kampala's Sanitary Regime: Whose Toilet Is It Anyway?' in *Infrastructural Lives: Urban Infrastructure in Context,* ed. S. Graham and C. McFarlane (London: Routledge

-Earthscan, 2015), 153–73; McFarlane, C., and Silver, J., 'Navigating the City: Dialectics of Everyday Urbanism,' *Transactions of the Institute for British Geographers* 42, no. 3 (2017): 458–71; Lombard, M., 'Discursive Constructions of Low-Income Neighbourhoods,' *Geography Compass* 9 (2015): 648–59.

86. Kagenda, 'KCCA's Night Raiders.'

87. Wiig, A., and Silver, J., 'Turbulent Presents, Precarious Futures: Urbanization and the Deployment of Global Infrastructure,' *Regional Studies* 53, no. 6 (2019): 912–23.

88. Brown, 'Kampala's Sanitation Regime.'

89. We worked with a range of people who reflected some of the diversity of the neighborhood: two widowed women with children to support (one younger and one older, with grandchildren); one young man in his late teens who had lost his parents and depended on extended family; two men in their late thirties who had young families but different levels of income security; and one older man who was economically the most secure and politically well-connected. This is not a "representative sample" of this incredibly diverse neighborhood, and caution needs to be used in building generalizations about life in Namuwongo from a small group. Nonetheless, the stories that emerge reveal how different residents mobilize and use practices that enter into the making of everyday life in the area.

Our initial interviewing was extended into mobile methods through "follow along participant observation" (FAPO). This included trips with residents as they navigated the city, observing from a distance or sometimes in close proximity how they negotiated a series of everyday topographies, and how those experiences were shaped in part through issues ranging from family crises to traffic jams, dealing with the authorities, and income generation. We worked with local photographer Josephine Namukisa, who provided a visual documentation of the navigations that served both as a means of pinpointing key moments, encounters, and other significant processes, and as a resource that then leveraged into different conversations with the residents about ways of portraying their and other urban navigations. We then brought the residents into focus groups and workshops that discussed, debated, and shared the initial findings. FAPOs are a particularly useful means for better understanding the intersections between lived densities and their interconnections with fragments in a daily basis.

Our mixed-method approach—interviews, focus groups, workshops, follow-along, and an exhibition (which I discuss later in the book)—echoes approaches aimed at building insight through different forms of data on precarious lives in other cities. See, for example, Gough, K., Chigunta, F., and Langevang, T., 'Expanding the Scales and Domains of (In)security: Youth Employment in Urban Zambia,' *Environment and Planning A* 48, no. 2 (2016): 348–66; Vigh, H., 'Motion Squared: A Second Look at the Concept of Social Navigation,' *Anthropological Theory* 9, no.4 (2009): 419–38. This includes the use of "walkabout" methodologies: Katri Gadd's work with street children in Pelotas, Brazil, which draws on actor-network theory (Gadd, K.J., 'Street Children's Lives and Actor-Networks,' *Children's Geographies* 14, no. 3 [2016]: 295–309); Hägerstrand's time geography, to understand the encounters, spaces, and networks through which street children, over a seven-year period, differently navigated the challenges and possibilities of urban life (Hägerstrand, T., 'Time-Geography: Focus on Corporeality of Man, Society and Environment,' in *The Science and Praxis of Complexity,* ed. S. Aida [Tokyo: United Nations University, 1985]: 193–216); Latour, B., *Reassembling the Social: An Introduction to Actor-Network-Theory* (Oxford: Oxford University Press, 2005). Others draw attention to the "tactics of social navigation" for youth, and consider how mobility can be brought explicitly to the fore of methodological considerations. See, for instance, Jones, P., and Evans, J., 'Rescue Geography: Place-making, Affect and Regeneration,' *Urban Studies* 49 (2012): 2315–30.

90. Martin, A., Myers, N., and Viseu, A., 'The Politics of Care in Technoscience,' *Social Studies of Science* 45, no. 5 (2015): 625–41.

91. Simone, *Improvised Lives,* 20.

92. Gill, L., *Teetering on the Rim: Global Restructuring, Daily Life, and the Armed Retreat of the Bolivian State* (New York: Columbia University Press, 2000); Moser, C., *Confronting Crisis: A Comparative Study of Household Responses to Poverty and Vulnerability in Four Poor Urban Communities* (Washington, DC: World Bank, 1996).

93. Moser, *Ordinary Families.*

94. Porter, G., ' "I think a woman who travels a lot is befriending other men and that's why she travels": Mobility Constraints and Their Implications for Rural Women and Girl Children in Sub-Saharan Africa,' *Gender, Place and Culture* 18, no. 1 (2011): 65–81; Porter, G., 'Mobilities in Rural Africa: New Connections, New Challenges,' *Annals of the Association of American Geographers* 106, no. 2 (2016): 434–41.

95. Day, C., and Evans, R., 'Managing Caring Responsibilities, Change and Transitions in Young People's Family Lives in Zambia,' *Journal of Comparative Family Studies* 46, no. 1 (2015): 137–52.

96. Honwana, A., *Time of Youth: Work, Social Change, and Politics in Africa* (West Hartford, CT: Kumarian Press, 2012); Dyson, J., *Working Childhoods: Youth, Agency and the Environment in India* (Cambridge: Cambridge University Press, 2014); Tranberg-Hansen, K., 'Getting Stuck in the Compound: Some Odds against Social Adulthood in Lusaka, Zambia,' *Africa Today* 51 (2005): 2–16; Jeffrey, C., *Timepass: Youth, Class, and the Politics of Waiting in India* Stanford, CA: Stanford University Press, 2010).

97. Uganda Country Progress Report, *HIV and AIDS,* Ministry of Health, Government of Uganda, Kampala, 2014.

98. Banks and Sulaiman, *Problem or Promise?* See also De Boeck, F., and Honwana, A., 'Children and Youth in Africa: Agency, Identity and Place,' in *Makers and Breakers: Children and Youth in Postcolonial Africa,* ed. A. Honwana and F. De Boeck (Oxford: James Currey, 2005).

99. Day and Evans, 'Managing Caring Responsibilities.'

KNOWING FRAGMENTS

Epigraph: Most, G. 'On Fragments,' in *The Fragment: An Incomplete History,* ed. W. Tronzo (Los Angeles: Getty Research Institute, 2009), 18.

1. Lefebvre, *The Production of Space.*

2. Simone, *Improvised Lives*, 10. See also Lancione, 'Assemblages of Care'; Lancione, *Rethinking Life at the Margins;* Srivastava, S., *Entangled Urbanism: Slum, Gated Community and Shopping Mall in Delhi and Gurgaon* (Delhi: Oxford University Press, 2015); Thieme, T., 'Navigating and Negotiating Ethnographies of Urban Hustle in Nairobi Slums,' *City* 21, no. 2 (2017): 219–31.

3. Lichtenstein, J., 'The Fragment: Elements of a Definition,' in *The Fragment: An Incomplete History,* ed. W. Tronzo (Los Angeles: Getty Research Institute, 2009), 115–29.

4. Adorno, T., *Minima Moralia: Reflections from a Damaged Life* (London: Verso, [1951] 2005); Balfour, I. 'The Whole Is the Untrue: On the Necessity of the Fragment (after Adorno),' in *The Fragment: An Incomplete History,* ed. W. Tronzo (Los Angeles: Getty Research Institute, 2009), 82–91, on 88.

5. Adorno, T., *Lectures on Negative Dialectics: Fragments of a Lecture Course, 1965/66,* ed. R. Tiedemann, trans. R. Livingstone (Cambridge: Polity Press, 2008).

6. Adorno, *Lectures on Negative Dialectics,* 69. And see Adorno, T., *Against Epistemology: A Metacritique* (Oxford: Wiley-Blackwell, 2013).

7. Balfour, 'The Whole Is the Untrue.'

8. Tiedemann, R., 'Additional Notes,' in Adorno, *Lectures on Negative Dialectics,* 247.

9. Tiedemann, 'Additional Notes,' 248.

10. Adorno, *Lectures on Negative Dialectics,* 72, 54.

11. This process led to the collapse of what Graham and Marvin called the "modernist infrastructural ideal"—standardized, monopolized, and integrated infrastructures for all—and, in the process, intensified inequalities across urban space. See Graham, S., and McFarlane, C., eds., *Infrastructural Lives: Urban Infrastructure in Context* (London: Routledge-Earthscan, 2015); Monstadt and Schramm, 'Toward the Networked City?'

12. On shards, see Mohammed, R., and Sidaway, J., 'Shards and Stages: Migrant Lives, Power, and Space Viewed from Doha, Qatar,' *Annals of the Association of American Geographers* 106, no. 6 (2016): 1397–417.

13. Chakrabarty, D., *Habitations of Modernity: Essays in the Wake of the Subaltern Studies* (Chicago: University of Chicago Press, 2002).

14. Chakrabarty, D., 'Marxism after Marx: History, Subalternity and Difference,' in *Marxism beyond Marxism,* ed. S. Makdisi, C. Casarino, and R. E. Karle (New York: Routledge, 1996), 60.

15. Chakrabarty, 'Marxism after Marx.' See also Derrida, J., *Positions,* trans. A. Bass (Chicago: Chicago University Press, 1981).

16. Napolitano, V., 'Anthropology and Traces,' *Anthropological Theory* 15, no. 1 (2014): 47–67.

17. Pandey, G., *Routine Violence: Nations, Fragments, Histories* (Stanford, CA: Stanford University Press, 2006), 66–67.

18. Smith, J.H., 'Relics: An Evolving Tradition in Latin Christianity,' in *Saints and Sacred Matter: The Cult of Relics in Byzantium and Beyond,* ed. C. Hahn and H. A. Klein, Series: Dumbarton Oaks Symposia and Colloquia (Cambridge, MA: Harvard University Press, 2015), 41–60, on 60.

19. Klein, H.A., 'Sacred Things and Holy Bodies: Collecting Relics from Late Antiquity to the Early Renaissance,' in *Treasures of Heaven: Saints, Relics, and Devotion in Medieval Europe*, ed. M. Bagnoli, H.A. Klein, G. Mann, and J. Robinson (New Haven, CT: Yale University Press, 2010).

20. Lichtenstein, 'The Fragment,' in Tronzo, *The Fragment*, 120.

21. Chapman, J., and Gaydarska, B., *Parts and Wholes: Fragmentation in Prehistoric Context* (Oxford: Oxbow Books, 2007).

22. Goldschmidt, N., ' "Orts, Scraps, and Fragments": Translation, Non-Translation, and the Fragments of Ancient Greece,' in *Modernism and Non-Translation*, ed. J. Harding and J. Nash (Oxford: Oxford University Press, 2019), 49–66.

23. Goldschmidt, ' "Orts, Scraps, and Fragments," ' 56.

24. Most, G., 'On Fragments,' in Tronzo, *The Fragment*.

25. Most, 'On Fragments.'

26. Tronzo, *The Fragment*.

27. Most, 'On Fragments,' in Tronzo, *The Fragment*, 18.

28. Goldschmidt, ' "Orts, Scraps, and Fragments," ' 66.

29. Leshem, N., *Life after Ruin: The Struggles over Israel's Depopulated Arab Spaces* (Cambridge: Cambridge University Press, 2016), 70.

30. Pamuk, O., *Istanbul: Memories and the City* (London: Faber and Faber, 2006), 231.

31. Edensor, T., 'Entangled Agencies, Material Networks and Repair in a Building Assemblage: The Mutable Stone of St Ann's Church, Manchester,' *Transactions of the Institute of British Geographers* 36 (2011): 238–52, on 250.

32. See, for example, Jacobs, J., *The Death and Life of Great American Cities* (London: Jonathan Cape, 1961).

33. Pacione, M. 'Housing Policies in Glasgow since 1880,' *Geographical Review* 69, no. 4 (1979): 395–412, on 402.

34. Johnstone, C., 'Housing and Class Struggles in Post-war Glasgow,' in *Class Struggle and Social Welfare*, ed. M. Lavalette and G. Mooney (London: Routledge, 2000).

35. Simone, 'Emergency Democracy and the "Governing Composite," ' 30.

36. Amin and Thrift, *Seeing Like a City*, 167; Kishik, D., *The Manhattan Project: A Theory of the City* (Stanford, CA: Stanford University Press, 2015).

37. Subaltern studies, like urban studies, is a theoretically diverse set of debates; for a good overview, see Chaturvedi, V., ed., *Mapping Subaltern Studies and the Postcolonial* (London: Verso, 2012). Indeed, the lack of any clear "subaltern theory," as Vivek Chibber among others have argued, has often been viewed as a weakness in prominent critiques of the literature. See Chibber, V., *Postcolonial Theory and the Specter of Capital* (London: Verso, 2013). While subaltern studies has always been focused on some key categories—such as the problem of how to identify and understand different forms of agency, subject position, and hegemony historically—theoretically this body of work increasingly diversified over time, taking it beyond its Gramscian and economic focus to include various strands of poststructuralist and cultural theory, in some cases as an explicitly Marxist project and in others as a decisive break from Marxism.

This theoretical multiplicity echoes the proliferation of approaches in urban studies, and has itself shaped the patchwork takeup of subaltern studies in urban studies research, in which the key influences have probably been Dipesh Chakrabarty's writings on provincialization, Partha Chatterjee's writings on political society, and Gayatri Spivak's conception of the subaltern.

The influence of subaltern studies on urban studies has taken two broad forms. First, as part of a wider impact of postcolonial thought and imperatives on research. See, for example, Bunnell, T., and Maringanti, A., 'Practising Urban Regional Research beyond Metrocentricity,' *International Journal of Urban and Regional Research* 34 (2010): 415–20; Robinson, J., *Ordinary Cities: Between Modernity and Development* (London: Routledge, 2006); Sidaway, J. D., Woon, C. Y., and Jacobs, J. M., 'Planetary Postcolonialism,' *Singapore Journal of Tropical Geography* 35, no. 1 (2014): 4–21. Second, as a more specific attempt to work with particular subaltern studies theorists or conceptualizations. Here, see Chattopadhyay, S., *Unlearning the City: Infrastructure in a New Optical Field* (Minneapolis: University of Minnesota Press, 2012); Gidwani, V., 'Capitalism's Anxious Whole: Fear, Capture and Escape in the *Grundrisse*,' *Antipode* 40, no. 5 (2008): 857–78; Gidwani, V., 'Subalternity,' in *International Encyclopedia of Human Geography,* ed. R. Kitchin and N. Thrift (London: Elsevier, 2009); Gidwani, V., 'Six Theses on Waste, Value and Commons,' *Social and Cultural Geography* 14, no. 7 (2013): 773–83; Roy, A., 'Slumdog Cities: Rethinking Subaltern Urbanism,' *International Journal of Urban and Regional Research* 35 (2011): 223–38. Three uses stand out: subaltern as a relation to "popular" political struggle; subaltern as simultaneously an epistemology of the urban subject and ethical challenge of representation; and subaltern as a name for the limits of urban theory rather than spaces of urban marginality alone.

For Swati Chattopadhyay, in her reconceptualization of infrastructure in relation to contemporary urbanism in India, subaltern practices exist on the "edges of visibility," beyond definition and representation and in excess of authority, but can become "popular" and visible to state and capital as they become agents of social change (*Unlearning the City,* 251–52). She draws on a rich array of routes through which this might take place, from familiar cultural practices like cricket and puja festivals to more explicitly political cultural acts like political wall writing or some forms of vehicular art. These practices can take ordinary spaces such as streets, neighborhoods, walls, or trucks and turn them, temporarily, into what she calls "spatial fragments" that belong "neither to the everyday nor to the exceptional . . . [they are] created out of a series of conjunctures, of bodies and objects, movements and views, noise and warmth, walls and roads, events and memories" (119). For Chattopadhyay, in the spaces and switches between subaltern and popular, of shifting rhythms, uses, and densities in urban space, lie a reconceptualization of infrastructure and a challenge to how urban theory might "unlearn the city" (252).

Vinay Gidwani has reflected on the appeal of "subaltern" in his work, and usefully identifies two senses that are deeply entwined: epistemological and ethical. Epistemologically, his work has examined how the subaltern subject, for example in relation to his work on urban waste and livelihoods, is both subjected to and subject of. See, for example, cowritten pieces by him on waste, livelihood, exploitation, and capital, including Gidwani, V., and Reddy, R. N., 'The Afterlives of Waste: Notes from India for a Minor History of Capitalist Surplus,' *Antipode* 43, no. 4 (2011): 1625–58, and Gidwani and Maringanti, 'The Waste-Value Dialectic.' Ethically—and here Gidwani chimes with a wider sense in which subaltern debates have impacted methodological and representational concerns in urban studies—Spivak's argument that to confront the subaltern is both to represent others and to represent ourselves is vital. See also Jazeel, T., 'Singularity: A Manifesto for Incomparable Geographies,' *Singapore Journal of Tropical Geography* 40, no. 1 (2018): 5–21; Jazeel, T., 'Subaltern Geographies: Geographical Knowledge and Postcolonial Strategy,' *Singapore Journal of Tropical Geography* 35, no. 1 (2014): 88–103; Jazeel, T., and Legg, S., 'Introducing Subaltern Geographies,' in *Subaltern Geographies: Subaltern Studies, Space, and the Geographical Imagination,* ed. T. Jazeel and S. Legg (Athens: University of Georgia Press, 2019); Jazeel, T., and McFarlane, C., 'The Limits of Responsibility: A Postcolonial Politics of Academic Knowledge Production,' *Transactions of the Institute of British Geographers* 35, no. 1 (2010): 109–24.

Ananya Roy, also drawing on Spivak, makes a different argument. While Roy is sympathetic to research that locates the subaltern in the "slum" of the megacity, she looks to shift subaltern urbanism beyond forms of thinking that "assign unique political agency to the mass of urban subalterns" ('Slumdog Cities,' 235). The subaltern, she argues, is not located in any pre-given territory, nor simply to be found in politically subversive practices. Writing against what she calls "ontological and topological readings of the subaltern," for Roy the subaltern is a more generalized category that "marks the limits of archival and ethnographic recognition" (231). Roy seeks to expand the realm of what she calls "subaltern urbanism" by, for example, examining how practices too often attributed to the "slum" alone, such as informal planning, are also to be found in state processes. We can think here too of important efforts to examine the connections and disconnections between the "slum" and more elite urbanisms in the same city, such as Sanjay Srivastava's *Entangled Modernities,* which brings informal neighborhoods into a shared conceptual and methodological space with the gated community and the shopping mall in his ethnography of Delhi. See Srivastava, *Entangled Urbanism;* Ghertner, A., 'Rule by Aesthetics'; Ghertner, A., 'When Is the State? Topology, Temporality, and the Navigation of Everyday State Space in Delhi,' *Annals of the American Association of Geographers* 107, no. 3 (2017): 731–50; Björkman, L., *Pipe Politics, Contested Waters.*

It is important to also note, however, the use of the term "subaltern urbanization" as a broad descriptor of neglected smaller urban formations which often fall out of focus in accounts that link the megacity to patterns of urbanization and urban life. For example, Partha Mukhopadhyaya et al. use "subaltern urbanization" to focus on the mix of relatively autonomous and distinctive smaller urban forms in India—"spaces outside the metropolitan shadow"—which need to be understood not simply as smaller versions of larger cities but on their own terms (29). These are patterns of urbanization found, for instance, along transit corridors extending beyond cities, sometimes connected to particular industrial sectors and networks. See Mukhopadhyay, P., Zerha, M-H., and Denis, E., 'Subaltern Urbanisation Revisited,' in *The Contemporary Urban*

Conundrum, ed. S. Patel and O. Goyal, IIC Quarterly, Winter–Spring (Delhi: Ravinder Datta for India International Centre, 2016), 28–44; Kundu, A., 'Rurbanisation: An Alternative Development Paradigm,' in Patel and Goyal, *The Contemporary Urban Conundrum*, 17–27; Roy, A., 'What Is Urban about Critical Urban Theory?' *Urban Geography* 37 (2015): 1–14.

As writing in this area shows, these spaces, often dense and underprovided, can have an ambivalent status between rural and urban, and if classified as "villages" are then eligible for different state service provisions than if they are "urban." There are costs either way—for instance, middle classes may seek urban status for the investment it might bring, while landed elites may worry about losing control over land speculation if an area is classified as urban, and poorer groups are sometimes concerned about the consequences of becoming urban for trading or residency. The larger point here is that while the strategy of delinking the subaltern from geographical forms is an important conceptual and political move, this does not mean that there isn't value in careful attempts to identify often neglected forms of urbanization and urban life through the category of the subaltern.

These three senses of the subaltern in urban studies—as a political struggle, as an epistemic and ethical challenge of researching urban space and subjects, and as a limit point not just of a group or a space but of urban theory more generally—mirror wider debates in the social sciences and humanities around how to define, conceptualize, research, and think politically about what has long been a slippery and daunting concept. Each of these accounts works with distinct definitions of the subaltern, but at least two cross-cutting issues emerge: first, a concern with the importance of representation, including who does the representation as much as who/what is being represented; and second, a concern with what those representations might mean for how we understand contemporary urbanism. There has, however, been less consideration of what the notion of the "fragment" in subaltern studies might mean for urban studies.

What I take from these accounts is less a concern with pinpointing the specificity of the subaltern, and more a challenge for how we encounter and conceptualize urban multiplicity, a theme that has run through this book. This imagination is alert to the challenge of the subaltern—i.e., to that which is barely visible, and which exists beyond dominant forms of knowing urbanism—but it seeks a wider canvas that exceeds the subaltern itself. It takes the concern with how we represent to include marginalized urban knowledges—knowledges that are themselves not necessarily subaltern but are nonetheless undervalued in the potentials they bring to mainstream urban theory.

38. Chatterjee, P., *The Nation and Its Fragments: Colonial and Postcolonial Histories* (Princeton, NJ: Princeton University Press, 1993).

39. Pandey, *Routine Violence*.

40. Pandey, G., 'In Defence of the Fragment: Writing about Hindu-Muslim Riots in India Today,' *Economic and Political Weekly*, March 1991, 559.

41. Chakrabarty, *Habitations of Modernity*.

42. Gramsci, A., *Selections from Prison Notebooks* (London: Lawrence and Wishart, 1971).

43. Chakrabarty, *Habitations of Modernity*, 34–35.

44. Chakrabarty, *Habitations of Modernity*, 274.

45. Chakrabarty, *Habitations of Modernity*.

46. Chakrabarty, *Habitations of Modernity*, 275.

47. Prakash, G., *Bonded Histories: Genealogies of Labour Servitude in Colonial India* (Cambridge: Cambridge University Press, 1990).

48. Jazeel, 'Singularity.'

49. Jazeel, 'Singularity.'

50. Roy, 'Slumdog Cities,' 231.

51. See Anand, N., *Hydraulic City: Water and the Infrastructures of Citizenship in Mumbai* (Durham, NC: Duke University Press, 2017); Chattopadhyay, *Unlearning the City;* McFarlane, *Learning the City;* Graham and McFarlane, *Infrastructural Lives;* Kooy, M., and Bakker, K., 'Technologies of Government: Constituting Subjectivities, Spaces, and Infrastructures in Colonial and Contemporary Jakarta,' *International Journal of Urban and Regional Research* 32 (2008): 375–91.

52. Jazeel, 'Singularity.'

53. Adorno, *Lectures on Negative Dialectics*, 9.

54. Adorno, T., *Negative Dialectics*, trans. E. B. Ashton (London: Routledge, [1966] 1973); Adorno, *Minima Moralia*.

55. Adorno, *Lectures on Negative Dialectics*, 70.

56. Adorno, *Lectures on Negative Dialectics*, 29

57. Adorno, *Lectures on Negative Dialectics*, 36, 40.

WRITING IN FRAGMENTS

First epigraph: Kishik, D., *The Manhattan Project: A Theory of the City* (Stanford, CA: Stanford University Press, 2015), 216, 95.

Second epigraph: Deleuze, G., and Parnet, C., *Dialogues II,* rev. ed. (New York: Columbia University Press, [1977] 2002), 55.

1. Ferris, D., 'Review of Howard Eiland and Michael W. Jennings (2014) *Walter Benjamin: A Critical Life*, Cambridge, Mass.: Harvard University Press,' *Critical Inquiry* 42, no. 3 (2016): 76–77.

2. Buck-Morss, S., *The Dialectics of Seeing: Walter Benjamin and the Arcades Project* (Cambridge, MA: MIT Press, 1991), 18.

3. Chaudhuri, A., 'Introduction,' in Benjamin, *Walter Benjamin: One Way Street and Other Writings,* trans. J. A. Underwood (London: Penguin Books, [1928] 2009), xv.

4. Lichenstein, 'The Fragment,' in Tronzo, *The Fragment*, 125.

5. Benjamin, W., *The Arcades Project,* trans. H. Eiland and K. McLaughlin (Cambridge, MA: Harvard University Press, 2003), 368.

6. Arendt, H., 'Introduction: Walter Benjamin, 1892–1940,' in *Illuminations: Essays and Reflections,* ed. H. Arendt (New York: Schocken Books, [1968] 2007), 11.

7. Buck-Morss, *The Dialectics of Seeing,* 225; Cowan, B., 'Walter Benjamin's Theory of Allegory,' *New German Critique* 22 (Winter 1981): 109–22.

8. Eiland, H., and Jennings, M., *Walter Benjamin: A Critical Life* (Cambridge, MA: Harvard University Press, 2016), 18.

9. Lash, S., *Another Modernity: A Different Rationality* (Oxford: Wiley-Blackwell, 1999), 246, 325; Roy, A. 'The Blockade of the World-Class City: Dialectical Images of Indian Urbanism,' in *Worlding Cities: Asian Experiments and the Art of Being Global,* ed. A. Roy and A. Ong (Oxford: Wiley-Blackwell, 2011), 259–78.

10. Buck-Morss, *The Dialectics of Seeing.*

11. Benjamin, *The Arcades Project,* 462.

12. Buck-Morss, *The Dialectics of Seeing,* 338; see also Gregory, D., *Geographical Imaginations* (Oxford: Blackwell, 1994).

13. Letter written by Benjamin in 1927 and reprinted in Smith, G., ed., *Walter Benjamin: Moscow Diary,* trans. R. Sieburth (Cambridge, MA: Harvard University Press, 1986), 132–33.

14. Leslie, E., *Walter Benjamin* (London: Reaktion Books, 2007), 82.

15. Adorno, T., 'A Portrait of Walter Benjamin,' in Adorno, *Prisms,* trans. S. and S. Weber (Cambridge, MA: MIT Press, [1967] 1997), 240.

16. Benjamin, 'One Way Street,' in Benjamin, *Walter Benjamin,* 54.

17. Solnit, R., *Wanderlust: A History of Walking* (London: Verso, 2002), 197.

18. Solnit, *Wanderlust,* 198.

19. Leslie, *Walter Benjamin.*

20. Leslie, E., *Walter Benjamin: Overpowering Conformism* (London: Pluto Press, 2000), 67–68.

21. Comaroff and Comaroff, *Theory from the South,* 48–49.

22. Kishik, *The Manhattan Project,* 216, 95.

23. Kishik, *The Manhattan Project,* 62.

24. Kishik, *The Manhattan Project,* 11.

25. Kishik, *The Manhattan Project,* 67.

26. Merrifield, A., *Metromarxism: A Marxist Tale of the City* (London: Routledge, 2002), 67.

27. Massey, D., *For Space* London: Sage, 2005).

28. See, for example, Pred, A., *Recognising European Modernities: A Montage of the Present* (London: Routledge, 1995); Pred, A., *Even in Sweden: Racisms, Racialized Spaces, and the Popular Geographical Imagination* (Berkeley: University of California Press, 2000).

29. Gregory, *Geographical Imaginations,* 253.

30. Pred, *Recognising European Modernities,* 27. Copyright permission was given for the use of the brief extract from Allan Pred's *Recognising European Modernities.*

31. Jukes, P., *A Shout in the Street: An Excursion into the Modern City* (Los Angeles: University of California Press, 1991), 55.

32. Jukes, *A Shout in the Street,* 44.

33. Vladislavic, *Portrait with Keys,* 205.

34. Vladislavic, *Portrait with Keys,* 201.

35. Vladislavic, *Portrait with Keys,* 54.

36. Vladislavic, *Portrait with Keys,* 185.

37. Ruffato, L., *There Were Many Horses,* trans. A. Doyle (Seattle: Amazon Crossing, [2001] 2014).

38. Ruffato, *There Were Many Horses,* 99, 100–101.

39. Sinclair, I., *London Overground: A Day's Walk around the Ginger Line* (London: Penguin, 2015), 109, 117.

40. Sinclair, *London Overground,* 238.

41. Sinclair, *London Overground,* 118.

42. Sinclair, *London Overground,* 140, 142.

43. Sinclair, *London Overground,* 161.

44. Sinclair, *London Overground,* 224, 239.

45. Sinclair, *London Overground,* 235.

46. Sinclair, *London Overground,* 243–44.

47. To cite a few works examining the shaping and politics of the intimate: Peake, L., and Rieker, M., eds., *Rethinking Feminist Interventions into the Urban* (New York: Routledge, 2013); Mountz, A., and Hyndman, J., 'Feminist Approaches to the Global Intimate,' *Women's Studies Quarterly* 34, nos. 1–2 (2006): 446–63; Pratt, G., and Rosner, V., eds., *The Global and the Intimate: Feminism in Our Time* (New York: Columbia University Press, 2012); Katz, C., *Growing Up Global: Economic Restructuring and Children's Everyday Lives* (Minneapolis: University of Minnesota Press, 2004). See also Geraldine Pratt's reflections on the space of feminist, queer, and postcolonial theory in recent theoretical debate on the nature of the urban, and the special issue of which it is a part: Pratt, G., 'One Hand Clapping: Notes towards a Methodology for Debating Planetary Urbanization,' *Environment and Planning D: Society and Space* 36, no. 3 (2018): 563–69.

48. Moten, F., *Black and Blur (Consent Not to Being Single)* (Durham, NC: Duke University Press: 2017), vii.

49. Moten, *Black and Blur,* vii, xii.

50. Moten, *Black and Blur,* 132–33.

51. Moten, *Black and Blur,* 271.

52. Sirmans, F., 'In the Cipher: Basquait and Hip-Hop Culture,' in *Basquait,* ed. M. Mayer (New York: Brooklyn Museum, [2005] 2010), 91–128, on 92.

53. Sirmans, 'In the Cipher.'

54. Sirmans, 'In the Cipher,' 94, 93.

55. Parker, K., 'Basquait, Jean-Michel,' www.scholarblogs.emory.edu (accessed February 27, 2020).

56. Jones, K. 'Lost in Translation: Jean-Michel in the (Re)Mix,' in Mayer, *Basquait,* 163–79.

57. Berman, M., *All That Is Solid Melts into Air: The Experience of Modernity* (Verso: London, [1982] 2010), 17.

58. Adorno, *Prisms,* 240.

59. Marcus, G., preface for Benjamin, W., *One-Way Street,* trans. M. Jenning (Cambridge, MA: Harvard University Press, 2016), 2.

60. Das, V., *Life and Words: Violence and the Descent into the Ordinary* (Los Angeles: University of California Press, 2007), 5–6.

61. Das, *Life and Words,* 7, 8.

62. Pandey, G., 'Voices from the Edge: The Struggle to Write Subaltern Histories,' in *Mapping Subaltern Studies and the Postcolonial,* ed. V. Chaturvedi (London: Verso, 2012), 281–99, on 289.

63. Baudrillard, J., *Fragments: Cool Memories III, 1990–1995,* trans. E. Agar (London: Verso, 1995), 133.

64. Baudrillard, *Fragments*, 8.

65. Baudrillard, *Fragments*, 8.

66. This is a phrase Benjamin used in a 1927 letter, reprinted in Smith, *Walter Benjamin: Moscow Diary*, 132.

POLITICAL FRAMINGS

Epigraph: Pandey, 'Voices from the Edge,' in Chaturvedi, *Mapping Subaltern Studies*, 296.

1. Name changed to protect anonymity.

2. Davis, M., *Planet of Slums* (London: Verso, 2006), 141.

3. Names changed to protect anonymity.

4. Anjaria, J.S., *The Slow Boil: Street Food, Rights, and Public Space in Mumbai* (Stanford, CA: Stanford University Press, 2016); Ghertner, 'When Is the State?'

5. McFarlane et al., 'Informal Urban Sanitation.'

6. De Boeck, 'Divining the City'; Schnitzler, A., 'Traveling Technologies: Infrastructure, Ethical Regimes, and the Materiality of Politics in South Africa,' *Cultural Anthropology* 28, no. 4 (2013): 670–93; Monstadt and Schramm, 'Toward the Networked City?'

7. Grosz, E., *Time Travels: Feminism, Nature, Power* (Crows Nest, NSW: Allen and Unwin, 2005), 2.

8. Simone, *City Life from Jakarta to Dakar*.

9. Massey, *For Space*.

10. Farías and Blok, *Urban Cosmopolitics*, 11.

11. Mbembe, A., and Nuttall, S., 'Writing the World from an African Metropolis,' *Public Culture* 16, no. 3 (2004): 349.

12. Fredericks, *Garbage Citizenship*.

13. Fredericks, *Garbage Citizenship*, 98.

14. See also Samson, M., 'Rescaling the State, Restructuring Social Relations: Local Government Transformation and Waste Management Privatization in Post-apartheid Johannesburg,' *International Feminist Journal of Politics* 10, no. 1 (2008): 119–43.

15. Fredericks, *Garbage Citizenship*, 120.

16. On social media and poverty, see Porter, 'Mobilities in Rural Africa.'

17. Latour, B., 'Networks, Societies, Spheres: Reflections of an Actor-Network Theorist,' *International Journal of Communication* 5 (2011), 4.

18. Thrift, N., 'The Promise of Urban Informatics: Some Speculations,' *Environment and Planning A* 46, no. 6 (2014): 1263–66.

19. Connolly, *A World of Becoming*.

20. De Boeck, 'Divining the City,' 51. See also Bayat, A., *Street Politics: Poor People's Movements in Iran* (New York: Columbia University Press, 1997); Bayat, A., *Life as Politics: How Ordinary People Change the Middle East* (Stanford, CA: Stanford University Press, 2010).

21. Bolongaro, K., 'Welcome to Syrian Berlin: A Refugee Tour of the City,' *Al Jazeera*, March 3, 2016, www.aljazeera.com/indepth/features/2016/02/syrian-berlin-refugee-tour-city-160211132536180.html (accessed May 23, 2019).

22. Jazeel, T., 'Singularity: A Manifesto for Incomparable Geographies,' *Singapore Journal of Tropical Geography* 40, no. 1 (2018): 5–21.

23. Robins, S., 'The 2011 Toilet Wars in South Africa: Justice and Transition between the Exceptional and the Everyday after Apartheid,' *Development and Change* 45, no. 3 (2014): 493.

24. Schnitzler, 'Travelling Technologies.'

25. Robins, S. 'Poo Wars as Matter Out of Place: "Toilets for Africa" in Cape Town,' *Anthropology Today* 30, no. 1 (2014): 1–3.

26. Robins, S., 'Slow Activism in Fast Times: Reflections on the Politics of Media Spectacles after Apartheid,' *Journal of Southern African Studies* 40, no. 1 (2014): 104.

27. Robins, 'The 2001 Toilet Wars,' 488.

28. Turok, I., 'Persistent Polarisation Post-apartheid? Progress towards Urban Integration in Cape Town,' *Urban Studies* 38, no. 13 (2001): 2349–77; Lemanski, C., 'Global Cities in the South: Deepening Social and Spatial Polarization in Cape Town,' *Cities* 24, no. 6 (2007): 448–61; Parnell and Pieterse, 'The "Right to the City"'; McDonald, D., *World City Syndrome: Neoliberalism and Inequality in Cape Town* (London: Routledge, 2006).

29. Crankshaw, O., 'Deindustrialization, Professionalization and Racial Inequality in Cape Town,' *Urban Affairs Review* 48, no. 6 (2012): 836–62; Lawson, V., 'Decentring Poverty Studies: Middle-Class Alliances and the Social Construction of Poverty,' *Singapore Journal of Tropical Geography* 33, no. 1 (2012): 12.

30. Comaroff and Comaroff, *Theory from the South*, 41, 39.

31. Mels, A., Castellano, D., Braadbaart, O., Veenstra, S., Dijkstra, I., Meulman, B., and Wilsenach, J. A. 'Sanitation Services for the Informal Settlements of Cape Town, South Africa,' *Desalination* 248, no. 1 (2009): 330–37.

32. Jaglin, S., 'Differentiating Networked Services in Cape Town: Echoes of Splintering Urbanism,' *Geoforum* 39 (2008): 1897–906; Parnell, S., Beall, J., and Crankshaw, O., 'A Matter of Timing: African Urbanisation and Access to Housing in Johannesburg,' in *African Urban Economies: Viability, Vitality or Vitiation?,* ed. D. Brycson and D. Potts (London: Palgrave Macmillan, 2005), 229–51; Social Justice Coalition (SJC), *Our Toilets Are Dirty: Report of the Social Audit into the Janitorial Service for Communal Flush Toilets in Khayelitsha, Cape Town* (Cape Town: SJC/Ndifuna Ukwazi, October 1, 2014).

33. Attwell, D., *Rewriting Modernity: Studies in Black South African Literary History* (Athens: Ohio University Press, 2006); Serote, M. W., *Yakhal'inkomo* (Johannesburg: Renoster Books, 1972), 47.

34. On Black poetry and liberation politics, see Attwell, *Rewriting Modernity;* Ngara, E., *Ideology and Form in African Poetry: Implications for Communication* (London: Heinemann Educational Books, 1990).

35. Heath, M. A., 'Defining Black Consciousness: Mongane Wally Serote's "What's in This Black 'Shit'",' *M. Ayodele Heath,* April 27, 2004, http://mayodeleheath.blogspot.co.uk/2005/04/defining-black-consciousness-mongane.html (accessed June 7, 2019).

36. Atwell, *Rewriting Modernity*, 148.

37. Kristeva, J., *The Powers of Horror: An Essay on Abjection,* trans. L. S. Roudiez (New York: Columbia University Press, 1982), 9.

38. Robins, 'The 2011 Toilet Wars'; McFarlane, C., and Silver, J., 'The Poolitical City: "Seeing Sanitation" and Making the Urban Political in Cape Town,' *Antipode* 49, no. 1 (2017): 125–44.

39. Benjamin, *The Arcades Project.*

40. Hansen, 'Benjamin's Gamble with Cinema.'

41. Jackson, S.J., 'Rethinking Repair,' in *Media Technologies: Essays on Communication, Materiality, and Society,* ed. T. Gillespie, P.J. Boczkowski, and K.A. Foot (Cambridge, MA: MIT Press, 2014), 221–39, on 237.

42. Benjamin, *The Arcades Project,* 405.

43. Hentschel, 'Postcolonialising Berlin.'

44. Sennett, R., *The Craftsmen* (London: Penguin Books, 2008).

45. Napolitano, 'Anthropology and Traces,' 57.

46. Fredericks, *Garbage Citizenship,* 131.

47. Attwell, *Rewriting Modernity.*

48. Drabinski, K., 'Poetics of the Mangrove,' in *Deleuze and Race,* ed. A. Saldanha and J.M. Adams (Edinburgh: Edinburgh University Press, 2013), 288–99; Hsiao L.C., ed., *"This Shipwreck of Fragments": Historical Memory, Imaginary Identities, and Postcolonial Geography in Caribbean Culture and Literature* (Newcastle, UK: Cambridge Scholars, 2009).

49. Fredericks, *Garbage Citizenship.*

50. Jensen, C.B., and Morita, A., 'Introduction: Infrastructures as Ontological Experiments *Ethnos,* 82, no. 4 (2017): 615–26.

51. Miranda, C.A., 'Noah Purifoy, An Artist Forged by Fire,' *Los Angeles Times,* August 13, 2015, www.latimes.com/entertainment/arts/la-ca-cm-noah-purifoy-20150816-story.html (accessed July 10, 2019).

52. Hunter, M.A., and Robinson, Z.F., *Chocolate Cities: The Black Map of American Life* (Oakland: University of California Press, 2018); and see Soja, E., *Seeking Spatial Justice* (Minneapolis: University of Minnesota Press, 2010).

53. Hunter and Robinson, *Chocolate Cities,* 142.

54. King, M.L., 'Beyond the Los Angeles Riots,' *Saturday Review,* November 13, 1965, 35.

55. Miranda, 'Noah Purifoy.'

56. Frank, C., 'Noah Purifoy and Migrating Assemblages,' *Warscapes,* February 16, 2016, www.warscapes.com/reviews/noah-purifoy-and-migrating-assemblages (accessed January 12, 2020); Purifoy, N., and Michel, T., *Junk Art: 66 Signs of Neon* (Los Angeles, 1966), 4; Chattopadhyay, C. 'Improvisation and Assemblage: Noah Purifoy Explores Contradictions and Cultures,' *Sculpture* (July–August 1997): 31–39.

57. Chattopadhyay, *Unlearning the City.*

58. Elder, A., 'Noah Purifoy: Dystopian Dadaism from Riot-Torn LA to Joshua Tree Still Resonates,' *The Guardian,* May 29, 2015, www.theguardian.com/artanddesign/2015/may/29/noah-purifoy-los-angeles-county-museum-of-art (accessed September 6, 2019).

59. Miranda, 'Noah Purifoy.'

60. Williams, *Why Cities Look the Way They Do,* 106.

61. Massumi, B., *Parables for the Virtual: Movement, Affect, Sensation* (Durham, NC: Duke University Press, 2002).

62. Benjamin, *The Arcades Project.*

63. Miranda, 'Noah Purifoy.'

64. Purifoy and Michel, *Junk Art,* 3.

65. Used courtesy of Noah Purifoy Foundation ©2020.

66. Shaw, C., 'Make Art Not War: Watts and the Junk Art Conversation,' *East of Borneo,* November 22, 2010, www.eastofborneo.org/articles/make-art -not-war-watts-and-the-junk-art-conversation/ (accessed July 10, 2019).

67. Cited in Miranda, 'Noah Purifoy.'

68. Hunter and Robinson, *Chocolate Cites,* 88.

69. McKittrick, K., 'Plantation Futures,' *Small Axe: A Caribbean Journal of Criticism* 17, no. 3 (2013): 1–15, on 5.

70. Roy, 'Dis/possessive Collectivism.'

71. Purifoy and Michel, *Junk Art,* 3.

72. Cited in Miranda, 'Noah Purifoy.'

73. Lichenstein, *The Fragment.*

74. Gurney, K., *The Art of Public Space: Curating and Re-imagining the Ephemeral City* (New York: Springer, 2015); Hawkins, H., *For Creative Geographies: Geography, Visual Arts and the Making of Worlds* (London: Routledge, 2013); Miles, M., *Art, Space and the City* (London: Routledge, 1997).

75. Atkinson, R., 'Domestication by Cappuccino or Revenge on Urban Space? Control and Empowerment in the Management of Public Spaces,' *Urban Studies* 40, no. 9 (2003): 1829–43; Cameron, S., and Coaffee, J., 'Art, Gentrification and Regeneration—From Artist as Pioneer to Public Arts,' *European Journal of Housing Policy* 5, no. 1 (2005): 39–58.

76. Amin and Thrift, *Seeing Like a City,* 167.

77. Slitine, M., 'Contemporary Art from a City at War: The Case of Gaza (Palestine),' *Cities,* 77, no. 1 (2018): 49–59; Guinard, P., and Margier, A., 'Art as a New Urban Norm: Between Normalization of the City through Art and Normalization of Art through the City in Montreal and Johannesburg,' *Cities* 77 (2018): 13–20.

78. Guinard, P., and Molina, G., 'Urban Geography of Arts: the Co-production of Arts and Cities,' *Cities* 77 (2018), 3.

79. Maher, D., '900 Miles to Paradise, and Other Afterlives of Architecture,' in *Architecture Post-mortem: The Diastolic Architecture of Decline, Dystopia and Death,* ed. D. Kunze, D. Bertolin, and S. Brott (London: Routledge, 2013), 219.

80. Green, P., 'A Master of Accumulation,' *New York Times,* January 23, 2013, www.nytimes.com/2013/01/24/garden/in-buffalo-one-mans-living-museum .html (accessed July 8, 2019).

81. Pommier, C., *The Art of* Viyé Diba: *The Intelligent Hand* (Vancouver, BC: Arts in Action Society; Dakar, Senegal: SudProd Senvision, 2003 (available at https://vimeo.com/68892833).

82. Pommier, *The Art of* Viyé Diba.

83. Pommier, *The Art of* Viyé Diba.

84. Grabski, J., 'Viyé Diba's *Tout Se Sait:* The Affective Experience of Urban Life,' *Journal of Contemporary African Art* 36, no. 2 (2015): 98.

85. Grabski, 'Viyé Diba's *Tout Se Sait,* 101.

86. Grabski, 'Viyé Diba's *Tout Se Sait,* 105–6.

87. October Gallery, *El Anatsui,* 2016, www.octobergallery.co.uk /exhibitions/tsiatsia.shtml (accessed August 17, 2019).

88. Ando, E., 'Njideka Akunyili Crosby,' *Bomb Magazine,* https:// bombmagazine.org/articles/njideka-akunyili-crosby/ (accessed April 20, 2020). I am grateful to Jen Bagelman for drawing my attention to Crosby's work, and to the work of Betty Acquah.

89. Ede, A., 'Art: Betty Acquah,' *Maple Tree Literary Supplement,* www .mtls.ca/issue17/art/ (accessed April 20, 2020).

90. Roy, T., 'Non-renewable Resources: The Poetics and Politics of Vivan Sunderam's *Trash,' Theory, Culture and Society* 30, nos. 7–8 (2013): 268; Sunderam, V., *Trash* (Mumbai: Chemould Prescott Road, 2008).

91. Roy, 'Non-renewable Resources,' 274.

92. Roy, 'Non-renewable Resources,' 273.

93. Chemould Prescott Road, *Vivan Sunderam, Trash,* Mumbai, 2008, www.gallerychemould.com/exhibitions/vivan-show-2008/ (accessed July 8, 2018); and see Sunderam, V., *Trash* (Mumbai: Chemould Prescott Road, 2008).

94. Weinstein, 'Mumbai's Development Mafias'; Weinstein, *The Durable Slum.*

95. Leslie, E., 'Recycling,' in *Restless Cities,* ed. M. Beaumont and G. Dart (London: Verso, 2010), 243.

96. Leslie, 'Recycling,' 240.

97. Leslie, 'Recycling,' 240.

98. Cited in Spencer, R., *Eduardo Paolozzi: Recurring Themes* (London: Trefoil Books, 1984), 20.

99. Foster, H., 'Erase, Deface, Transform,' *London Review of Books,* February, 16, 2017, 16.

100. Foster, 'Erase, Deface, Transform,' 17; such as Paolozzi's *Cyclops* (1957).

101. Foster, 'Erase, Deface, Transform,' 17.

102. Cited in Patel, V., 'Sanitation and Dignity,' *The Hindu,* September 24, 2013, www.thehindu.com/news/national/other-states/sanitation-and-dignity /article5160791.ece (accessed August 25, 2019).

103. Maharaj, K., 'Bombay High Court Makes Right to Clean Toilets a Fundamental Right for Women in India,' *Oxford Human Rights Hub,* February 8, 2016, http://ohrh.law.ox.ac.uk/bombay-high-court-makes-right-to-clean-toilets -a-fundamental-right-for-women-in-india/ (accessed July 29, 2019).

104. Pinto, R., 'Right to Pee Activists Return Award as Toilets Still Unclean,' *Times of India,* March 9, 2016, http://timesofindia.indiatimes.com/city/mumbai /Right-to-Pee-activists-return-award-as-toilets-still-unclean/articleshow/51318710 .cms (accessed May 10, 2019).

105. Faleiro, S., 'For Some Voters in Mumbai, This Election's All about Toilets,' *Quartz,* 2014, http://qz.com/196893/for-some-voters-in-mumbai-this -elections-all-about-toilets/ (accessed May 10, 2019).

106. Phadke et al., *Why Loiter?,* 79.

107. Björkman, *Pipe Politics, Contested Waters,* 231.

108. Grosz, *Time Travels.*

109. Deleuze, G., *Difference and Repetition* (London: Continuum, [1968] 2001).

110. Braidotti, R., 'Becoming Woman: Or Sexual Difference Revisited,' *Theory, Culture and Society* 20 (2003): 43–64; Colls, R., 'Feminism, Bodily Difference and Non-representational Geographies,' *Transactions of the Institute of British Geographers* 37 (2012): 430–45; Irigaray, L., *An Ethics of Sexual Difference,* trans. C. Burke and G. C. (London: Continuum, 2004).

111. McFarlane, *Learning the City.*

112. Gieseking, J. J., 'A Queer Geographer's Life as an Introduction to Queer Theory, Space, and Time,' in *Queer Geographies: Beirut, Tijuana, Copenhagen,* ed. L. Lau, M. Arsanios, F. Zúñiga-González, M. Kryger, and O. Mismar (Roskilde: Museum of Contemporary Art, 2013), 17.

113. Lancione and McFarlane, 'Life at the Urban Margins.'

114. Trilling, D., 'In Germany, Refugees Seek Fair Treatment,' *Al Jazeera,* April 2, 2014, www.aljazeera.com/indepth/features/2014/04/germany-refugees-seek-fair-treatment-berlin-oranienplatz-201442112531138114.html (accessed May 10, 2019).

115. Coldwell, W., 'Refugees Tell a Different Berlin Story,' *The Guardian,* November 28, 2015, www.theguardian.com/travel/2015/nov/28/refugees-tell-a-different-berlin-story (accessed May 10, 2019) 2015.

116. Langa, N., 'About the Refugee Movement in Kreuzberg, Berlin,' *Movements: Journal fur Migrations und Grenzregimeforschung* 1, no. 2 (2015); Sevcenco, M., 'Refugees Demanding Rights Continue 4-Month-Long Occupation in Berlin,' *Occupy Wall Street,* 2014, http://occupywallstreet.net/story/refugees-demanding-rights-continue-4-month-long-occupation-berlin (accessed May 10, 2019); Linek, L. ' "This Is Our Battleground": How a New Refugee Movement Is Challenging Germany's Racist Asylum Laws,' *Ceasefire,* March 20, 2013, https://ceasefiremagazine.co.uk/this-battleground-germanys-refugee-movement-challenges-racist-asylum-laws/ (accessed May 10, 2019); Ladry, O., ' "Wir Sind Alle Oranienplatz!": Space for Refugees and Social Justice in Berlin,' *Seminar: A Journal of Germanic Studies* 51, no. 4 (2015): 398–413.

117. Cash, M., 'A Safe Space of One's Own,' *Mama Cash,* November 12, 2015, www.mamacash.org/news/a-safe-space-of-ones-own/ (accessed May 11, 2018).

118. Krawczyk, D., 'Not Everything Works Out as Planned,' *Political Critique: Central European Magazine for Politics and Culture,* February 4, 2016, http://politicalcritique.org/world/eu/2016/refugees-berlin-ohlauer-school/ (accessed May 11, 2019).

119. Krawczyk, 'Not Everything Works Out as Planned.'

120. Butler, J., *Notes toward a Performative Theory of Assembly* (Cambridge, MA: Harvard University Press, 2018); Butler, J., and Athanasiou, A., *Dispossession: The Performative in the Political* (Cambridge: Polity Press, 2013); Butler, J., *The Force of Nonviolence: An Ethico-Political Bind* (London: Verso Books, 2020).

121. Watt, P., 'A Nomadic War Machine in the Metropolis: En/countering London's 21st-Century Housing Crisis with Focus E15,' *City* 20, no. 2 (2016): 297–320; Deleuze, G., and Guattari, F., *Anti-Oedipus* (London: Continuum,

[1972] 2004); Deleuze, G., and Guattari, F., *A Thousand Plateaus* (London: Bloomsbury, [1980] 2013).

122. Coldwell, 'Refugees tell a Different Berlin Story'; Langa, *About the Refugee Movement,* described her experience in a piece for the German journal *Movements.*

123. Riceburg, J., 'Just Let the Refugees Stay!', *John Riceburg,* July 2, 2014, https://johnriceburg.wordpress.com/2014/07/02/just-let-the-refugees-stay/ (accessed May 11, 2019).

124. Cash, 'A Safe Space of One's Own.'

125. Vasudevan, *Metropolitan Preoccupations;* Sim, D., 'Controversial Oranienplatz Refugee Camp Demolished,' *International Business Times,* April 9, 2014, www.ibtimes.co.uk/controversial-oranienplatz-berlin-refugee-camp-demolished-1444043 (accessed May 10, 2019).

126. Riceburg, 'Just Let the Refugees Stay!'

127. Comaroff and Comaroff, *Theory from the South.*

128. Vasudevan, *Metropolitan Preoccupations,* 199. See also Vasudevan, *The Autonomous City.*

129. Vasudevan, *Metropolitan Preoccupations.*

130. Farías and Blok, *Urban Cosmopolitics,* 2; Latour, B. 'Whose Cosmos, Which Cosmopolitics? Comments on the Peace Terms of Ulrich Beck,' *Common Knowledge* 10, no. 3 (2004): 450; Stengers, I., 'A Cosmopolitical Proposal,' in *Making Things Public: Atmospheres of Democracy,* ed. B. Latour and P. Weibel (Cambridge, MA: MIT Press, 2005; Stengers, I., *Cosmopolitics, Vol. 2* (Minneapolis: University of Minnesota Press, 2011).

131. Amin, A., and Thrift, N., *Arts of the Political: New Openings for the Left* (Durham, NC: Duke University Press, 2013); Bergen, V., 'Politics as the Orientation of Every Assemblage,' *New Formations* (2009): 34–41.

132. Bagelman, J., *Sanctuary City: A Suspended State* (London: Palgrave, 2016); Damai, P., 'Messianic-City: Ruins, Refuge and Hospitality in Derrida,' *Discourse* 27, nos. 2–3 (2005): 68–94.

133. Roy, A., 'The City in the Age of Trumpism: From Sanctuary to Abolition,' *Environment and Planning D: Society and Space* 37, no. 5 (2019): 761–78; Bagelman, *Sanctuary City.*

134. Vasagar, J., 'Berlin's Refugee Chaos Erodes German Reputation for Efficiency,' *Financial Times,* December 11, 2015, www.ft.com/cms/s/0/aa243aa0-9f52-11e5-8613-08e211ea5317.html#axzz49TiY8LuH (accessed May 23, 2019).

135. Juran, S., and Broer, P.N., 'A Profile of Germany's Refugee Populations,' *Population and Development Review* 43, no. 1 (2017): 149–57.

136. Bergfeld, M., 'Germany's *Willkommenskultur:* Trade Unions, Refugees and Labour Market Integration,' *Global Labour Journal* 8, no. 1 (2017): 80–89.

137. Katz et al., 'Cities and Refugees.'

138. Bergfeld, 'Germany's *Willkommenskultur*'; Amnesty International, 'Leben in Unsicherheit—Wie Deutschland Die Opfer Rassistischer Gewalt Im Stich Lässt,' June 2016, www.amnesty.de/files/Amnesty-Bericht-Rassistische-Gewalt-in-Deutschland-Juni2016.pdf (accessed March 16, 2017).

139. Anonymous, 'Who'd Live in a Nazi Town in Germany? I Do—It's Terrifying,' *The Guardian,* October 31, 2018, 10.

140. Katz et al., 'Cities and Refugees.'

141. Katz et al., 'Cities and Refugees.'

142. Katz et al., 'Cities and Refugees.' Soederberg, S., 'Governing Global Displacement in Austerity Urbanism: The Case of Berlin's Refugee Crisis,' *Development and Change* 50, no. 4 (2018): 923–947.

143. Darling, J., 'Asylum and the Post-political: Domopolitics, Depoliticisation and Acts of Citizenship,' *Antipode* 46, no. 1 (2014): 72–91; Darling, J., 'Forced Migration and the City: Irregularity, Informality, and the Politics of Presence,' *Progress in Human Geography* 41 (2017): 178–98.

144. Yiftachel, O., 'Critical Theory and "Gray Space": Mobilization of the Colonized,' *City* 13, nos. 2–3 (2009): 240–56.

145. Lefebvre, *The Urban Revolution.*

146. Amin, A., *Land of Strangers* (Cambridge: Polity Press, 2012), 11.

147. Darling, 'Forced Migration'; Amin, *Land of Strangers;* and on sanctuary cities, see Bagelman, *Sanctuary City;* Roy, 'The City in the Age of Trumpism.'

148. Uzar, F., 'Social Participation of Turkish and Arabic Immigrants in the Neighbourhood: Case Study of Moabit West, Berlin,' *Journal of Identity and Migration Studies* 1, no. 2 (2007), www.e-migration.ro/jims/Vol1_no2_2007/JIMS_vol1_no2_2007_UZAR.pdf (accessed May 23, 2019).

149. In 2016, LaGeSo became the Landesamt fur Fluchtlingsungelegenheiten, or State Office for Refugee Affairs.

150. One of the most striking aspects of Berlin's encounter with refugees is that it is not only seasoned activists who have been inspired to act, but residents like Christiane who were previously living quite different lives. At Tempelhof Airport—the old Nazi-era monolith that is now the largest refugee camp in the city, with over two thousand inhabitants—I spoke to Jon, who had gone from no involvement in activism at all to taking on an important organizational role distributing clothes and basic provisions for refugees. "I wasn't political at all," he reflected. "But the refugee crisis—or what the news calls a 'crisis'—has made us [people living in Germany] political. If this is going to work, we all need to play a part . . . It's ordinary people, seeing pictures in the news, and getting together with friends and on Facebook and doing something. So, it's a different kind of activism."

151. Trilling, 'In Germany, Refugees Seek Fair Treatment.'

152. Sevcenco, 'Refugees Demanding Rights.'

153. Vasagar, 'Berlin's Refugee Chaos.'

154. Hinze, A.M., *Turkish Berlin: Integration Policy and Urban Space* (Minneapolis: University of Minnesota Press, 2013).

155. Barfield, T., 'Berlin Refugee Boss Resigns in Disgrace,' *The Local,* December 10, 2015, www.thelocal.de/20151210/berlin-refugee-boss-leaves-in-disgrace (accessed May 23, 2019).

156. Hinze, *Turkish Berlin;* Ree X., 'Are Refugees Really Welcome? Inside the Fight to Save Berlin's Wagenplatz Kanal,' *Open Democracy,* April 21, 2016, www.opendemocracy.net/transformation/ree-x/inside-fight-to-save-berlins-wagenplatz-kanal (accessed August 26, 2019).

157. Katz et al., 'Cities and Refugees.'

158. Darling, 'Forced Migration and the City.'

159. Kishik, *The Manhattan Project.*

160. Schindler, 'Towards a Paradigm of Southern Urbanism'; Goldman, 'Speculating on the Next World City,' in Roy and Ong, *Worlding Cities,* 229–58.

161. Goldman, 'Speculating on the Next World City'; Bhan, *In the Public's Interest;* Ghertner, *Rule by Aesthetics.*

162. Mayne, *Slums.*

163. Merrifield, *The New Urban Question,* 41. And see Merrifield, A., *The Politics of the Encounter: Urban Theory and Protest under Planetary Urbanization* (Athens: University of Georgia Press, 2013).

164. Massumi, B., *99 Theses on the Revaluation of Value: A Postcapitalist Manifesto* (Minneapolis: University of Minnesota Press, 2018).

165. Simone, *Improvised Lives.*

166. Gibson-Graham, J.K., *A Postcapitalist Politics* (Minneapolis: University of Minnesota Press, 2006).

167. Simone, *Improvised Lives.*

168. Roy, 'Non-renewable Resources,' 267, 274.

169. Ongwec, J., 'Namuwongo: Key to Kampala's Present and Future Development,' *Africa at LSE,* May 28, 2015, http://blogs.lse.ac.uk/africaatlse /2015/05/28/namuwongo-key-to-kampalas-present-and-future-development / (accessed August 12, 2018).

170. Ongwec, J., 'Namuwongo'; Hueler, H., 'Uganda Fears Unprecedented Rise in Mob Justice,' *VOA News,* June 6, 2014, www.voanews.com/a/uganda-fears-unprecedented-rise-in-mob-justice/1931384.html 2014 (accessed January 16, 2018).

171. Latour, B., 'From Realpolitik to Dingpolitik, or How to Make Things Public,' in *Making Things Public: Atmospheres of Democracy,* ed. B. Latour and P. Weibel (Cambridge, MA: MIT Press, 2008), 31.

172. Jacobs, J.M., 'Comparing Comparative Urbanisms,' *Urban Geography* 33, no. 6 (2012b): 904–14.

173. Sennett, R., 'The City of Fragments,' *Cityscapes: Rethinking Urban Things,* African Centre for Cities, no. 5 (2013), www.cityscapesdigital.net/2014 /07/19/city-fragments/ (accessed July 6, 2019).

174. Ongwec, 'Namuwongo.'

175. Yiftachel, 'Critical Theory and "Gray Space".'

176. Appadurai, A., 'Deep Democracy: Urban Government and the Horizon of Politics,' *Public Culture* 14, no. 1 (2002): 21–47; King, S., 'Increasing the Power of the Poor? NGO-Led Social Accountability Initiatives and Political Capabilities in Uganda,' *European Journal of Development Research* 27 (2015): 887–902.

177. Simone, A., 'City of Potentialities: An Introduction,' *Theory, Culture and Society* 33, nos. 7–8 (2016): 5–29.

WALKING CITIES

Epigraph: Benjamin, W., *Berlin Childhood around 1900,* trans. H. Eiland (Cambridge, MA: Belknap Press, 2006), 53–54.

1. Pierce, J., and Lawhon, M.. 'Walking as Method: Toward Methodological Forthrightness and Comparability in Urban Geographical Research,' *Professional Geographer* 67, no. 4 (2015): 655–62; Wylie, J., 'A Single Day's Walking: Narrating Self and Landscape on the South West Coast Path,' *Transactions of the Institute of British Geographers* 30, no. 2 (2005): 234–47.

2. See also Merriman, P., 'Rethinking Mobile Methods,' *Mobilities* 9, no. 2 (2014): 167–87.

3. De Certeau, M., *The Practice of Everyday Life* (Berkeley: University of California Press, 1984).

4. De Certeau, *The Practice of Everyday Life,* 91.

5. De Certeau, *The Practice of Everyday Life,* 93.

6. De Certeau, *The Practice of Everyday Life,* 93.

7. See Solnit, *Wanderlust,* 199.

8. Benjamin, *Arcades,* 420.

9. Benjamin, *Arcades,* 420.

10. Benjamin, *Arcades,* 537.

11. Edensor, T., 'Walking in Rhythms: Place, Regulation, Style and the Flow of Experience,' *Visual Studies* 25 (2010): 69–79.

12. Amin and Thrift, *Arts of the Political,* 40.

13. Solnit, *Wanderlust,* 206.

14. Solnit, *Wanderlust,* 206.

15. Amin and Thrift, *Arts of the Political,* 427.

16. Simone and Pieterse, *New Urban Worlds,* xvii; see also Pierce and Lawhon, 'Walking as Method.'

17. Benjamin, *Berlin Childhood around 1900,* 53–54.

18. Solnit, R., *A Field Guide to Getting Lost* (Edinburgh: Canongate, 2006), 6.

19. Sondzi, P., 'Hope in the Past: On Walter Benjamin,' in Benjamin, *Berlin Childhood around 1900,* 26.

20. Quoted in Irving, I., 'ArtAttack Interviews Korean Artist, Kyung Hwa Shon,' *ArtAttack,* February 8, 2016, https://artattackapp.wordpress.com/2016/02/08/artattack-interview-kyung-hwa-shon-london-art-fair/ (accessed July 7, 2019).

21. Wunderlich, F. M., 'Walking and Rhythmicity: Sensing Urban Space,' *Journal of Urban Design* 13 (2008): 125–39; Wunderlich, F. M., 'Place-Temporality and Urban Place-Rhythms in Urban Analysis and Design: An Aesthetic Akin to Music,' *Journal of Urban Design* 18, no. 3 (2013): 383–408; Coverley, M., *Psychogeography* (London: Pocket Essentials, 2006).

22. Solnit, *Wanderlust,* 213.

23. Coverley, *Psychogeography,* 123,

24. Davis, L. H., ed., *The Disability Studies Reader,* 4th ed. (London: Routledge, 2013).

25. Elkin, L., *Flâneuse: Women Walk the City, in Paris, New York, Tokyo, Venice and London* (London: Chatto and Windus, 2017); Middleton, J., 'Sense and the City: Exploring the Embodied Geographies of Urban Walking,' *Social and Cultural Geography* 11 (2010): 575–96; Warren, S., 'Pluralising the Walking Interview: Researching (Im)mobilities with Muslim Women,' *Social and Cultural Geography* 18, no. 6 (2016): 786–807.

26. Dreyer, E., and McDowall, E., 'Imagining the Flâneur as a Woman,' *Communicatio: South African Journal for Communication Theory and Research* 38, no. 1 (2012): 30–44, on 41.

27. Benjamin, *The Arcades Project,* 17.

28. Benjamin, *The Arcades Project,* 83.

29. Benjamin, *The Arcades Project,* 334.

30. Solnit, *Wanderlust,* 209.

31. Solnit, *Wanderlust.*

32. Solnit, *Wanderlust,* 241.

33. Laing, O., *The Lonely City: Adventures in the Art of Being Alone* (Edinburgh: Canongate, 2017), 222.

34. Laing, *The Lonely City,* 224.

35. Parent, L., 'The Wheeling Interview: Mobile Methods and Disability,' *Mobilities* 11, no. 4 (2016): 521–32.

36. Parent, 'The Wheeling Interview,' 530.

37. Benjamin, *The Arcades Project,* 429.

38. Elkin, *Flâneuse.*

39. Hessel, F., *Walking in Berlin: A Flaneur in the Capital* (London: Scribe, [1929] 2016), 7.

40. Shulze, W., and Schneider, R., *Heimkehr ins Leben, Berlin 1945–1960* (Berlin: Aufbau-Verlag, 2005).

41. Shulze and Schneider, *Heimkehr ins Leben,* 126, 128.

42. Jukes, *A Shout in the Street,* 52.

43. Colomb, C., 'The Trajectory of Berlin's "Interim Spaces": Tensions and Conflicts in the Mobilisation of "Temporary Uses" of Urban Space in Local Economic Development,' in *Transience and Permanence in Urban Development,* ed. J. Henneberry (Chichester: Wiley Blackwell, 2017), 131–49; Collinson, P. 'Berlin Tops the World as City with the Fastest Rising Property Prices,' *The Guardian,* April 10, 2018, www.theguardian.com/world/2018/apr/10 /berlin-world-fastest-rising-property-prices (accessed July 18, 2018).

44. Leslie, 'Recycling,' in Beaumont and Dart, *Restless Cities,* 241.

45. Huyssen, A., 'The Voids of Berlin,' *Critical Inquiry* 24, no. 1 (1997): 57–81.

46. Shelton, B., Karakiexicz, J., and Khan, T., *The Making of Hong Kong: From Vertical to Volumetric* (London: Routledge, 2011), 4.

47. Shelton et al., *The Making of Hong Kong,* 16; see also Alexander, C., 'The City Is Not a Tree,' *Design* 206 (1966): 46–55.

48. Shelton et al., *The Making of Hong Kong,* 161.

49. Singh, J. T., 'Sunday in the Park: Domestic Workers and Public Space in Hong Kong,' *Cities of Migration,* July 29, 2013, http://citiesofmigration.ca /good_idea/sunday-in-the-park/.

50. Society for Community Organization (SoCo), 2016, www.soco.org.hk /trapped/index.htm (accessed August 15, 2019).

51. Lau, J., 'Rooftop Slums Are a Stark Reminder of Hong Kong's Social and Housing Problems,' *South China Morning Post,* October 8, 2016, www.scmp .com/news/hong-kong/education-community/article/2026112/rooftop-slums- are-stark-reminder-hong-kongs (accessed August 16, 2019).

52. Xue, C. Q., Manuel, K. K., and Chung, R., 'Public Space in the Old Derelict City Area—A Case Study of Mong Kok, Hong Kong,' *Urban Design International* 6, no. 1 (2001): 16–31; Reuters, 'The World's Most Crowded Place,' *Reuters,* n.d., www.reuters.com/news/picture/the-worlds-most-crowded-place?articleId = USRTR2SRF6 (accessed July 15, 2019).

53. Keegan, M., 'Hong Kong's "Cardboard Grannies": The Elderly Box Collectors Living in Poverty,' *The Guardian,* April 24, 2018, www.theguardian.com/cities/2018/apr/24/hong-kong-cardboard-grannies-elderly-box-collectors-recycling-poverty (accessed January 6, 2019).

54. Mattern, S., 'Maintenance and Care,' *Places,* November 2018, https://placesjournal.org/article/maintenance-and-care/?cn-reloaded = 1 (accessed July 9, 2019).

55. Merriman, 'Rethinking Mobile Methods.'

56. Wolf, M., *Tokyo Compression* (Peperoni Books, 2010); Wolf, M., *Architecture of Density* (Peperoni Books, 2012).

57. O'Hagan, S., 'How Photographer Michael Wolf Captured the Melancholy of Our Teeming Cities,' *The Guardian,* April 26, 2019, www.theguardian.com/artanddesign/2019/apr/26/how-photographer-michael-wolf-captured-the-planets-teeming-city-life (accessed May 3, 2019).

58. Wolf, M., *Informal Solutions: Observations in Hong Kong Back Alleys* (WE Press, 2016).

59. Feustel, M., 'Farewell to Michael Wolf (1954–2019),' *The Eye of Photography,* April 29, 2019, https://loeildelaphotographie.com/en/farewell-to-michael-wolf-1954–2019-bb/ (accessed May 5, 2019). See also Feustel's website for this piece on Wolf: www.marcfeustel.com/michael-wolf-informal-solutions, and Wolf, *Informal Solutions.*

60. Cited in Feustel, 'Farewell to Michael Wolf.'

61. Rigg, N., 'Interview: Michael Wolf's Best Photographs: Four Plucked Ducks in Hong Kong,' *The Guardian,* April 19, 2017, www.theguardian.com/artanddesign/2017/apr/19/michael-wolf-best-photograph-hong-kong-dead-ducks-interview (accessed May 17, 2019).

62. Benjamin, W., and Lacis, A., 'Naples,' in Benjamin, *Walter Benjamin,* 414–21.

63. Benjamin and Lacis, 'Naples,' 420.

64. Benjamin and Lacis, 'Naples,' 416.

65. Benjamin and Lacis, 'Naples,' 416.

66. Benjamin and Lacis, 'Naples,' 420.

67. Benjamin and Lacis, 'Naples,' 416.

68. Wolf interviewed in Booker, M., 'These Unbelievable Photos Make Hong Kong Look Like Abstract Art,' *The New Republic,* October 16, 2013, https://newrepublic.com/article/115209/michael-wolf-photography-hong-kongs-architecture-density, (accessed May 5, 2019).

69. Keegan, M. 'Pipe Dreams: Can "Nano Apartments" Solve Hong Kong's Housing Crisis?' *The Guardian,* May 21, 2018, www.theguardian.com/cities/2018/may/21/nano-apartments-hong-kong-housing-crisis (accessed August 29, 2018). See also Hammond, G., 'Could You Live in a Micro-Flat?' *Financial*

Times, May 2, 2019, www.ft.com/content/03a9343e-6b35-11e9-80c7 –60ee53e6681d (accessed May 6, 2019).

70. Hammond, 'Could You Live in a Micro-Flat?'

71. See also Marcuse, P., and Madden, D., *In Defense of Housing: The Politics of Crisis* (London: Verso, 2016).

72. Speed, B., 'Manhattan's Population Density Is Changing—and Not in the Way You'd Expect,' *CityMetric,* November 12, 2014, www.citymetric.com /horizons/manhattan-s-population-density-changing-and-not-way-you-d -expect-468 (accessed November 12, 2018); Smith, *The New Urban Frontier.*

73. Marcuse and Madden, *In Defense of Housing.*

74. Wolf-Powers, L., 'New York City's Community-Based Housing Movement: Achievements and Prospects,' in *Community Action and Planning: Contexts, Drivers and Outcomes,* ed. N. Gallent and D. Ciaffi (Bristol: Policy Press, 2014), 217–35; Stein, S., 'Progress for Whom, toward What? Progressive Politics and New York City's Mandatory Inclusionary Housing,' *Journal of Urban Affairs* 40, no. 6 (2018): 770–81.

75. Mattern, 'Maintenance and Care.'

76. Knowles, S. G., 'Learning from Disaster? The History of Technology and the Future of Disaster Research,' *Technology and Culture* 55, no. 4 (2014): 773–84.

77. Klinenberg, *Palaces for the People,* 47.

78. BAN (Brooklyn Anti-Gentrification Network), 2018, https://bangentrification.org/about/ (accessed August 8, 2018).

79. BARN (Bushwick Action Research Collective), 'Neighbourhood Change in Bushwick,' http://bushwickactionresearch.org/about-gentrification/ (accessed August 7, 2018).

80. Collinson, 'Berlin Tops the World.'

81. Baker, K., 'The Death of a Once Great City: The Fall of New York and the Urban Crisis of Affluence,' *Harper's Magazine,* July 18, 2018, https:// harpers.org/archive/2018/07/the-death-of-new-york-city-gentrification/ (accessed November 12, 2018).

82. Williams, *Why Cities Look the Way They Do,* 46

83. Akasegawa, G., *Hyperart: Thomasson,* trans. M. Fargo (Kaya Press [1985] 2010).

84. Vladislavic, *Portrait with Keys,* 176.

85. Vladislavic, *Portrait with Keys,* 173.

86. Vladislavic, *Portrait with Keys,* 173.

87. Vladislavic, *Portrait with Keys,* 176. And see Gibson, J.J., *The Ecological Approach to Visual Perception* (Boston: Houghton Mifflin, 1979).

88. Vladislavic, *Portrait with Keys,* 173.

89. Whitney, K. (2017) '"A Brave New World": What Happened to Newcastle's Dream for a Vertical City?', *The Guardian,* February 7, 2017, www .theguardian.com/cities/2017/feb/07/brave-new-world-newcastle-dream-for-vertical-city (accessed February 10 2020).

90. The film can be seen at https://vimeo.com/80787092 (accessed February 10, 2020).

91. Harris, A., 'Engineering Formality: Flyover and Skywalk Construction in Mumbai,' *International Journal of Urban and Regional Research* 42, no. 2 (2018): 295–314. See also Graham, S., *Vertical: The City from Satellites to Bunkers* (London: Verso, 2016).

IN COMPLETION

Epigraph: Benjamin, W., 'Hashish in Marseilles,' in *Walter Benjamin: One Way Street and Other Writings*, 49.

1. Parker, C., 'Avoided Object,' in Tronzo, *The Fragment*, 91.
2. Scanlan, J., *On Garbage* (London: Reaktion, 2005), 100, 119.
3. Lefebvre, *The Urban Revolution*, 174.
4. Connolly, *A World of Becoming*.
5. Nylund, P., and Cohen, B., 'Collision Density: Driving Growth in Urban Entrepreneurial Ecosystems,' *International Entrepreneurship and Management Journal* 13 (2017): 757–76.
6. Anand, *Hydraulic City*; Björkman, *Pipe Politics, Contested Waters*; Schnitzler, *Travelling Technologies*; Truelove, '(Re-)Conceptualising Water Inequality in Delhi, India.'
7. Guma P. K., 'The Governance and Politics of Urban Space in the Postcolonial City: Kampala, Nairobi and Dar es Salaam,' *Africa Review* 8 (2016): 31–43.
8. Branch and Mampilly, *Africa Uprising*; Goodfellow, T., 'Taming the "Rogue" Sector: Studying State Effectiveness in Africa through Informal Transport Politics,' *Comparative Politics* 47 (2015): 127–47.
9. Dobson, S., Nyamweru, H., and Dodman, D., 'Local and Participatory Approaches to Building Resilience in Informal Settlements in Uganda,' *Environment and Urbanization* 27 (2015): 605–20.
10. Klinenburg, *Palaces for the People*, 16.
11. Branch and Mampilly, *Africa Uprising*.
12. Turok, I., 'Persistent Polarisation Post-apartheid?'
13. Dobson et al., 'Local and Participatory Approaches.'
14. Satterthwaite, D., and Mitlin, D., *Reducing Urban Poverty in the Global South* (London: Routledge, 2014); Elwood, S., Lawson, V., and Sheppard, E., 'Geographical Relational Poverty Studies,' *Progress in Human Geography* 41, no. 6 (2016): 745–65.
15. See also Graham, S., and Thrift, N., 'Out of Order: Understanding Repair and Maintenance,' *Theory, Culture and Society* 24, no. 3 (2007): 1–25; Mattern, S., 'Maintenance and Care.'
16. See, for example, Srivastava, *Entangled Urbanism*.
17. See Joyce, *The Rule of Freedom*; Marcuse and Madden, *In Defense of Housing*; Merrifield, *The New Urban Question*.
18. Amin, A., and Howell, P., *Releasing the Commons: Rethinking the Futures of the Commons* (London: Routledge, 2016); Jeffrey, A., McFarlane, C., and Vasudevan, A., 'Rethinking Enclosure: Space, Subjectivity, and the Commons,' *Antipode* 44 (2012): 1247–67.

19. Acuto, M., Dinardi, C., and Marx, C., 'Transcending (In)formal Urbanism,' *Urban Studies* 3, no. 56 (2019): 475–87.

20. Amin and Thrift, *Seeing Like a City;* Magnusson, *Politics of Urbanism;* Valverde, M., 'Seeing Like a City: The Dialectic of Modern and Premodern Ways of Seeing in Urban Governance,' *Law and Society Review* 45, no. 2 (2011): 277–312.

21. Bagelman, *Sanctuary City;* Darling, 'Asylum and the Post-political'; Roy, 'The City in the Age of Trumpism'; see also Spivak, G.S., *Outside in the Teaching Machine* (New York: Routledge, 1993).

22. Kishik, *The Manhattan Project,* 222.

23. Amin and Thrift, *Seeing Like a City;* Magnusson, *Politics of Urbanism.*

24. See, for example, numerous reports on their website, urbz.net.

Bibliography

Acuto, M., Dinardi, C., and Marx, C. 'Transcending (In)formal Urbanism.' *Urban Studies* 3, no. 56 (2019): 475–87.

Adorno, T. *Negative Dialectics*. Translated by E. B. Ashton. London: Routledge, [1966] 1973.

Adorno, T. 'A Portrait of Walter Benjamin.' In Adorno, T., *Prisms*, 227–42. Translated by S. and S. Weber. Cambridge, MA: MIT Press, [1967] 1997.

Adorno, T. *Minima Moralia: Reflections from a Damaged Life*. London: Verso, [1951] 2005.

Adorno, T. *Lectures on Negative Dialectics: Fragments of a Lecture Course, 1965/66*. Edited by R. Tiedemann, translated by R. Livingstone. Cambridge: Polity Press, 2008.

Adorno, T. *Against Epistemology: A Metacritique*. Oxford: Wiley-Blackwell, 2013.

Agarwal, S. 'Gleaning the Dumps of Deonar: "I Was Born in Garbage, I Will Die in Garbage."' *Counterpunch,* November 29, 2019. Accessed December 3, 2019. www.counterpunch.org/2019/11/29/gleaning-the-dumps-of-deonar-i-was-born-in-garbage-i-will-die-in-garbage/.

Akasegawa, G. *Hyperart: Thomasson*. Translated by M. Fargo. Los Angeles: Kaya Press, [1985] 2010.

Alexander, C. 'The City Is Not a Tree.' *Design* 206 (1966): 46–55.

Alsayyad, N., and Roy, A. 'Medieval Modernity: On Citizenship and Urbanism in a Global Era.' *Space and Polity* 10, no. 1 (2006): 1–20.

Amin, A. *Land of Strangers*. Cambridge: Polity Press, 2012.

Amin, A. 'The Urban Condition: A Challenge to Social Science.' *Public Culture* 25, no. 2 (2013): 201–8.

Amin, A. 'Lively Infrastructure.' *Theory, Culture and Society* 31, nos. 7–8 (2014): 137–61.

Amin, A., and Howell, P. *Releasing the Commons: Rethinking the Futures of the Commons*. London: Routledge, 2016.

Amin, A., and Thrift, N. *Arts of the Political: New Openings for the Left*. Durham, NC: Duke University Press, 2013.

Amin, A., and Thrift, N. *Seeing Like a City*. Cambridge: Polity Press, 2017.

Amnesty International. 'Leben in Unsicherheit—Wie Deutschland Die Opfer Rassistischer Gewalt Im Stich Lässt.' *Amnesty International,* June 2016. Accessed March 16, 2017. www.amnesty.de/files/Amnesty-Bericht -Rassistische-Gewalt-in-Deutschland-Juni2016.pdf.

Anand, N. *Hydraulic City: Water and the Infrastructures of Citizenship in Mumbai*. Durham, NC: Duke University Press, 2017.

Angel, S., Blei, A.M., Parent, J., Lamson-Hall, P., and Galarza-Sanchez, N., with Civco, D.L., Qian Lei, R., and Thom, K. *Atlas of Urban Expansion—2016 Edition, Volume 1: Areas and Densities,* 2016. Accessed November 15, 2019. www.atlasofurbanexpansion.org.

Angel, S., Liu, Y., Blei, A.M., Lamson-Hall, P., Galarza-Sanchez, N., and Arango-Franco, S. *The New Urban Peripheries, 1990–2014: Selected Findings from a Global Sample of Cities,* Working Paper 40, June 2018. Accessed November 15, 2019. https://marroninstitute.nyu.edu/uploads/content/New _Urban_Peripheries_Working_Paper.pdf.

Angel, S., Parent, J., Civco, D.L., and Blei, A. 'The Persistent Decline in Urban Densities: Global and Historical Evidence of "Sprawl".' Working Paper, *Lincoln Institute of Land Policy,* 2010. www.lincolninst.edu/publications /working-papers/persistent-decline-urban-densities.

Anjaria, J.S. *The Slow Boil: Street Food, Rights, and Public Space in Mumbai*. Stanford, CA: Stanford University Press, 2016.

Anonymous. 'Who'd Live in a Nazi Town in Germany? I Do—It's Terrifying.' *The Guardian,* October 31, 2018, 10.

Appadurai, A. 'Deep Democracy: Urban Government and the Horizon of Politics.' *Public Culture* 14, no. 1 (2002): 21–47.

Appadurai, A. *Fear of Small Numbers: An Essay of the Geography of Anger*. Durham, NC: Duke University Press, 2006.

Arendt, H. 'Introduction: Walter Benjamin, 1892–1940.' In Arendt, H., ed., *Illuminations: Essays and Reflections,* 1–55. New York: Schocken Books, [1968] 2007.

Atkinson, R. 'Domestication by Cappuccino or Revenge on Urban Space? Control and Empowerment in the Management of Public Spaces.' *Urban Studies* 40, no. 9 (2003): 1829–43.

Atlas of Urban Expansion. *Kampala,* 2019. Accessed July 5, 2019. www.atlaso- furbanexpansion.org/cities/view/Kampala.

Attwell, D. *Rewriting Modernity: Studies in Black South African Literary History*. Athens: Ohio University Press, 2006.

Bagelman, J. *Sanctuary City: A Suspended State*. London: Palgrave, 2016.

Baker, K. 'The Death of a Once Great City: The Fall of New York and the Urban Crisis of Affluence.' *Harper's Magazine,* July 18, 2018. Accessed November 12, 2018. https://harpers.org/archive/2018/07/the-death-of-new -york-city-gentrification/.

Balfour, I. 'The Whole Is the Untrue: On the Necessity of the Fragment (after Adorno).' In Tronzo, W., ed., *The Fragment: An Incomplete History*, 82–91. Los Angeles: Getty Research Institute, 2009.

BAN (Brooklyn Anti-Gentrification Network). Accessed August 8, 2018. https://bangentrification.org/about/.

Banks, N. 'Livelihood Limitations: The Political Economy of Urban Poverty in Dhaka, Bangladesh.' *Development and Change* 47, no. 2 (2016): 266–92.

Banks, N., and Sulaiman, M. *Problem or Promise? Harnessing Youth Potential in Uganda*. Youthwatch, 2012. Accessed August 1, 2016. www.research.manchester.ac.uk/portal/files/33714156/full_text.pdf.

Barfield, T. 'Berlin Refugee Boss Resigns in Disgrace.' *The Local*, December 10, 2015. Accessed May 23, 2017. www.thelocal.de/20151210/berlin-refugee-boss-leaves-in-disgrace.

BARN (Neighbourhood Change in Bushwick). *Bushwick Action Research Collective*, 2018. Accessed August 7, 2018. http://bushwickactionresearch.org/about-gentrification/.

Baudrillard, J. *Fragments. Cool Memories III, 1990–1995*. Translated by E. Agar. London: Verso, 1995.

Bayat, A. *Street Politics: Poor People's Movements in Iran*. New York: Columbia University Press, 1997.

Bayat, A. 'From "Dangerous Classes" to "Quiet Rebels": Politics of the Urban Subaltern in the Global South.' *International Sociology* 15, no. 3 (2000): 533–55.

Bayat, A. *Life as Politics: How Ordinary People Change the Middle East*. Stanford, CA: Stanford University Press, 2010.

Bebbington, A. 'Capitals and Capabilities: A Framework for Analysing Peasant Viability, Rural Livelihoods and Poverty.' *World Development* 27, no. 12 (1999): 2021–44.

Benjamin, W. *The Arcades Project*. Translated by H. Eiland and K. McLaughlin. Cambridge, MA: Harvard University Press, 2003.

Benjamin, W. *Berlin Childhood around 1900*. Boston, MA: Harvard University Press, 2006.

Benjamin, W. 'Hashish in Marseilles.' In *Walter Benjamin: One Way Street and Other Writings*, 116–25. Translated by J. A. Underwood. London: Penguin Books, [1928] 2009.

Benjamin, W. 'One Way Street.' In *Walter Benjamin: One Way Street and Other Writings*. Translated by J. A. Underwood. London: Penguin Books, [1928] 2009.

Benjamin, W., and Lacis, A. 'Naples.' In W. *Walter Benjamin: One Way Street and Other Writings*, 414–21. Translated by J. A. Underwood. London: Penguin Books, [1928] 2009.

Bergen, V. 'Politics as the Orientation of Every Assemblage.' *New Formations* (2009): 34–41.

Bergfeld, M. 'Germany's *Willkommenskultur:* Trade Unions, Refugees and Labour Market Integration.' *Global Labour Journal* 8, no. 1 (2017): 80–89.

Berliner, P. F. *Thinking in Jazz: The Infinite Art of Improvisation*. Chicago: University of Chicago Press, 1994.

Berman, M. *All That Is Solid Melts into Air: The Experience of Modernity.* Verso: London, [1982] 2010.

Bhan, G. *In the Public's Interest: Eviction, Citizenship and Inequality in Contemporary Delhi.* Athens: University of Georgia Press, 2016.

Bhan, G. 'Notes on a Southern Urban Practice.' *Environment & Urbanization* 31, no. 2 (2019): 1–16.

Björkman, L. *Pipe Politics, Contested Waters: Embedded Infrastructures of Millennial Mumbai.* Durham, NC: Duke University Press, 2015.

Blok, A., and Farías, I. 'Whose Urban Cosmos, Which Urban Cosmopolitics? Assessing the Route Travelled and the One Ahead.' In Blok, A., and Farías, I., eds., *Urban Cosmopolitics: Agencements, Assemblies, Atmospheres,* 227–44. London: Routledge, 2016.

Bolongaro, K. 'Welcome to Syrian Berlin: A Refugee Tour of the City.' *Al Jazeera,* March 3, 2016. Accessed May 23, 2019. www.aljazeera.com/indepth /features/2016/02/syrian-berlin-refugee-tour-city-160211132536180.html.

Booker, M. 'These Unbelievable Photos Make Hong Kong Look Like Abstract Art.' *The New Republic,* October 16, 2013. Accessed May 5, 2019. https:// newrepublic.com/article/115209/michael-wolf-photography-hong-kongs -architecture-density.

Braidotti, R. 'Becoming Woman; Or Sexual Difference Revisited.' *Theory, Culture and Society* 20 (2003): 43–64.

Branch, A., and Mampilly, Z. *Africa Uprising: Popular Protest and Political Change.* London: Zed Books, 2015.

Brenner, N. 'Theses on Urbanization.' *Public Culture* 25, no. 1 (2013): 85–114.

Brenner, N. 'Debating Planetary Urbanization: For an Engaged Pluralism.' *Environment and Planning D: Society and Space* 36, no. 3 (2018): 570–90.

Brenner, N., and Schmid, C. 'Planetary Urbanization.' In Gandy, M., ed., *Urban Constellations,* 10–13. Berlin: Jovis, 2012.

Brenner, N., and Schmid, C. 'Towards a New Epistemology of the Urban?' *City* 19, nos. 2–3 (2015): 151–82.

Brickell, K., Arrigoittia, F., and Vasudevan, A. *Geographies of Forced Eviction: Dispossession, Violence, Resistance.* London: Palgrave, 2017.

Brillembourg, A., and Klumpner, H. 'Past.' In Urban Think Tank, *Torre David: Informal Vertical Communities,* 70–129. Zurich: Lars Muller, 2012.

Brillembourg, A., and Klumpner, H. 'Potential.' In Urban Think Tank, *Torre David: Informal Vertical Communities,* 360–83. Zurich: Lars Muller, 2012.

Brown, S. T. 'Kampala's Sanitary Regime: Whose Toilet Is It Anyway?' In Graham, S., and McFarlane, C., eds., *Infrastructural Lives: Urban Infrastructure in Context,* 153–73. London: Routledge-Earthscan, 2015.

Buck-Morss, S. *The Dialectics of Seeing: Walter Benjamin and the Arcades Project.* Cambridge, MA: MIT Press, 1991.

Buckley, M., and Strauss, K. 'With, against and beyond Lefebvre: Planetary Urbanization and Epistemic Plurality.' *Environment and Planning D: Society and Space* 34, no. 4 (2016). https://doi.org/10.1177%2F0263775816628872.

Bulkeley, H. *Accomplishing Climate Governance.* Cambridge: Cambridge University Press, 2015.

Bulkeley, H. 'Navigating Climate's Human Geographies: Exploring the Whereabouts of Climate Politics.' *Dialogues in Human Geography* 9, no. 3 (2019): 3–17.

Bunnell, T., and Maringanti, A. 'Practising Urban Regional Research beyond Metrocentricity.' *International Journal of Urban and Regional Research* 34 (2010): 415–20.

Butler, J. *Notes toward a Performative Theory of Assembly.* Cambridge, MA: Harvard University Press, 2018.

Butler, J., and Athanasiou, A. *Dispossession: The Performative in the Political.* Cambridge: Polity Press, 2013.

Butler, J. *The Force of Nonviolence: An Ethico-Political Bind.* London: Verso Books, 2020.

Butler, P. 'More than a Million People Living in Destitution, Study Shows.' *The Guardian,* April 27, 2016. Accessed August 15, 2018. www.theguardian. com/society/2016/apr/27/million-people-uk-living-destitution-joseph-rowntree-foundation?CMP = share_btn_tw.

Caldeira, T. *City of Walls: Crime, Segregation, and Citizenship in São Paulo.* Berkeley: University of California Press, 2000.

Caldeira, T. 'Peripheral Urbanization: Autoconstruction, Transversal Logics, and Politics in Cities of the Global South.' *Environment and Planning D: Society and Space* 35, no. 1 (2017): 3–20.

Cameron, S., and Coaffee, J. 'Art, Gentrification and Regeneration—From Artist as Pioneer to Public Arts.' *European Journal of Housing Policy* 5, no. 1 (2005): 39–58.

Cash, M. 'A Safe Space of One's Own.' *Mama Cash,* November 12, 2015. Accessed May 11, 2018. www.mamacash.org/news/a-safe-space-of-ones -own/.

Chakrabarty, D. 'Marxism after Marx: History, Subalternity and Difference.' In Makdisi, S., Casarino, C., and Karle, R. E., eds., *Marxism beyond Marxism.* New York: Routledge, 1996.

Chakrabarty, D. *Habitations of Modernity: Essays in the Wake of the Subaltern Studies.* Chicago: University of Chicago Press, 2002.

Chakrabarty, D. 'Radical Histories and Question of Enlightenment Rationalism: Some Recent Critiques of *Subaltern Studies.*' In Chaturvedi, V., ed., *Mapping Subaltern Studies and the Postcolonial.* London: Verso, [2000] 2012.

Chapman, J., and Gaydarska, B. *Parts and Wholes: Fragmentation in Prehistoric Context.* Oxford: Oxbow Books, 2007.

Chatterjee, P. *The Nation and Its Fragments: Colonial and Postcolonial Histories.* Princeton, NJ: Princeton University Press, 1993.

Chatterjee, P. *The Politics of the Governed: Reflections on Popular Politics in Most of the World.* New Delhi: Permanent Black, 2004.

Chattopadhyay, C. 'Improvisation and Assemblage: Noah Purifoy Explores Contradictions and Cultures.' *Sculpture* (July–August 1997): 31–39.

Chattopadhyay, S. *Unlearning the City: Infrastructure in a New Optical Field.* Minneapolis: University of Minnesota Press, 2012.

Chaturvedi, V., ed. *Mapping Subaltern Studies and the Postcolonial*. London: Verso, 2012.

Chaudhuri, A. 'Introduction.' In *Walter Benjamin: One Way Street and Other Writings*, vii–xv. Translated by J. A. Underwood. London: Penguin Books, 2009.

Chemould Prescott Road. *Vivan Sunderam, Trash*. Mumbai, 2008. Accessed July 8, 2018. www.gallerychemould.com/exhibitions/vivan-show-2008/.

Chibber, V. *Postcolonial Theory and the Specter of Capital*. London: Verso, 2013.

Cohen, B. *The Emergence of the Urban Entrepreneur: How the Growth of Cities and the Sharing Economy Are Driving a New Breed of Innovators*. Santa Barbara, CA: Praeger, 2016.

Cohen, B., Almirall, E., and Chesbrough, H. 'The City as a Lab: Open Innovation Meets the Collaborative Economy.' *California Management Review* 59, no. 1 (2016): 5–13.

Cohen, D. A. 'Seize the Hamptons.' *Jacobin,* November 2014. Accessed August 24, 2019. www.jacobinmag.com/2014/10/seize-the-hamptons/.

Coldwell, W. 'Refugees Tell a Different Berlin Story.' *The Guardian,* November 28, 2015. Accessed May 10, 2019. www.theguardian.com/travel/2015/nov/28/refugees-tell-a-different-berlin-story.

Collinson, P. 'Berlin Tops the World as City with the Fastest Rising Property Prices.' *The Guardian,* April 10, 2018. Accessed July 18, 2018. www.theguardian.com/world/2018/apr/10/berlin-world-fastest-rising-property-prices.

Colls, R. 'Feminism, Bodily Difference and Non-representational Geographies.' *Transactions of the Institute of British Geographers* 37 (2012): 430–45.

Colomb, C. 'The Trajectory of Berlin's "Interim Spaces": Tensions and Conflicts in the Mobilisation of "Temporary Uses" of Urban Space in Local Economic Development.' In Henneberry, J., ed., *Transience and Permanence in Urban Development,* 131–49. Chichester: Wiley-Blackwell, 2017.

Comaroff, J., and Comaroff, J. *Theory from the South; Or, How Euro-America Is Evolving toward Africa*. London: Paradigm, 2012.

Connolly, W. E. *A World of Becoming*. Durham, NC: Duke University Press, 2011.

Connor, P. 'Nearly 1 in 100 Worldwide Are Now Displaced from Their Homes.' Pew Research Center, 2016. Accessed August 7, 2016. www.pewresearch.org/fact-tank/2016/08/03/nearly-1-in-100-worldwide-are-now-displaced-from-their-homes/.

Coutard, O., and Rutherford, J., eds. *Beyond the Networked City: Infrastructure Reconfigurations and Urban Change in the North and South*. London: Routledge, 2015.

Coverley, M. *Psychogeography*. London: Pocket Essentials, 2006.

Cowan, B. 'Walter Benjamin's Theory of Allegory.' *New German Critique* 22 (Winter 1981): 109–22.

Crankshaw, O. 'Deindustrialization, Professionalization and Racial Inequality in Cape Town.' *Urban Affairs Review* 48, no. 6 (2012): 836–62.

Damai, P. 'Messianic-City: Ruins, Refuge and Hospitality in Derrida.' Discourse 27, nos. 2–3 (2005): 68–94.

Darling, J. 'Asylum and the Post-political: Domopolitics, Depoliticisation and Acts of Citizenship.' *Antipode* 46, no. 1 (2014): 72–91.

Darling, J. 'Forced Migration and the City: Irregularity, Informality, and the Politics of Presence.' *Progress in Human Geography* 41 (2017): 178–98.

Das, V. *Life and Words: Violence and the Descent into the Ordinary.* Los Angeles: University of California Press, 2007.

Dawson, A. *Extreme Cities: The Peril and Promise of Urban Life in the Age of Climate Change.* London: Verso, 2017.

Davidson, M., and Iveson, K., 'Beyond City Limits: A Conceptual and Political Defense of "the City" as an Anchoring Concept for Critical Urban Theory.' *City* 19, no. 5 (2015).

Davis, L. H., ed. *The Disability Studies Reader,* 4th ed. London: Routledge, 2013.

Davis, M. *City of Quartz: Excavating the Future in Los Angeles.* London: Verso, 1999.

Davis, M. *Planet of Slums.* New York: Verso, 2006.

Day, C., and Evans, R. 'Managing Caring Responsibilities, Change and Transitions in Young People's Family Lives in Zambia.' *Journal of Comparative Family Studies* 46, no. 1 (2015): 137–52.

De Boeck, F. 'Divining the City: Rhythm, Amalgamation and Knotting as Forms of Urbanity.' *Social Dynamics* 41, no. 1 (2015): 47–58.

De Boeck, F., and Baloji, S. *Suturing the City: Living Together in Congo's Urban Worlds.* London: Autograph, 2016.

De Boeck, F., and Honwana, A. 'Children and Youth in Africa: Agency, Identity and Place.' In Honwana, A., and De Boeck, F., eds., *Makers and Breakers: Children and Youth in Postcolonial Africa.* Oxford: James Currey Oxford, 2005.

De Certeau, M. *The Practice of Everyday Life.* Berkeley: University of California Press, 1984.

Dear, M., and Flusty, S. 'Postmodern Urbanism.' *Annals of the Association of American Geographers* 88, no. 1 (1998): 50–72.

Deleuze, G. *Difference and Repetition.* London: Continuum, [1968] 2001.

Deleuze, G., and Parnet, C. *Dialogues II,* rev. ed. New York: Columbia University Press, [1977] 2002.

Deleuze, G., and Guattari, F. *Anti-Oedipus.* London: Continuum, [1972] 2004.

Deleuze, G., and Guattari, F. *A Thousand Plateaus.* London: Bloomsbury, [1980] 2013.

Derrida, J. *Positions.* Translated by A. Bass. Chicago: Chicago University Press, 1981.

Dikeç, M. *Urban Rage: The Revolt of the Excluded.* New Haven, CT: Yale University Press, 2018.

Dobson, S., Nyamweru, H., and Dodman, D. 'Local and Participatory Approaches to Building Resilience in Informal Settlements in Uganda.' *Environment and Urbanization* 27 (2015): 605–20.

Dorling, D. *All That Is Solid: How the Great Housing Disaster Defines Our Times, and What We Can Do about It.* London: Penguin, 2015.

Doshi, S. 'The Politics of the Evicted: Redevelopment, Subjectivity, and Difference in Mumbai's Slum Frontier.' *Antipode* 45, no. 4 (2013): 844–65.

Dossal, M. *Theatre of Conflict, City of Hope*. New Delhi: Oxford University Press, 2010.

Dovey, K. 'Informal Urbanism and Complex Adaptive Assemblages.' *International Development Planning Review* 34, no. 4 (2012): 349–68.

Drabinski, K. 'Poetics of the Mangrove.' In Saldanha, A., and Adams J.M., eds., *Deleuze and Race*, 288–99. Edinburgh: Edinburgh University Press, 2013.

Dreyer, E., and McDowall, E. 'Imagining the Flâneur as a Woman.' *Communicatio: South African Journal for Communication Theory and Research* 38, no. 1 (2012): 30–44.

Dyson, J. *Working Childhoods: Youth, Agency and the Environment in India*. Cambridge: Cambridge University Press, 2014.

Easterling, K. *Extrastatecraft: The Power of Infrastructure Space*. London: Verso, 2016.

Edensor, T. 'Walking in Rhythms: Place, Regulation, Style and the Flow of Experience.' *Visual Studies* 25 (2010): 69–79.

Edensor, T. 'Entangled Agencies, Material Networks and Repair in a Building Assemblage: The Mutable Stone of St Ann's Church, Manchester.' *Transactions of the Institute of British Geographers* 36, no. 2 (2011): 238–52.

Eiland, H., and Jennings, M. *Walter Benjamin: A Critical Life*. Cambridge, MA: Harvard University Press, 2016.

Elder, A. 'Noah Purifoy: Dystopian Dadaism from Riot-Torn LA to Joshua Tree Still Resonates.' *The Guardian*, May 29, 2015. Accessed September 6, 2019. www.theguardian.com/artanddesign/2015/may/29/noah-purifoy-los-angeles-county-museum-of-art.

Elkin, L. *Flâneuse: Women Walk the City, in Paris, New York, Tokyo, Venice and London*. London: Chatto and Windus, 2017.

Elwood, S., Lawson, V., and Sheppard, E. 'Geographical Relational Poverty Studies.' *Progress in Human Geography* 41, no. 6 (2017): 745–65.

Faleiro, S. 'For Some Voters in Mumbai, This Election's All about Toilets.' *Quartz*, 2014. Accessed May 10, 2019. http://qz.com/196893/for-some-voters-in-mumbai-this-elections-all-about-toilets/.

Farías, I., and Blok, A. 'Introducing Urban Cosmopolitics: Multiplicity and the Search for a Common World.' In Blok, A., and Farías, I., eds., *Urban Cosmopolitics: Agencements, Assemblies, Atmospheres*, 1–22. London: Routledge, 2016.

Fernandes, N. *City Adrift: A Short Biography of Bombay*. New Delhi: Adelph, 2013.

Ferris, D. 'Review of Howard Eiland and Michael W. Jennings (2014) *Walter Benjamin: A Critical Life*, Cambridge, Mass.: Harvard University Press.' *Critical Inquiry* 42, no. 3 (2016): 76–77.

Feustel, M. 'Farewell to Michael Wolf (1954–2019).' *The Eye of Photography*, April 29, 2019. Accessed May 5, 2019. https://loeildelaphotographie.com/en/farewell-to-michael-wolf-1954–2019-bb/.

Florida, R. *The Rise of the Creative Class Revisited*. New York: Basic Books, 2011.

Foster, H. 'Erase, Deface, Transform.' *London Review of Books*, February 16, 2017, 16–17.

Fredericks, R. *Garbage Citizenship: Vital Infrastructures of Labor in Dakar, Senegal.* Durham, NC: Duke University Press, 2018.

Gadd, K.J. 'Street Children's Lives and Actor-Networks.' *Children's Geographies* 14, no. 3 (2016): 295–309.

Gandy, M. *The Fabric of Space: Water, Modernity, and the Urban Imagination.* Cambridge, MA: MIT Press, 2014.

Garthwaite, K. *Hunger Pains: Life inside Foodbank Britain.* Bristol: Policy Press, 2016.

Ghertner, A. 'Rule by Aesthetics: World-Class City Making in Delhi.' In Roy, A., and Ong, A., eds., *Worlding Cities: Asian Experiments and the Art of Being Global,* 279–306. Oxford: Wiley-Blackwell, 2011.

Ghertner, A. 'When Is the State? Topology, Temporality, and the Navigation of Everyday State Space in Delhi.' *Annals of the American Association of Geographers* 107, no. 3 (2017): 731–50.

Gibbs, D., Krueger, R., and MacLeod, G. 'Grappling with Smart City Politics in an Era of Market Triumphalism.' *Urban Studies* 50, no. 11 (2013): 2151–57.

Gibson, J.J. *The Ecological Approach to Visual Perception.* Boston: Houghton Mifflin, 1979.

Gibson-Graham, J.K. *A Postcapitalist Politics.* Minneapolis: University of Minnesota Press, 2006.

Gidwani, V. 'Capitalism's Anxious Whole: Fear, Capture and Escape in the *Grundrisse.'* *Antipode* 40, no. 5 (2008): 857–78.

Gidwani, V. 'Subalternity.' In Kitchin, R., and Thrift, N., eds., *International Encyclopedia of Human Geography.* London: Elsevier, 2009.

Gidwani, V. 'Six Theses on Waste, Value and Commons.' *Social and Cultural Geography* 14, no. 7 (2013): 773–83.

Gidwani, V., and Reddy, R.N. 'The Afterlives of Waste: Notes from India for a Minor History of Capitalist Surplus.' *Antipode* 43, no. 4 (2011): 1625–58.

Gidwani, V., and Maringanti, A. 'The Waste-Value Dialectic: Lumpen Urbanization in Contemporary India.' *Comparative Studies of South Asia, Africa and the Middle East* 36 (2016): 112–33.

Gieseking, J.J. 'A Queer Geographer's Life as an Introduction to Queer Theory, Space, and Time.' In Lau, L., Arsanios, M., Zúñiga-González, F., Kryger, M. and Mismar, O., eds., *Queer Geographies: Beirut, Tijuana, Copenhagen,* 4–21. Roskilde: Museum of Contemporary Art, 2013.

Gill, L. *Teetering on the Rim: Global Restructuring, Daily Life, and the Armed Retreat of the Bolivian State.* New York: Columbia University Press, 2000.

Gillespie, T. 'From Quiet to Bold Encroachment: Contesting Dispossession in Accra's Informal Sector.' *Urban Geography* 38, no. 7 (2017): 974–92.

Goldman, M. 'Speculating on the Next World City.' In Roy, A., and Ong, A., eds., *Worlding Cities: Asian Experiments and the Art of Being Global,* 229–58. Oxford: Wiley-Blackwell, 2011.

Goldschmidt, N. ' "Orts, Scraps, and Fragments": Translation, Non-Translation, and the Fragments of Ancient Greece.' In Harding, J., and Nash, J., eds., *Modernism and Non-Translation,* 49–66. Oxford: Oxford University Press, 2019.

Goodfellow, T. 'The Institutionalisation of "Noise" and "Silence" in Urban Politics: Riots and Compliance in Uganda and Rwanda.' *Oxford Development Studies* 41, no. 4 (2013): 436–54.

Goodfellow, T. 'Taming the "Rogue" Sector: Studying State Effectiveness in Africa through Informal Transport Politics.' *Comparative Politics* 47 (2015): 127–47.

Gore, C.D., and Muwanga, N.K. 'Decentralization Is Dead, Long Live Decentralization! Capital City Reform and Political Rights in Kampala, Uganda.' *International Journal of Urban and Regional Research* 38, no. 8 (2014): 2201–16.

Gough, K., Chigunta, F., and Langevang, T. 'Expanding the Scales and Domains of (In)security: Youth Employment in Urban Zambia.' *Environment and Planning A* 48, no. 2 (2016): 348–66.

Grabski, J. 'Viyé Diba's *Tout Se Sait:* The Affective Experience of Urban Life.' *Journal of Contemporary African Art* 36, no. 2 (2015): 94–107.

Graham, S. *Cities under Siege: The New Military Urbanism.* London: Verso, 2010.

Graham, S., and Marvin, S. *Splintering Urbanism: Networked Infrastructures, Technological Mobilities and the Urban Condition.* Oxford: Blackwell, 2001.

Graham, S., and McFarlane, C., eds. *Infrastructural Lives: Urban Infrastructure in Context.* London: Routledge-Earthscan, 2015.

Graham, S., and Thrift, N. 'Out of Order: Understanding Repair and Maintenance.' *Theory, Culture and Society* 24, no. 3 (2007): 1–25.

Graham, S., Desai, R., and McFarlane, C. 'Water Wars in Mumbai.' *Public Culture* 25 (2013): 115–41.

Gramsci, A. *Selections from Prison Notebooks.* London: Lawrence and Wishart, 1971.

Green, P. 'A Master of Accumulation.' *New York Times,* January 23, 2013. Accessed July 8, 2019. www.nytimes.com/2013/01/24/garden/in-buffalo-one-mans-living-museum.html.

Gregory, D. *Geographical Imaginations.* Oxford: Blackwell, 1994.

Gregson, N., Crang, M., Ahamed, F., Akhtar, N., and Ferdous, R. 'Following Things of Rubbish Value: End-of-Life Ships, "Chock-Chocky" Furniture and the Bangladeshi Middle-Class Consumer.' *Geoforum* 41 (2010): 846–54.

Grosz, E. *Time Travels: Feminism, Nature, Power.* Crows Nest, NSW: Allen and Unwin, 2005.

Guinard, P., and Margier, A. 'Art as a New Urban Norm: Between Normalization of the City through Art and Normalization of Art through the City in Montreal and Johannesburg.' *Cities* 77 (2018): 13–20.

Guinard, P., and Molina, G. 'Urban Geography of Arts: The Co-production of Arts and Cities.' *Cities* 77 (2018): 1–3.

Guma, P.K. 'The Governance and Politics of Urban Space in the Postcolonial City: Kampala, Nairobi and Dar es Salaam.' *Africa Review* 8 (2016): 31–43.

Gurney, K. *The Art of Public Space: Curating and Re-imagining the Ephemeral City.* New York: Springer, 2015.

Hägerstrand, T. 'Time-Geography: Focus on Corporeality of Man, Society and Environment.' In Aida, S., ed., *The Science and Praxis of Complexity.* 193–216. Tokyo: United Nations University, 1985.

Hall, P. *Cities of Tomorrow: An Intellectual History of Urban Planning and Design since 1880*, 4th ed. Oxford: Wiley Blackwell, 2014.

Hall, S. *City, Street and Citizen: The Measure of the Ordinary*. London: Routledge, 2012.

Hammond, G. 'Could You Live in a Micro-Flat?' *Financial Times*, May 2, 2019. Accessed May 6, 2019. www.ft.com/content/03a9343e-6b35-11e9-80c7-60ee53e6681d.

Hansen, M. B. 'Benjamin's Gamble with Cinema.' *October* 109 (2004): 3–45.

Harris, A. 'Concrete Geographies: Assembling Global Mumbai through Transport Infrastructure.' *City* 17, no. 3 (2013): 343–60.

Harris, A. 'Engineering Formality: Flyover and Skywalk Construction in Mumbai.' *International Journal of Urban and Regional Research* 42, no. 2 (2018): 295–314.

Harvey, D. *Social Justice in the City*. Baltimore: Johns Hopkins University Press, 1973.

Hasan, A. 'Karachi, Informal Settlements and COVID-19.' *International Institute for Environment and Development*, guest blog, May 6, 2020. Accessed October 7, 2020. www.iied.org/karachi-informal-settlements-covid-19.

Hawkins, H. *For Creative Geographies: Geography, Visual Arts and the Making of Worlds*. London: Routledge, 2013.

Heath, M. A. 'Defining Black Consciousness: Mongane Wally Serote's "What's in This Black 'Shit'."' *M. Ayodele Heath*, April 27, 2005. Accessed June 7, 2019. http://mayodeleheath.blogspot.co.uk/2005/04/defining-black-consciousness-mongane.html.

Hentschel, C. 'Postcolonialising Berlin and the Fabrication of the Urban.' *International Journal of Urban and Regional Research* 39, no. 1 (2014): 79–91.

Hessel, F. *Walking in Berlin: A Flaneur in the Capital*. London: Scribe, [1929] 2016.

Hickey, S. 'Rethinking Poverty Analysis from the Margins: Insights from Northern Uganda.' *Afriche e Orienti* 11, no. 2 (2009): 119–36.

Hinze, A. M. *Turkish Berlin: Integration Policy and Urban Space*. Minneapolis: University of Minnesota Press, 2013.

Honwana, A. *Time of Youth: Work, Social Change, and Politics in Africa*. West Hartford, CT: Kumarian Press, 2012.

Hsiao, L. C., ed. *'This Shipwreck of Fragments': Historical Memory, Imaginary Identities, and Postcolonial Geography in Caribbean Culture and Literature*. Newcastle, UK: Cambridge Scholars, 2009.

Hueler, H. 'Uganda Fears Unprecedented Rise in Mob Justice.' *VOA News*, June 6, 2014. Accessed January 16, 2018. www.voanews.com/a/uganda-fears-unprecedented-rise-in-mob-justice/1931384.html.

Hunter, M. A., and Robinson, Z. F. *Chocolate Cities: The Black Map of American Life*. Oakland: University of California Press, 2018.

Huyssen, A. 'The Voids of Berlin.' *Critical Inquiry* 24, no. 1 (1997): 57–81.

Indorewala, H. 'Indian Cities Have Been Reduced to Just Real Estate."' *The Wire*, October 9, 2019. Accessed December 6, 2020. https://thewire.in/urban/our-cities-prior-itise-real-estate-over-ecological-sustain-ability.

Irigaray, L. *An Ethics of Sexual Difference*. Translated by C. Burke and G. C. Gill. London: Continuum, 2004.

Irving, I. 'ArtAttack Interviews Korean Artist, Kyung Hwa Shon.' *ArtAttack*, February 8, 2016. Accessed July 7, 2019. https://artattackapp.wordpress .com/2016/02/08/artattack-interview-kyung-hwa-shon-london-art-fair/.

Jackson, S. J. 'Rethinking Repair.' In Gillespie, T., Boczkowski, P. J., and Foot, K. A., *Media Technologies: Essays on Communication, Materiality, and Society*, 221–39. Cambridge, MA: MIT Press, 2014.

Jacobs, J. *The Death and Life of Great American Cities*. London: Jonathan Cape, 1961.

Jacobs, J. M. 'Comparing Comparative Urbanisms.' *Urban Geography* 33, no. 6 (2012): 904–14.

Jacobs, J. M. 'Urban Geography I: Still Thinking Cities Relationally I.' *Progress in Human Geography* 36, no. 3 (2012): 412–22.

Jaglin, S. 'Differentiating Networked Services in Cape Town: Echoes of Splintering Urbanism.' *Geoforum* 39 (2008): 1897–906.

Jazeel, T. 'Subaltern Geographies: Geographical Knowledge and Postcolonial Strategy.' *Singapore Journal of Tropical Geography* 35, no. 1 (2014): 88–103.

Jazeel, T. 'Urban Theory with an Outside.' *Environment and Planning D: Society and Space* 36, no. 3 (2018): 405–19.

Jazeel, T., 'Singularity: A Manifesto for Incomparable Geographies.' *Singapore Journal of Tropical Geography* 40, no. 1 (2018): 5–21.

Jazeel, T., and Legg. S. 'Introducing Subaltern Geographies.' In Jazeel, T., and Legg, S., eds., *Subaltern Geographies: Subaltern Studies, Space, and the Geographical Imagination*. Athens: University of Georgia Press, 2019.

Jazeel, T., and McFarlane, C. 'The Limits of Responsibility: A Postcolonial Politics of Academic Knowledge Production.' *Transactions of the Institute of British Geographers* 35, no. 1 (2010): 109–24.

Jeffrey, C. *Timepass: Youth, Class, and the Politics of Waiting in India*. Stanford, CA: Stanford University Press, 2010.

Jeffrey, A., McFarlane, C., and Vasudevan, A. 'Rethinking Enclosure: Space, Subjectivity, and the Commons.' *Antipode* 44 (2012): 1247–67.

Jensen, C. B., and Morita, A. 'Introduction: Infrastructures as Ontological Experiments.' *Ethnos* 82, no. 4 (2017): 615–26.

Johnstone, C. 'Housing and Class Struggles in Post-war Glasgow.' In Lavalette, M., and Mooney, G., eds., *Class Struggle and Social Welfare*. London: Routledge, 2000.

Jones, P., and Evans, J. 'Rescue Geography: Place-making, Affect and Regeneration.' *Urban Studies* 49 (2012): 2315–30.

Joyce, P. *The Rule of Freedom: Liberalism and the Modern City*. London: Verso, 2002.

Jukes, P. *A Shout in the Street: An Excursion into the Modern City*. Los Angeles: University of California Press, 1991.

Juran, S., and Broer, P. N., 'A Profile of Germany's Refugee Populations.' *Population and Development Review* 43, no. 1 (2017): 149–57.

Kagenda, P. 'KCCA's Night Raiders.' *The Independent,* August 18, 2014. Accessed February 10, 2019. www.independent.co.ug/news/news-analysis/9244-kccas-night-raiders.

Kareem, B., and Lwasa, S. 'From Dependency to Interdependencies: The Emergence of a Socially Rooted but Commercial Waste Sector in Kampala City, Uganda.' *African Journal of Environmental Science and Technology* 5, no. 2 (2011): 136–42.

Katz, B., Noring, L., and Garrelts, N. 'Cities and Refugees: The German Experience.' *Brookings,* September 18, 2016. Accessed March 16, 2019. www.brookings.edu/research/cities-and-refugees-the-german-experience/.

Keegan, M. 'Hong Kong's "Cardboard Grannies": The Elderly Box Collectors Living in Poverty.' *The Guardian,* April 24, 2018. Accessed January 6, 2019. www.theguardian.com/cities/2018/apr/24/hong-kong-cardboard-grannies-elderly-box-collectors-recycling-poverty.

Keegan, M. 'Pipe Dreams: Can "Nano Apartments" Solve Hong Kong's Housing Crisis?' *The Guardian,* May 21, 2018. Accessed August 29, 2018. www.theguardian.com/cities/2018/may/21/nano-apartments-hong-kong-housing-crisis.

Keil, R. 'Extended Urbanization, "Disjunct Fragments" and Global Suburbanisms.' *Environment and Planning D: Society and Space* 36, no. 3 (2018), 494–511.

Keil, R. *Suburban Planet.* Cambridge: Polity, 2018.

Khan, B. 'BMC Official Holds NGOs Responsible for Mankhurd Toilet Collapse.' *DNA,* 2015. Accessed September 10, 2019. http://54.254.97.154/locality/mumbai-north-east/bmc-official-holds-ngos-responsible-mankhurd-toilet-collapse-54794.

King, S. 'Increasing the Power of the Poor? NGO-Led Social Accountability Initiatives and Political Capabilities in Uganda.' *European Journal of Development Research* 27 (2015): 887–902.

Kimar, W. 'On Raids and Connecting Favela Resistances in Kenya and Brazil.' *LSE,* 2014. Accessed August 2, 2019. http://blogs.lse.ac.uk/favelasatlse/.

Kishik, D. *The Manhattan Project: A Theory of the City.* Stanford, CA: Stanford University Press, 2015.

Klinenberg, E. *Palaces for the People: How to Build a More Equal and United Society.* London: The Bodley Head, 2018.

Klein, H. A. 'Sacred Things and Holy Bodies: Collecting Relics from Late Antiquity to the Early Renaissance.' In Bagnoli, M., Klein, H. A., Mann, G., and Robinson, J., eds., *Treasures of Heaven: Saints, Relics, and Devotion in Medieval Europe.* New Haven, CT: Yale University Press, 2010.

Knowles, S. G. 'Learning from Disaster? The History of Technology and the Future of Disaster Research.' *Technology and Culture* 55, no. 4 (2014): 773–84.

Kooy, M., and Bakker, K. 'Technologies of Government: Constituting Subjectivities, Spaces, and Infrastructures in Colonial and Contemporary Jakarta.' *International Journal of Urban and Regional Research* 32 (2008): 375–91.

Koppikar, S. 'Death-Trap Toilets: The Hidden Dangers of Mumbai's Poorest Slums.' *The Guardian,* February 27, 2017. Accessed December 11, 2019. www.theguardian.com/global-development-professionals-network/2017 /feb/27/death-trap-toilets-mumbai-india-slums.

Krawczyk, D. 'Not Everything Works Out as Planned.' *Political Critique: Central European Magazine for Politics and Culture,* February 4, 2016. Accessed May 11, 2019. http://politicalcritique.org/world/eu/2016/refugees-berlin -ohlauer-school/.

Kristeva, J. *Powers of Horror: An Essay on Abjection.* Translated by L.S. Roudiez. New York: Columbia University Press, 1982.

Kumari, S., and Singh, A.K. 'Working Women in Informal Sector: Geographical Perspective.' *Journal of the Anthropological Survey of India* 65, no. 2 (2016): 185–99.

Kundu, A. 'Rurbanisation: An Alternative Development Paradigm.' In Patel, S., and Goyal, O., eds., *The Contemporary Urban Conundrum,* IIC Quarterly (Winter–Spring 2016), 17–27. Delhi: Ravinder Datta for India International Centre.

Ladry, O. '"Wir Sind Alle Oranienplatz!" Space for Refugees and Social Justice in Berlin.' *Seminar: A Journal of Germanic Studies* 51, no. 4 (2015): 398–413.

Laing, O. *The Lonely City: Adventures in the Art of Being Alone.* Edinburgh: Canongate, 2017.

Lancione, M. 'Assemblages of Care and the Analysis of Public Policies on Homelessness in Turin, Italy.' *City* 18 (2014): 25–40.

Lancione, M., ed. *Rethinking Life at the Margins: The Assemblage of Contexts, Subjects and Politics.* London: Routledge, 2016.

Lancione, M. 'Revitalising the Uncanny: Challenging Inertia in the Struggle against Forced Evictions.' *Environment and Planning D: Society and Space* 35, no. 6 (2017): 1012–32.

Lancione, M. 'Radical Housing: On the Politics of Dwelling as Difference.' *International Journal of Housing Policy* 20, no. 2 (2019): 273–89.

Lancione, M., and McFarlane, C. 'Life at the Urban Margins: Sanitation Infra-making and the Potential of Experimental Comparison.' *Environment and Planning A* 48, no. 12 (2017). https://doi.org/10.1177%2F0308518X16659772.

Lancione, M., and McFarlane, C., eds. *Global Urbanism: Knowledge, Power and the City.* London: Routledge, 2021.

Langa, N. 'About the Refugee Movement in Kreuzberg, Berlin.' *Movements: Journal fur Migrations und Grenzregimeforschung* 1, no. 2 (2015).

Larkin, B. *Signal and Noise: Media, Infrastructure, and Urban Culture in Nigeria.* Durham, NC: Duke University Press, 2008.

Larkin, B. 'The Politics and Poetics of Infrastructure.' *Annual Review of Anthropology* 42 (2013): 327–43.

Lash, S. *Another Modernity: A Different Rationality.* Oxford: Wiley-Blackwell, 1999.

Latour, B. 'Whose Cosmos, Which Cosmopolitics? Comments on the Peace Terms of Ulrich Beck.' *Common Knowledge* 10, no. 3 (2004): 450.

Latour, B. *Reassembling the Social: An Introduction to Actor-Network-Theory.* Oxford: Oxford University Press, 2005.

Latour, B. 'From Realpolitik to Dingpolitik, or How to Make Things Public.' In Latour, B., and Weibel, P., eds., *Making Things Public: Atmospheres of Democracy*, 14–41. Cambridge, MA: MIT Press, 2008.

Latour, B. 'Networks, Societies, Spheres: Reflections of an Actor-Network Theorist.' *International Journal of Communication* 5 (2011): 796–810.

Lau, J. 'Rooftop Slums Are a Stark Reminder of Hong Kong's Social and Housing Problems.' *South China Morning Post*, October 8, 2016. Accessed August 16, 2019. www.scmp.com/news/hong-kong/education-community /article/2026112/rooftop-slums-are-stark-reminder-hong-kongs.

Lawhon, M., and Truelove, Y. 'Disambiguating the Southern Urban Critique: Propositions, Pathways and Possibilities for a More Global Urban Studies.' *Urban Studies* 57, no. 1 (2020). https://doi.org/10.1177%2F0042098019829412.

Lawson, V. 'Decentring Poverty Studies: Middle Class Alliances and the Social Construction of Poverty.' *Singapore Journal of Tropical Geography* 33, no. 1 (2012): 1–19.

Lees, L., Slater, T., and Wyly, E. *Gentrification*. Routledge: New York, 2008.

Lefebvre, H. *The Critique of Everyday Life, Volume 1*. Translated by J. Moore. London: Verso, [1958] 1991.

Lefebvre, H. *The Production of Space*. Oxford: Blackwell, [1974] 1991.

Lefebvre, H. *The Urban Revolution*. Minneapolis: University of Minnesota Press, [1970] 2003.

Lefebvre, H. *The Critique of Everyday Life: The One Volume Edition*. Translated by J. Moore. London: Verso, 2014.

Lefebre, C. 'The Complete City: Why Density and Amenities Are Essential to Everyday Urban Living.' *Minnpost*, July 16, 2014. Accessed August 19, 2019. www.minnpost.com/the-line/2014/07/complete-city-why-density-and -amenities-are-essential-everyday-urban-living/.

Legg, S. *Spaces of Colonialism: Delhi's Urban Governmentalities*. Oxford: Wiley-Blackwell, 2008.

Lemanski, C. 'Global Cities in the South: Deepening Social and Spatial Polarization in Cape Town.' *Cities* 24, no. 6 (2007): 448–61.

Leshem, N. *Life after Ruin: The Struggles over Israel's Depopulated Arab Spaces*. Cambridge: Cambridge University Press, 2016.

Leslie, E. *Walter Benjamin: Overpowering Conformism*. London: Pluto Press, 2000.

Leslie, E. *Walter Benjamin*. London: Reaktion Books, 2007.

Leslie, E. 'Recycling.' In Beaumont, M., and Dart, G., eds., *Restless Cities*, 233–56. London: Verso, 2010.

Lichenstein, J. 'The Fragment: Elements of a Definition.' In Tronzo, W., ed., *The Fragment: An Incomplete History*, 115–29. Los Angeles: Getty Research Institute.

Lindel, I., and Ampaire, C. 'The Untamed Politics of Urban Informality: "Gray Space" and Struggles for Recognition in an African City.' *Theoretical Inquiries in Law* 17 (2016): 257–82.

Linek, L. ' "This Is Our Battleground": How a New Refugee Movement Is Challenging Germany's Racist Asylum Laws.' *Ceasefire*, March 20, 2013.

Accessed May 10, 2019. https://ceasefiremagazine.co.uk/this-battleground-germanys-refugee-movement-challenges-racist-asylum-laws/.

Lombard, M. 'Discursive Constructions of Low-Income Neighbourhoods.' *Geography Compass* 9 (2015): 648–59.

Lwasa, S. 'Sustainable Urban Development: Managing City Development in Uganda.' *Global Urbanization* (2011): 276–93.

Magnusson, W. *Politics of Urbanism: Seeing Like a City*. New York: Routledge, 2011.

Maharaj, K. 'Bombay High Court Makes Right to Clean Toilets a Fundamental Right for Women in India.' *Oxford Human Rights Hub*, February 8, 2016. Accessed July 29, 2019. http://ohrh.law.ox.ac.uk/bombay-high-court-makes-right-to-clean-toilets-a-fundamental-right-for-women-in-india/.

Maher, D. '900 Miles to Paradise, and Other Afterlives of Architecture.' In Kunze, D., Bertolin, D., and Brott, S., eds., *Architecture Post-mortem: The Diastolic Architecture of Decline, Dystopia and Death*, 219–40. London: Routledge, 2013.

Mann, D., and Andabati, D. *The Informal Settlement of Namuwongo: A Baseline Survey for the PECTIS Project*, May 2014. Accessed September 14, 2018. http://suda-africa.org/wp-content/uploads/2014/05/PECTIS_Baseline-Survey-Report_Validation-Draft_reduced.pdf.

Marcus, G. 'Preface' for Benjamin, W., *One-Way Street*. Translated by M. Jenning. Cambridge, MA: Harvard University Press, 2016.

Marcuse, P., and Madden, D. *In Defense of Housing: The Politics of Crisis*. London: Verso, 2016.

Marshall, C. 'How David Bowie Used William S. Burrough's Cut-up Method to Write His Unforgettable Lyrics.' *Open Culture*, May 7, 2019. www.openculture.com/2019/05/how-david-bowie-used-william-s-burroughs-cut-up-method-to-write-his-unforgettable-lyrics.html.

Martin, A., Myers, N., and Viseu, A. 'The Politics of Care in Technoscience.' *Social Studies of Science* 45, no. 5 (2015): 625–41.

Marvin, S., Luque-Ayala, A. and McFarlane, C., eds. *Smart Urbanism: Utopian Vision or False Dawn?* London: Routledge, 2015.

Massey, D. *Spatial Divisions of Labour: Social Structures and the Geography of Production*. New York: Macmillan, 1984.

Massey, D. *For Space*. London: Sage, 2005.

Massey, D. *World City*. Cambridge: Polity Press, 2007.

Massumi, B. *Parables for the Virtual: Movement, Affect, Sensation*. Durham, NC: Duke University Press, 2002.

Massumi, B. *99 Theses on the Revaluation of Value: A Postcapitalist Manifesto*. Minneapolis: University of Minnesota Press, 2018.

Mattern, S. 'Maintenance and Care.' *Places*, November 2018. Accessed July 9, 2019. https://placesjournal.org/article/maintenance-and-care/?cn-reloaded = 1.

Mayer, M., ed. *Basquiat*. New York: Brooklyn Museum, [2005] 2010.

Mayne, A. *Slums: The History of Global Injustice*. London: Reaktion Books, 2017.

Mbembe, A., and Nuttall, S. 'Writing the World from an African Metropolis.' *Public Culture* 16, no. 3 (2004): 347–72.

McDonald, D. *World City Syndrome: Neoliberalism and Inequality in Cape Town.* London: Routledge, 2006.

McFarlane, C. *Learning the City: Knowledge and Translocal Assemblage.* Oxford: Wiley-Blackwell, 2011.

McFarlane, C. 'The Entrepreneurial Slum: Civil Society, Mobility, and the Co-production of Urban Development.' *Urban Studies* 49 (2012): 2926–47.

McFarlane, C. 'The Geographies of Urban Density: Topology, Politics and the City.' *Progress in Human Geography* 40 (2016): 629–38.

McFarlane, C., Desai, R., and Graham, S. 'Informal Urban Sanitation: Everyday Life, Comparison and Poverty.' *Annals of the Association of American Geographers* 104 (2014): 989–1011.

McFarlane, C., and Silver, J. 'The Poolitical City: "Seeing Sanitation" and Making the Urban Political in Cape Town.' *Antipode* 49, no. 1 (2017): 125–44.

McFarlane, C., and Silver, J. 'Navigating the City: Dialectics of Everyday Urbanism.' *Transactions of the Institute for British Geographers* 42, no. 3 (2017): 458–71.

McKittrick, K. *Demonic Grounds: Black Women and the Cartographies of Struggle.* Minneapolis: University of Minnesota Press, 2006.

McKittrick, K. 'Plantation Futures.' *Small Axe: A Caribbean Journal of Criticism* 17, no. 3 (2013): 1–15.

McNeill, D. 'The volumetric city.' *Progress in Human Geography,* 44, no. 5 (2019): 815–831.

Mels, A., Castellano, D., Braadbaart, O., Veenstra, S., Dijkstra, I., Meulman, B., and Wilsenach, J. A. 'Sanitation Services for the Informal Settlements of Cape Town, South Africa.' *Desalination* 248, no. 1 (2009): 330–37.

Menon, M. 'Maharashtra Faces Growing Urban Malnutrition.' *The Hindu,* April 22, 2012. Accessed July 5, 2019. www.thehindu.com/news/national /article3342953.ece.

Menon, N. 'Deonar Dumping Ground Is Making Children Sick.' *Mumbai Mirror,* June 2, 2009, 7.

Merrifield, A. *Metromarxism: A Marxist Tale of the City.* London: Routledge, 2002.

Merrifield, A. *The Politics of the Encounter: Urban Theory and Protest under Planetary Urbanization.* Athens: University of Georgia Press, 2013.

Merrifield, A. *The New Urban Question.* London: Pluto Press, 2014.

Merriman, P. 'Rethinking Mobile Methods.' *Mobilities* 9, no. 2 (2014): 167–87.

Michael, C. 'Has Tokyo Reached "Peak City"?' *The Guardian,* June 14, 2019. Accessed June 20, 2019. www.theguardian.com/cities/2019/jun/14/has -tokyo-reached-peak-city.

Middleton, J. 'Sense and the City: Exploring the Embodied Geographies of Urban Walking.' *Social and Cultural Geography* 11 (2010): 575–96.

Miles, M. *Art, Space and the City.* London: Routledge, 1997.

Miranda, C. A. 'Noah Purifoy, An Artist Forged by Fire.' *Los Angeles Times,* August 13, 2015. Accessed July 10, 2019. www.latimes.com/entertainment /arts/la-ca-cm-noah-purifoy-20150816-story.html.

Mitlin, D., and Satterthwaite, D. *Urban Poverty in the Global South: Scale and Nature.* London: Routledge, 2013.

Mohammed, R., and Sidaway, J. 'Shards and Stages: Migrant Lives, Power, and Space Viewed from Doha, Qatar.' *Annals of the Association of American Geographers* 106, no.6 (2016): 1397–417.

Monstadt, J., and Schramm, S. 'Toward the Networked City? Translating Technological Ideals and Planning Models in Water and Sanitation Systems in Dar es Salaam.' *International Journal of Urban and Regional Research* 41, no. 4 (2017): 104–25.

Monteith, W., and Lwasa, S. 'The Participation of Urban Displaced Populations in (In)Formal Markets: Contrasting Experiences in Kampala, Uganda.' *Environment and Urbanization* 29, no. 2 (2016): 383–402.

Moody, R. 'Swinging Modern Sounds 44: And Another Day.' *The Rumpus,* April 25, 2013. https://therumpus.net/2013/04/swinging-modern-sounds-44-and-another-day/.

Morland, I., and Willox, D. *Queer Theory.* London: Palgrave, 2004.

Moser, C. *Confronting Crisis: A Comparative Study of Household Responses to Poverty and Vulnerability in Four Poor Urban Communities.* Washington, DC: World Bank, 1996.

Moser, C. *Ordinary Families, Extraordinary Lives: Assets and Poverty Reduction in Guayaquil, 1978–2004.* Washington, DC: Brookings Institute Press, 2009.

Moser, C., and McIlwaine, C. 'Editorial: New Frontiers in Twenty-First Century Urban Conflict and Violence.' *Environment and Urbanization* 26, no. 2 (2014): 331–44.

Moten, F. *Black and Blur (Consent Not to Being Single).* Durham, NC: Duke University Press: 2017.

Mukhopadhyay, P., Zerha, M-H., and Denis, E. 'Subaltern Urbanisation Revisited.' In Patel, S., and Goyal, O., eds., *The Contemporary Urban Conundrum.* IIC Quarterly (Winter–Spring), 28–44. Delhi: Ravinder Datta for India International Centre, 2016.

Mumbai Human Development Report (HDR). *Mumbai Human Development Report, 2009.* New Delhi: Oxford University Press, 2009.

Murali, M., Cummings, C., Feyertag, J., Gelb, S., Hart, T., Khan, A., Langdown, I., and Lucci, P. *10 Things to Know about the Impacts of Urbanization.* London: Overseas Development Institute, 2018.

Murray, M. *The Urbanism of Exception: The Dynamics of Global City Building in the Twenty-First Century.* Cambridge: Cambridge University Press, 2017.

Myers, G. *African Cities: Alternative Visions of Urban Theory and Practice.* London: Zed Books, 2011.

Napolitano, V. 'Anthropology and Traces.' *Anthropological Theory* 15, no. 1 (2014): 47–67.

National Slum Dwellers Federation, Mahila Milan, and Sparc in India. *Toilet Talk,* 1997. Accessed December 11, 2019. https://knowyourcity.info/wp-content/uploads/2018/09/Toilet-Talk-with-photos.pdf.

Ngara, E. *Ideology and Form in African Poetry: Implications for Communication.* London: Heinemann Educational Books, 1990.

Nylund, P., and Cohen, B. 'Collision Density: Driving Growth in Urban Entrepreneurial Ecosystems.' *International Entrepreneurship and Management Journal* 13 (2017): 757–76.

October Gallery. *El Anatsui*, 2016. Accessed August 17, 2019. www.october-gallery.co.uk/exhibitions/tsiatsia.shtml.

O'Hagan, S. 'How Photographer Michael Wolf Captured the Melancholy of Our Teeming Cities.' *The Guardian*, April 26, 2019. Accessed May 3, 2019. www .theguardian.com/artanddesign/2019/apr/26/how-photographer-michael-wolf -captured-the-planets-teeming-city-life.

O'Reilly, K., 'Combining Sanitation and Women's Participation in Water Supply: An Example from Rajasthan.' *Development in Practice* 20, no. 1 (2010): 45–56.

Ongwec, J. 'Namuwongo: Key to Kampala's Present and Future Development.' *LSE*, May 28, 2015. Accessed August 12, 2018. http://blogs.lse.ac.uk /africaatlse/2015/05/28/namuwongo-key-to-kampalas-present-and-future-development/.

Oswin, N. 'Planetary Urbanization: A View from Outside.' *Environment and Planning D: Society and Space* 36, no. 3 (2018). https://doi.org/10.1177% 2F0263775816675963.

Pacheco-Vega, R. 'Urban Wastewater Governance in Latin America: Panorama and Reflections for a Research Agenda.' In Aguilar-Barajas, I., Mahlknecht, J., Kaledin, J., Kjellen, J., and Meija-Betancourt, A., eds., *Water and Cities in Latin America: Challenges for Sustainable Development*, 102–16. London: Routledge, 2015.

Pacione, M. 'Housing Policies in Glasgow since 1880.' *Geographical Review* 69, no. 4 (1979): 395–412.

Pamuk, O. *Istanbul: Memories and the City*. London: Faber and Faber, 2006.

Pandey, G. 'In Defence of the Fragment: Writing about Hindu-Muslim Riots in India Today.' *Economic and Political Weekly*, March 1991, 559–72.

Pandey, G. *Routine Violence: Nations, Fragments, Histories*. Stanford, CA: Stanford University Press, 2006.

Panjabi, K. 'Report on M-East Ward Reveals the Poor Picture of Mumbai's Unequal Development.' *DNA*, April 30, 2015. Accessed August 12, 2019. www.dnaindia.com/locality/mumbai-north-east/report-meast-ward-reveals-poor-picture-mumbai's-unequal-development-58740.

Parent, L. 'The Wheeling Interview: Mobile Methods and Disability.' *Mobilities* 11, no. 4 (2016): 521–32.

Parker, C. 'Avoided Object.' In Tronzo, W., ed., *The Fragment: An Incomplete History*, 91–113. Los Angeles: Getty Research Institute, 2009.

Parnell, S. 'Defining a Global Urban Development Agenda.' *World Development* 78 (2016): 529–40.

Parnell, S., and Pieterse, E. 'The "Right to the City": Institutional Imperatives of a Developmental State.' *International Journal of Urban and Regional Research* 34, no. 1 (2010): 146–62.

Parnell, S., and Robinson, J. '(Re)theorising Cities from the Global South: Looking beyond Neoliberalism.' *Urban Geography* 33, no. 4 (2012): 593–617.

Parnell, S., Beall, J., and Crankshaw, O. 'A Matter of Timing: African Urbanisation and Access to Housing in Johannesburg.' In Brycson, D., and Potts, D., eds., *African Urban Economies: Viability, Vitality or Vitiation?*, 229–51. London: Palgrave Macmillan, 2005.

Patel, V. 'Sanitation and Dignity.' *The Hindu,* September 24, 2013. Accessed August 25, 2019. www.thehindu.com/news/national/other-states/sanitation-and-dignity/article5160791.ece.

Peake, L. 'The Twenty-First Century Quest for Feminism and the Global Urban.' *International Journal of Urban and Regional Research* 40, no. 1 (2016): 219–27.

Peck, J. 'Austerity Urbanism.' *City* 16, no. 6 (2012): 626–55.

Perlman, J. 'The Metamorphosis of Marginality in Rio De Janeiro.' *Latin American Research* (2004).

Perlman, J. *Favela: Four Decades of Living on the Edge in Rio.* Oxford: Oxford University Press, 2010.

Pfeiffer, J., and Chapman, R. 'Anthropological Perspectives on Structural Adjustment and Public Health.' *Annual Review of Anthropology* 39 (2010): 149–65.

Phadke, S., Khan, S., and Ranade, S. *Why Loiter? Women and Risk on Mumbai's Streets.* Penguin: New Delhi, 2011.

Pierce, J., and Lawhon, M. 'Walking as Method: Toward Methodological Forthrightness and Comparability in Urban Geographical Research.' *Professional Geographer* 67, no. 4 (2015): 655–62.

Pieterse, E. 'Rethinking African Urbanism from the Slum.' *LSE Cities,* 2011. Accessed July 11, 2019. http://lsecities.net/media/objects/articles/rethinking-african-urbanism-from-the-slum/en-gb/.

Pinder, D. 'Reconstituting the Possible: Lefebvre, Utopia and the Urban Question.' *International Journal of Urban and Regional Research* 39, no. 1 (2015): 28–45.

Pinto, R. 'Right to Pee Activists Return Award as Toilets Still Unclean.' *Times of India,* March 9, 2016. Accessed May 10, 2019. http://timesofindia.indiatimes.com/city/mumbai/Right-to-Pee-activists-return-award-as-toilets-still-unclean/articleshow/51318710.cms.

Pommier, C. *The Art of* Viyé Diba: The *Intelligent Hand.* Vancouver, BC: Arts in Action Society; Dakar, Senegal: SudProd Senvision, 2003. Available at https://vimeo.com/68892833.

Porter, G. ' "I think a woman who travels a lot is befriending other men and that's why she travels": Mobility Constraints and Their Implications for Rural Women and Girl Children in Sub-Saharan Africa.' *Gender, Place and Culture* 18, no. 1 (2011): 65–81.

Porter, G. 'Mobilities in Rural Africa: New Connections, New Challenges.' *Annals of the Association of American Geographers* 106, no. 2 (2016): 434–41.

Prakash, G. *Bonded Histories: Genealogies of Labour Servitude in Colonial India.* Cambridge: Cambridge University Press, 1990.

Pred, A. *Recognising European Modernities: A Montage of the Present.* London: Routledge, 1995.

Pred, A. *Even in Sweden: Racisms, Racialized Spaces, and the Popular Geographical Imagination.* Berkeley: University of California Press, 2000.

Purifoy, N., and Michel, T. *Junk Art: 66 Signs of Neon.* Los Angeles, 1966.

Putnam, R. D. *Bowling Alone: The Collapse and Revival of American Community.* New York: Simon and Schuster, 2001.

Raghunath, P. '1000 Evicted Families Rebuild Homes.' *Gulf News India,* June 20, 2015. Accessed May 10, 2019. http://gulfnews.com/news/asia/india /1000-evicted-families-rebuild-homes-1.1537995.

Rahman, P. 'Exploring Urban Resilience: Violence and Infrastructure Provision in Katachi.' Master's thesis, Massachusetts Institute of Technology, Boston, 2012.

Ranganathan, M. 'Storm Drains as Assemblages: The Political Ecology of Flood Risk in Post-Colonial Bangalore.' *Antipode* 47, no. 5 (2015): 1300–1320.

Ranganathan, M. 'Beyond "Third World" Comparisons: America's Geography of Water, Race, and Poverty.' *International Journal of Urban and Regional Research,* 2018. www.ijurr.org/spotlight-on-overview/parched-cities-parched -citizens/beyond-third-world-comparisons/.

Rao, V. 'Proximate Distances: The Phenomenology of Density in Mumbai.' *Built Environment* 33, no. 2 (2007): 227–48.

Rao, V. 'Infra-City: Speculations on Flux and History in Infrastructure-Making.' In Graham, S., and McFarlane, C., eds., *Infrastructural Lives: Urban Infrastructure in Context,* 39–58. London: Routledge-Earthscan, 2015.

Ree X. 'Are Refugees Really Welcome? Inside the Fight to Save Berlin's Wagenplatz Kanal.' *Open Democracy,* April 21, 2016. Accessed August 26, 2019. www.opendemocracy.net/transformation/ree-x/inside-fight-to-save-berlins-wagenplatz-kanal.

Reuters. 'The World's Most Crowded Place.' *Reuters,* n.d. Accessed July 15, 2019. www.reuters.com/news/picture/the-worlds-most-crowded-place?articleId = USRTR2SRF6.

Riceburg, J. 'Just Let the Refugees Stay!' *John Riceburg,* July 2, 2014. Accessed May 11, 2019. https://johnriceburg.wordpress.com/2014/07/02/just-let-the -refugees-stay/.

Rigg, Natalie. 'Interview: Michael Wolf's Best Photographs: Four Plucked Ducks in Hong Kong.' *The Guardian,* April 19, 2017. Accessed May 17, 2019. www.theguardian.com/artanddesign/2017/apr/19/michael-wolf-best -photograph-hong-kong-dead-ducks-interview.

Robins, S. 'The 2011 Toilet Wars in South Africa: Justice and Transition between the Exceptional and the Everyday after Apartheid.' *Development and Change* 45, no. 3 (2014): 479–501.

Robins, S. 'Poo Wars as Matter Out of Place: 'Toilets for Africa in Cape Town.' *Anthropology Today,* 30, no. 1 (2014): 1–3.

Robins, S. 'Slow Activism in Fast Times: Reflections on the Politics of Media Spectacles after Apartheid.' *Journal of Southern African Studies* 40, no. 1 (2014): 91–110.

Robinson, J. *Ordinary Cities: Between Modernity and Development.* London: Routledge, 2006.

Rosen, P. 'Introduction to "Benjamin Now: Critical Encounters with *The Arcades Project."' Boundary* 2 30, no. 1 (2003): 1–15.

Roy, A. 'Slumdog Cities: Rethinking Subaltern Urbanism.' *International Journal of Urban and Regional Research* 35 (2011): 223–38.

Roy, A. 'The Blockade of the World-Class City: Dialectical Images of Indian Urbanism.' In Roy, A., and Ong, A., eds., *Worlding Cities: Asian*

Experiments and the Art of Being Global, 259–78. Oxford: Wiley-Blackwell, 2011.

Roy, A. *Capitalism: A Ghost Story.* London: Verso, 2014.

Roy, A. 'What Is Urban about Critical Urban Theory?' *Urban Geography* 37 (2015): 1–14.

Roy, A. 'Who's Afraid of Postcolonial Theory?' *International Journal of Urban and Regional Research* 40, no. 1 (2016): 200–209.

Roy, A. 'Dis/possessive Collectivism: Property and Personhood at City's End.' *Geoforum* 80 (2017): A1–11.

Roy, A. 'The City in the Age of Trumpism: From Sanctuary to Abolition.' *Environment and Planning D: Society and Space* 37, no. 5 (2019): 761–78.

Roy, A., and Ong, A., eds., *Worlding Cities: Asian Experiments and the Art of Being Global.* Oxford: Wiley-Blackwell, 2011.

Roy, T. 'Non-renewable Resources: The Poetics and Politics of Vivan Sunderam's *Trash.' Theory, Culture and Society* 30, nos. 7–8 (2013): 265–75.

Ruffato, L. *There Were Many Horses.* Translated by A. Doyle. Seattle: Amazon Crossing, [2001] 2014.

Samson, M. 'Rescaling the State, Restructuring Social Relations: Local Government Transformation and Waste Management Privatization in Post-apartheid Johannesburg.' *International Feminist Journal of Politics* 10, no. 1 (2008): 119–43.

Sassen, S. *Expulsions: Brutality and Complexity in the Global Economy.* Cambridge, MA: Harvard University Press, 2014.

Satterthwaite, D., and Mitlin, D. *Reducing Urban Poverty in the Global South.* London: Routledge, 2014.

Satterthwaite, D., Mitlin, D., and Bartlett, S. *Key Sanitation Issues: Commitments, Coverage, Choices, Context, Co-production, Costs, Capital, City-wide Coverage.* Environment and Urbanization Brief no. 31. London: IIED, 2015.

Scanlan J. *On Garbage.* London: Reaktion, 2005.

Schindler, S. 'Towards a Paradigm of Southern Urbanism.' *City* 21, no. 1 (2017): 47–64.

Schnitzler, A. 'Traveling Technologies: Infrastructure, Ethical Regimes, and the Materiality of Politics in South Africa.' *Cultural Anthropology* 28, no. 4 (2013): 670–93.

Schreker, T., and Bambra, C. *Neoliberal Epidemics: How Politics Makes Us Sick.* London: Palgrave Macmillan, 2015.

Scott, A. J., and Soja, E. W., eds. *The City: Los Angeles and Urban Theory at the End of the Twentieth Century.* Berkeley: University of California Press, 1996.

Seabrook, J., and Siddiqui, A. *People without History: India's Muslim Ghettos.* London: Pluto Press, 2011.

Sennett, R. *The Craftsmen.* London: Penguin Books, 2008.

Sennett, R. 'The City of Fragments.' *Cityscapes: Rethinking Urban Things,* July 19, 2014. African Centre for Cities, no. 5. Accessed July 6, 2019. www.cityscapesdigital.net/2014/07/19/city-fragments/.

Serote, M. W. *Yakhal'inkomo.* Johannesburg: Renoster Books, 1972.

Sevcenco, M. 'Refugees Demanding Rights Continue 4-Month-Long Occupation in Berlin.' *Occupy Wall Street*, 2014. Accessed May 10, 2019. http://occupywallstreet.net/story/refugees-demanding-rights-continue-4-month-long-occupation-berlin.

Sharma R. N., and Bhide, A. 'World Bank Funded Slum Sanitation Programme in Mumbai: Participatory Approach and Lessons Learnt.' *Economic and Political Weekly* 40, no. 17 (April 23–29, 2005): 1784–89.

Shaw, C. 'Make Art Not War: Watts and the Junk Art Conversation.' *East of Borneo*, November 22, 2010. Accessed July 10, 2019. www.eastofborneo.org/articles/make-art-not-war-watts-and-the-junk-art-conversation/.

Shelton, B., Karakiexicz, J., and Khan, T. *The Making of Hong Kong: From Vertical to Volumetric*. London: Routledge, 2011.

Sheppard, E., Leitner, H., and Maringanti, A. 'Provincializing Global Urbanism: A Manifesto.' *Urban Geography* 34 (2015): 893–900.

Shin, H. B. 'Theorising from Where? Reflections on De-centring Global (Southern) Urbanism.' In *Global Urbanism: Knowledge, Power, and the City*. London: Routledge, forthcoming.

Shulze, W., and Schneider, R. *Heimkehr ins Leben, Berlin 1945–1960*. Berlin: Aufbau-Verlag, 2005.

Sidaway, J. D., Woon, C. Y., and Jacobs, J. M. 'Planetary Postcolonialism.' *Singapore Journal of Tropical Geography* 35, no. 1 (2014): 4–21.

Silver, J. 'Incremental Infrastructures: Material Improvisation and Social Collaboration across Post-colonial Accra.' *Urban Geography* 35, no. 6 (2014): 788–804.

Sim, D. 'Controversial Oranienplatz Refugee Camp Demolished.' *International Business Times*, April 9, 2014. Accessed May 10, 2019. www.ibtimes.co.uk/controversial-oranienplatz-berlin-refugee-camp-demolished-1444043.

Simone, A. 'People as Infrastructure: Intersecting Fragments in Johannesburg.' *Public Culture* 16, no. 3 (2004): 407–29.

Simone, A. 'Emergency Democracy and the "Governing Composite".' *Social Text* 95, no. 2 (2008): 13–33.

Simone, A. 'The Politics of the Possible: Making Urban Life in Phnom Penh.' *Singapore Journal of Tropical Geography* 29, no. 2 (2008): 186–204.

Simone, A. *City Life from Jakarta to Dakar: Movements at the Crossroads*. London: Routledge, 2009.

Simone, A. 'The Surfacing of Urban Life.' *City* 15, nos. 3–4 (2011): 355–64.

Simone, A. 'City of Potentialities: An Introduction.' *Theory, Culture and Society* 33, nos. 7–8 (2016): 5–29.

Simone, A. *Improvised Lives: Rhythms of Endurance in an Urban South*. Cambridge: Polity Press, 2018.

Simone, A., and Pieterse, E. *New Urban Worlds: Inhabiting Dissonant Times*. Cambridge: Polity Press, 2017.

Sinclair, I. *London Overground: A Day's Walk around the Ginger Line*. London: Penguin, 2015.

Singh, J. T. 'Sunday in the Park: Domestic Workers and Public Space in Hong Kong.' *Cities of Migration*, July 29, 2013. http://citiesofmigration.ca/good_idea/sunday-in-the-park/.

Singh, G., Vithayathil, T., and Pradhan, K. C. 'Recasting Inequality: Residential Segregation by Caste over Time in Urban India.' *Environment and Urbanization* 31, no. 2 (2019): 615–34.

Slitine, M. 'Contemporary Art from a City at War: The Case of Gaza (Palestine).' *Cities* 77, no. 1 (2018): 49–59.

Smith, G., ed. *Walter Benjamin: Moscow Diary*. Translated by R. Sieburth. Cambridge, MA: Harvard University Press, 1986.

Smith, J. H. 'Relics: An Evolving Tradition in Latin Christianity.' In Hahn, C., and Klein, H. A., eds., *Saints and Sacred Matter: The Cult of Relics in Byzantium and Beyond*. Dumbarton Oaks Symposia and Colloquia. Cambridge, MA: Harvard University Press, 2015.

Smith, N. *The New Urban Frontier: Gentrification and the Revanchist City*. London: Routledge, 1996.

Social Justice Coalition (SJC). *Our Toilets Are Dirty: Report of the Social Audit into the Janitorial Service for Communal Flush Toilets in Khayelitsha, Cape Town*, October 1, 2014. Cape Town: SJC/Ndifuna Ukwazi.

Society for Community Organization (SoCo). 2016. Accessed August 15, 2019. www.soco.org.hk/trapped/index.htm.

Söderström, O. *Cities in Relations: Trajectories of Urban Development in Hanoi and Ouagadougo*. Oxford: Wiley-Blackwell, 2014.

Soederberg, S. 'Governing Global Displacement in Austerity Urbanism: The Case of Berlin's Refugee Crisis.' *Development and Change* 50, no. 4 (2018): 923–947.

Soja, E. 'Taking Los Angeles Apart: Some Fragments of a Critical Human Geography.' *Environment and Planning D: Society and Space* 4, no. 3 (1986): 255–72.

Soja, E. *Postmodern Geographies: The Reassertion of Space in Critical Social Theory*. London: Verso, 1989.

Soja, E. *Seeking Spatial Justice*. Minneapolis: University of Minnesota Press, 2010.

Solnit, R. *Wanderlust: A History of Walking*. London: Verso, 2002.

Solnit, R. *A Field Guide to Getting Lost*. Edinburgh: Canongate, 2006.

Sondzi, P. 'Hope in the Past: On Walter Benjamin.' In Benjamin, W., *Berlin Childhood around 1900*, 1–36. Boston, MA: Harvard University Press, 2006.

Speed, B. 'Manhattan's Population Density Is Changing—And Not in the Way You'd Expect.' *CityMetric*, November 12, 2014. Accessed November 12, 2018. www.citymetric.com/horizons/manhattan-s-population-density-changing-and-not-way-you-d-expect-468.

Spencer, R. *Eduardo Paolozzi: Recurring Themes*. London: Trefoil Books, 1984.

Spivak, G. S. *Outside in the Teaching Machine*. New York: Routledge, 1993.

Spivak, G. S. *Death of a Discipline*. New York: Columbia University Press, 2005.

Srivastava, S. *Entangled Urbanism: Slum, Gated Community and Shopping Mall in Delhi and Gurgaon*. Delhi: Oxford University Press, 2015.

Stanek, L. *Henri Lefebvre on Space: Architecture, Urban Research, and the Production of Theory*. Minneapolis: University of Minnesota Press, 2013.

Stein, S. 'Progress for Whom, Toward What? Progressive Politics and New York City's Mandatory Inclusionary Housing.' *Journal of Urban Affairs* 40, no. 6 (2018): 770–81.

Stein, S. *Capital City: Gentrification and the Real Estate State*. London: Verso, 2019.

Stengers, I. 'A Constructivist Reading of Process and Reality.' *Theory, Culture and Society* 25, no. 4 (2008): 91–110.

Stengers, I. 'A Cosmopolitical Proposal.' In Latour, B., and Weibel, P., eds. *Making Things Public: Atmospheres of Democracy*. Cambridge, MA: MIT Press, 2005.

Stengers, I. *Cosmopolitics, Vol. 2*. Minneapolis: University of Minnesota Press, 2011.

Sunderam, V. *Trash*. Mumbai: Chemould Prescott Road, 2008.

Tacoli, C. 'Editorial: The Urbanization of Food Insecurity and Malnutrition.' *Environment and Urbanization* 31, no. 2 (2019): 371–74.

Thieme, T. 'Navigating and Negotiating Ethnographies of Urban Hustle in Nairobi Slums.' *City* 21, no. 2 (2017): 219–31.

Thrift, N. 'The Promise of Urban Informatics: Some Speculations.' *Environment and Planning A* 46, no. 6 (2014): 1263–66.

Tiedemann, R. 'Additional Notes.' In Adorno, T., *Lectures on Negative Dialectics: Fragments of a Lecture Course, 1965/66*. Edited by R. Tiedemann, translated by R. Livingstone, 178–82. Cambridge: Polity Press, 2008.

Tindall, G. *City of Gold*. New Delhi: Penguin Books, 1992.

Tranberg-Hansen, K. 'Getting Stuck in the Compound: Some Odds against Social Adulthood in Lusaka, Zambia.' *Africa Today* 51 (2005): 2–16.

Trilling, D. 'In Germany, Refugees Seek Fair Treatment.' *Al Jazeera*, April 2, 2014. Accessed May 10, 2019. www.aljazeera.com/indepth/features/2014/04/germany-refugees-seek-fair-treatment-berlin-oranienplatz-20144211253138114.html.

Tronzo, W., ed. *The Fragment: An Incomplete History*. Los Angeles: Getty Research Institute, 2009.

Truelove, Y. '(Re-)Conceptualising Water Inequality in Delhi, India through a Feminist Political Ecology Framework.' *Geoforum* 42 (2011): 143–52.

Turok, I. 'Persistent Polarisation Post-apartheid? Progress towards Urban Integration in Cape Town.' *Urban Studies* 38, no. 13 (2001): 2349–77.

Uganda Bureau of Statistics. *ILRI Poverty Report, 2007*. www.ubos.org/onlinefiles/uploads/ubos/pdf%20documents/ILRI%20Poverty%20Report%202007.pdf.

Uganda Ministry of Health. *The HIV and AIDS Uganda Country Progress Report, 2014*. Kampala: Government of Uganda, 2014.

UN-Habitat. *Urban Profile of Kampala*. Nairobi: UN-Habitat, 2011.

United Nations. ' "Nobody Left Outside" Campaign Launched as UN Warns of Dire Shelter Conditions for Refugees.' May 18, 2016. Accessed June 28, 2019. www.un.org/apps/news/story.asp?NewsID = 53964#.V3JIBXidL8t.

United Nations. *Sustainable Development Goals: Goal 11—Sustainable Cities and Communities, n.d.* Accessed May 1, 2019. www.un.org/sustainabledevelopment/cities/.

Urban Think Tank. *Torre David: Informal Vertical Communities*. Zurich: Lars Muller, 2012.

Uzar, F. 'Social Participation of Turkish and Arabic Immigrants in the Neighbourhood: Case Study of Moabit West, Berlin.' *Journal of Identity and*

Migration Studies 1, no. 2 (2007). Accessed May 23, 2019. www.e-migration.ro/jims/Vol1_no2_2007/JIMS_vol1_no2_2007_UZAR.pdf.

Valverde, M. 'Seeing Like a City: The Dialectic of Modern and Premodern Ways of Seeing in Urban Governance.' *Law and Society Review* 45, no. 2 (2011): 277–312.

Varshney, A. 'People in This Mumbai Slum Barely Make It to Age 40.' *Mongabay,* April 2019. Accessed December 3, 2019. https://india.mongabay.com/2019/04/people-in-this-mumbai-slum-barely-make-it-to-age-40/.

Vasagar, J. 'Berlin's Refugee Chaos Erodes German Reputation for Efficiency.' *Financial Times,* December 11, 2015. Accessed May 23, 2019. www.ft.com/cms/s/0/aa243aa0–9f52–11e5–8613–08e211ea5317.html#axzz49TiY8LuH.

Vasudevan, A. *Metropolitan Preoccupations: The Spatial Politics of Squatting in Berlin.* Oxford: Wiley-Blackwell, 2015.

Vasudevan, A. *The Autonomous City: A History of Squatting.* London: Verso, 2017.

Vigh, H. 'Motion Squared: A Second Look at the Concept of Social Navigation.' *Anthropological Theory* 9, no. 4 (2009): 419–38.

Vince, G. *Adventures in the Anthropocene: A Journey to the Heart of the Planet We Made.* London: Chatto and Windus, 2014.

Vladislavic, I. *Portrait with Keys: Joburg and What-What.* Johannesburg: Umuzi, [2006] 2017.

Wallman, S. *Kampala Women Getting By: Well-Being in the Time of AIDS.* Athens: Ohio University Press, 1996.

Warren, S. 'Pluralising the Walking Interview: Researching (Im)mobilities with Muslim Women.' *Social and Cultural Geography* 18, no. 6 (2016): 786–807.

Watson, V. 'African Urban Fantasies: Dreams or Nightmares?' *Environment and Urbanization* 26, no. 1 (2014): 215–31.

Watt, P. 'A Nomadic War Machine in the Metropolis: En/countering London's 21st Century Housing Crisis with Focus E15.' *City* 20, no. 2 (2016): 297–320.

Weinstein, L. 'Mumbai's Development Mafias: Globalization, Organized Crime and Land Development.' *International Journal of Urban and Regional Research* 32, no. 1 (2008): 22–39.

Weinstein, L. *The Durable Slum: Dharavi and the Right to Stay Put in Globalizing Mumbai.* Minneapolis: University of Minnesota Press, 2013.

Wiig, A., and Silver, J. 'Turbulent Presents, Precarious Futures: Urbanization and the Deployment of Global Infrastructure.' *Regional Studies* 53, no. 6 (2019): 912–23.

Wilke, J. *Understanding the Asset-Based Approach to Community Development.* Working chapter, 2006. Accessed August 2, 2019. www.neighboraustin.com/PDF/Understanding%20the%20Asset-based%20Approach%20to%20Community%20%20Development.pdf.

Williams, R. *Why Cities Look the Way They Do.* Cambridge: Polity, 2019.

Wolf, Michael. *Informal Solutions: Observation in Hong Kong Back Alleys.* WE Press, 2016.

Wolf-Powers, L. 'New York City's Community-Based Housing Movement: Achievements and Prospects.' In Gallent, N., and Ciaffi, D., eds., *Commu-*

nity Action and Planning: Contexts, Drivers and Outcomes, 217–35. Bristol: Policy Press, 2014.

World Resources Institute. *Upward and Outward Growth: Managing Urban Expansion for More Equitable Cities in the Global South.* Washington, DC: World Resources Institute, 2019.

Wunderlich, F. M. 'Walking and Rhythmicity: Sensing Urban Space.' *Journal of Urban Design* 13 (2008): 125–39.

Wunderlich, F. M. 'Place-Temporality and Urban Place-Rhythms in Urban Analysis and Design: An Aesthetic Akin to Music.' *Journal of Urban Design* 18, no. 3 (2013): 383–408.

Xue, C. Q., Manuel, K. K., and Chung, R. 'Public Space in the Old Derelict City Area—A Case Study of Mong Kok, Hong Kong.' *Urban Design International* 6, no. 1 (2001): 16–31.

Yiftachel, O. 'Critical Theory and "Gray Space": Mobilization of the Colonized.' *City* 13, nos. 2–3 (2009): 240–56.

Yiftachel, O. '"Conceptual Topography" and the City.' *Urban Forum* 31 (2020): 443–51.

Zeiderman, A. 'Beyond the Enclave of Urban Theory.' *International Journal of Urban and Regional Research* 42, no. 6 (2018): 1114–26.

Index

www.ingramcontent.com/pod-product-compliance
Lightning Source LLC
Chambersburg PA
CBHW020457270326
41926CB00008B/642